Praise for
Acceleration for Gifted Learners, K–5

Each chapter is an in-depth manual on how to sensitively and effectively achieve acceleration collaboratively with parents, educators, and students.

—Susan G. Assouline, Associate Director,
The Belin-Blank Center for Gifted Education, The University of Iowa

The nation and our schools are finally taking a more measured look at acceleration as a viable intervention on behalf of high-ability students. Gives readers excellent step-by-step guidance on extensive ways to provide appropriate acceleration.

—Nicholas Colangelo, Myron and Jacqueline Blank Professor
of Gifted Education, Belin-Blank International
Center for Gifted Education, The University of Iowa

A must-read resource. Parents and teachers will value highly the content of this book on acceleration as they work together to address the needs of children who are gifted and talented.

—Julia Link Roberts, Director,
The Center for Gifted Studies, Western Kentucky University

A practical guide for all stakeholders in gifted education: parents, teachers, counselors and administrators. A "how to" with heart and compassion focusing on the whole child that addresses the social and emotional aspects of effective acceleration. Offers practical guidance in developing appropriate academic acceleration using delightful examples of gifted kids.

—Dorothy Sisk, Professor and
Conn Chair for Gifted Children, Lamar University

Goes beyond currently available resources to provide a wealth of information on many important topics, including attention to the social-emotional needs of candidates for acceleration, as well as concrete strategies regarding ways to provide appropriately challenging curricular experiences. I believe this book is a critically important addition to the professional libraries of all persons who support gifted young people in their quest for an excellent education.

—Susan Winebrenner, Author and Staff Development Specialist,
Education Consulting Service, Inc.

A renewed interest in acceleration and powerful support from the research community have triggered a need for practical guidance necessary to effectively implement acceleration practices. This book provides teachers with the tools for assessing individual students' academic strengths and differentiating classroom practices to accommodate the needs of highly able learners.

—Joseph S. Renzulli, Director,
The National Research Center on the
Gifted and Talented, University of Connecticut Board
of Trustees Distinguished Professor, Raymond and
Lynn Neag Professor of Gifted Education and Talent Development

Acceleration

for Gifted Learners, K–5

*We dedicate our work to three pioneers, Nicholas Colangelo, Susan G. Assouline,
and Miraca U. M. Gross. They resolved to release barriers to learning that adhered to
traditional practices. In assimilating existing research results, they enabled all of us to recognize
immense benefits through acceleration. They gave our brightest, most competent children a voice.*

Acceleration
for Gifted Learners, K–5

**Joan Franklin Smutny • Sally Y. Walker
Elizabeth A. Meckstroth**

CORWIN PRESS
A SAGE Publications Company
Thousand Oaks, CA 91320

For information:

 Corwin Press
A Sage Publications Company
2455 Teller Road
Thousand Oaks, California 91320
www.corwinpress.com

Sage Publications Ltd.
1 Oliver's Yard
55 City Road
London EC1Y 1SP
United Kingdom

Sage Publications India Pvt. Ltd.
B-42, Panchsheel Enclave
Post Box 4109
New Delhi 110 017 India

Printed in the United States of America.

Library of Congress Cataloging-in-Publication Data

Smutny, Joan F.
Acceleration for gifted learners, K–5 / Joan Franklin Smutny,
Sally Y. Walker, Elizabeth A. Meckstroth.
        p. cm.
Includes bibliographical references and index.
ISBN 1-4129-2566-5 or 978-1-412925-66-2 (cloth)
ISBN 1-4129-2567-3 or 978-1-412925-67-9 (pbk.)
    1. Gifted children—Education—United States. 2. Educational acceleration.
I. Walker, Sally Yahnke, 1942- II. Meckstroth, Elizabeth A. III. Title.
LC3993.9.S579 2007
371.95—dc22   2006020223

This book is printed on acid-free paper.

06 07 08 09 10 11 9 8 7 6 5 4 3 2 1

Acquisitions Editor:	Allyson P. Sharp
Editorial Assistant:	Nadia Kashper
Production Editor:	Diane S. Foster
Copy Editor:	Diana Breti
Typesetter:	C&M Digitals (P) Ltd.
Proofreader:	Sally Jaskold
Indexer:	Molly Hall
Cover Designer:	Audrey Snodgrass

Contents

Preface

During 2003 and 2004, I had the great pleasure and privilege of working with two fine scholars and good friends of many years, Dr. Nicholas Colangelo and Dr. Susan Assouline of the Connie Belin and Jocelyn N. Blank International Center for Gifted Education and Talent Development, at the University of Iowa, on a major report that investigated the status of acceleration in America's schools and colleges and why, despite the wealth of research that supports the use of acceleration with academically gifted students, educators are so wary of using it.

The report, *A Nation Deceived: Why Schools Hold Back America's Brightest Students* (Colangelo, Assouline, & Gross, 2004), was generously funded by the John Templeton Foundation of Pennsylvania. We developed the report in two companion volumes. Volume 2 consists of 11 chapters written by international experts on acceleration who presented the findings of many hundreds of research studies on 18 forms of academic acceleration. Volume 1 is a distillation of the principal findings of Volume 2, written to present the key facts about acceleration and the reasons for its underusage to teachers, parents, building principals, school board members, and educational administrators—the people who make the day-to-day decisions about how individual students should be educated. The report can be accessed at its Web site: http://www.nationdeceived.org.

A Nation Deceived has aroused wide national and, indeed, international interest. Educators and parents are beginning to recognize that acceleration can be much more than a simple grade-skip. Teachers are beginning to consider whether bright students in their classes might possibly be candidates for some form of acceleration. Families of gifted and talented students are beginning to ask themselves, "It seems to have worked for other children—could it be an answer for ours?"

The book you are holding, written by Joan Smutny, Sally Walker, and Elizabeth Meckstroth, is intended as a practical guidebook on acceleration to assist teachers, parents, school administrators, and counselors working with gifted children in the kindergarten and primary school years. It is written in three Parts and, appropriately, it begins and ends with the children themselves—chapters in which the focus is specifically directed at the characteristics and needs of gifted students who might benefit from one or more of the 18 forms of acceleration identified in *A Nation Deceived*.

Part I examines the range of accelerative practices appropriate for use with gifted children in the kindergarten and primary school years and discusses *how* and *why* these practices work. It asks and answers the critical questions that Nick, Susan, and I found were most frequently posed about acceleration. It looks at an issue that is not often enough addressed: the use of acceleration with groups of gifted students who are traditionally underserved, such as the urban poor and twice-exceptional children. It includes a section on the critical issue of assessment.

Part II provides a useful introduction to differentiating the curriculum by modifying content, process, and product. The provision of a developmentally appropriate curriculum is important for *all* children, not only the gifted, and for *all* gifted students, not only those who are to be accelerated, and the authors emphasize that acceleration is much more than a speedier progress through school. It must be accompanied by a curriculum designed to meet the learning needs of the individual child.

Part III covers a range of issues in social-emotional development, including the complexities of asynchrony—the many ways in which intellectually gifted students can be "out of synch" with their age peers—and also discusses family issues that may need to be considered when a child is accelerated.

Intellectually gifted children differ from their age peers of average ability in their capacity to learn, the ways in which they learn, the speed at which they learn, their feelings about learning, and their perceptions of themselves as learners. But, as the final Part of this book emphasizes, there is much more to it than that. They also differ in many aspects of their social and emotional development. They tend to be more socially and emotionally mature than their age peers. Many possess a capacity for empathy—the capacity to understand and feel, within themselves, the feelings of others—that is not usually found in children of their age. Their conceptions and expectations of friendship tend to be different from those of their age peers and more closely aligned with the friendship conceptions of older children. Even their hobbies and interests tend to be those of children some years older. Not surprisingly, many gifted children have little in common with their age peers. Many gravitate toward older children with whom they share more commonalities of interest—and commonalities of development. This developmental advancement—intellectual, academic, and emotional—is what makes gifted learners such excellent candidates for acceleration.

In an early chapter of this book, the authors quote David Elkind (2001), author of *The Hurried Child*, who pointed out that acceleration may actually be the wrong word to describe the many procedures by which a gifted child may be permitted to advance through school at a faster pace. I agree. As a driver, when I want my car to speed up, I step on what my American colleagues call the gas pedal, but which we in Australia call the accelerator. It is my decision, not the car's, to go faster—and to do so, I literally put pressure on my car to accelerate. By contrast, when, in my years as a classroom teacher and school administrator, I allowed gifted students to accelerate through school, I was *removing* the academic and social pressure that required the child to slow down her natural speed of progress. We call this "acceleration," but what I was actually doing, in essence, was taking my foot off the brake.

Some teachers may assume that the provision of a challenging, enriched, individualized, fast-paced curriculum is the essence of acceleration and that little more is required. They would be wrong. *All* students need a challenging, enriched curriculum through which they can work at their own natural pace of learning. The essence of acceleration is, in my view, a developmentally appropriate curriculum married to a developmentally appropriate *placement*. This means placing the gifted child with other students who are at similar stages of academic and emotional maturity. Sometimes this can be accommodated in a setting in which the gifted child remains with age peers—one example given in this book is acceleration through cluster grouping—but except in a minority of cases where issues in the child's development or environmental circumstances indicate otherwise (the book provides some thoughtfully presented examples of these), acceleration works best when the gifted student works with children who are older, either full time, as in grade advancement or early entrance, or for part of the day, as in subject acceleration.

Many teachers think of acceleration as "removing" a child from his or her natural setting, "taking her away" from her peers, or "bumping him up" a grade. These perceptions arise from a misunderstanding of the nature of acceleration and the nature of giftedness. There is nothing "natural" about keeping an academically gifted six-year-old with other six-year-olds with whom she has little or nothing in common except the chronological accident that they were all born in the same 12-month period, and insisting that she "work through" a curriculum that is developmentally suited to her classmates but that she mastered a year, or several years, before.

It is not preordained that six-year-olds must work with other six-year-olds. As Nick, Susan, and I pointed out in *A Nation Deceived,* until comparatively recently in America's history, students progressed through school grades on the basis of their individual ability and motivation. The decision to shift away from this recognition of the individual, and to move children through school in lockstep progression based on age rather than competence, was not an educational decision; it was a management decision made by an increasingly industrialized society increasingly preoccupied with "progress." Sadly, this "progress" stopped many gifted children in their tracks.

This book is written to assist educators and parents who want to restore to gifted students the right to progress at their natural pace of learning.

—Miraca U. M. Gross,
Director of the Gifted Education Research,
Resource, and Information Centre (GERRIC),
The University of New South Wales,
Sydney, Australia

Acknowledgments

Without the contributions of countless parents, educators, researchers, and writers who provided the essence of experience comprising the material for *A Nation Deceived: How Schools Hold Back America's Brightest Students* (Colangelo et al., 2004), this book would not have come about. The Templeton Report ignited the education field in a way that few books do. We also wish to thank the gifted children and young people in our lives whose determination to aspire and hope for change have spurred us on throughout the writing process. This book tells their stories. It expresses, as well, the practical wisdom and experiences of many parents and teachers who have the courage and foresight to go above and beyond prescribed practice and protocol to advocate for and apply acceleration.

No book can be published without editors. We are grateful for our discerning, competent editors, Sarah E. von Fremd, Julia Mossbridge, and Dee Stiffler, who wholeheartedly and expertly crafted our information and writings into a cohesive experience. We would also like to express our appreciation for Corwin Press editors Kylee Liegl and Allyson Sharp and their assistant, Nadia Kashper, for their knowledge, encouragement, and support of this book.

The contributions of the following reviewers are gratefully acknowledged:

Jane D. Adair
Resource Specialist
Long Beach Unified School District
Long Beach, CA

Margaret H. Blackwell
Executive Director, Exceptional Children & Student Services
Chapel Hill-Carrboro City Schools
Chapel Hill, NC

Richard M. Cash
Director of Gifted Programs
Bloomington Public Schools
Bloomington, MN

Michael C. Pyryt
Director, Centre for Gifted Education
University of Calgary
Calgary, Alberta, Canada

Julia Link Roberts
Mahurin Professor of Gifted Studies
Director of the Center for Gifted Studies
Western Kentucky University
Bowling Green, KY

Michael Sayler
Associate Professor, College of Education
University of North Texas
Denton, TX

Joseph Staub
Resource Specialist Teacher
Thomas Starr King Middle School
Los Angeles, CA

About the Authors

Joan Franklin Smutny is founder and director of the Center for Gifted at National-Louis University. Each year, she directs programs for thousands of gifted children from all socioeconomic and cultural backgrounds—age four through Grade 10. She teaches creative writing to children in her programs and offers parent seminars that take place concurrently with these programs. At the university level, she teaches graduate courses on gifted education for teachers in Illinois. Joan regularly leads workshops for teachers and parents on such topics as identification of gifted children and their unique learning needs, principles and practices of gifted education, differentiated instruction, parent and teacher advocacy, and the needs of underserved gifted. She is editor of the *Illinois Association for Gifted Children Journal;* contributing editor for *Understanding Our Gifted* and the *Roeper Review;* and a writer for *The Gifted Education Communicator* and *Parenting for High Potential.*

Joan Smutny has authored, coauthored, and edited many articles and books on gifted education for teachers and parents, including *Teaching Young Gifted Children in the Regular Classroom: Identifying, Nurturing, and Challenging Ages 4–9* (with Sally Walker and Elizabeth Meckstroth, 1997); *The Young Gifted Child: Potential and Promise, an Anthology* (1998); *Gifted Girls* (1998); *Stand Up for Your Gifted Child: How to Make the Most of Kids' Strengths at School and at Home* (2001); *Underserved Gifted Populations: Responding to Their Needs and Abilities* (2003); *Differentiated Instruction (Fastback)* (2003); *Designing and Developing Programs for Gifted Children* (2003); *Gifted Education: Promising Practices* (2003); and *Differentiating for the Young Child: Teaching Strategies Across the Content Areas (K–3)* (with S. E. von Fremd, 2004). In 1996, she won the National Association for Gifted Children (NAGC) Distinguished Service Award for outstanding contribution to the field of gifted education.

Sally Y. Walker is the executive director of the Illinois Association for Gifted Children (IAGC). She works throughout the state of Illinois to promote awareness and to advocate for gifted children, their parents, and educators. She has been to Washington D.C. to work on federal legislation for gifted education.

Sally also works as a consultant in the field of gifted education, providing seminars and technical assistance to schools across the United States.

For 12 years, Sally worked with a Regional Office of Education in Illinois, assisting schools in northern Illinois with meeting state mandates, providing professional development, and implementing gifted programming. Before working at the Regional Office of Education, Sally was a teacher in Rockford's Centralized Gifted Program and parent educator for the gifted program. She has taught kindergarten through college-level classes.

Sally is the author of *Survival Guide for Parents of Gifted Kids* (2002). She has co-authored *Teaching Young Gifted Children in the Regular Classroom: Identifying, Nurturing, and Challenging Ages 4–9* (1997) and *Making Memories, A Parent Portfolio* (1997). Sally has also co-authored *A Guide for Parents: Overseeing Your Gifted Child's Education* (2003) and written numerous articles.

She is a professional achievement mentor for the NAGC, working with mentees involved in professional development. She is on the advisory board for The California Association for the Gifted's *The Gifted Education Communicator* and Open Space Communication's *Understanding Our Gifted*. She currently serves as the chair of the Illinois Gifted Advisory Council for the Illinois State Board of Education.

Sally has a B.S. in psychology and education, an M.S. in guidance and counseling and educational administration, postgraduate work in early childhood, gifted, and parent education, and a Ph.D. in education. Sally works with parents and educators to recognize and program for the special needs of students.

 **Elizabeth A. Meckstroth** is a senior fellow with the Institute for Educational Advancement. She is on the National Advisory Board for *The Gifted Education Communicator* and a contributing editor on the advisory board of *Roeper Review.*

She coordinated development of Supporting Emotional Needs of the Gifted (SENG) and is a co-author of *Teaching Young Gifted Children in the Regular Classroom: Identifying, Nurturing, and Challenging Ages 4–9* (1997) and *Guiding the Gifted Child* (1989), awarded "Best Book" by the American Psychological Association. Betty has written numerous book chapters and articles, including the "Parenting" column for *Understanding Our Gifted* for three years. She pioneered parent support groups and has facilitated discussion groups since 1981. In private practice, she conducted intelligence and personality/learning style assessments for hundreds of gifted children, then coached parents to advocate for their children. She served on the executive committees of the Parent and Community and Counseling and Guidance Divisions of the NAGC, and is past co-chair of their Global Awareness Division. She was a family consultant for the Davidson Institute and received the Ohio Association for Gifted Children's Civic Leadership award. She has given hundreds of presentations and is a frequent speaker at national, state, and world conferences.

Betty earned an M.Ed. from the University of Dayton, license as a professional counselor, a certificate in analytical psychology from the C. G. Jung Institute of Chicago, and an M.S.W. in clinical social work from Loyola University in Chicago.

Her recent interests include Myers-Briggs interpretation, alternative healing modes, exotic travel, and floral art.

Introduction

No bird flies too high if he soars with his own wings.

—Ralph Waldo Emerson

At one time or another, most adults have had the experience of sitting in a classroom only to discover that they already know most of the material to be covered. They try to attend to the teacher but soon drift off, doodling in the margins of their empty notebook, staring at the clock. When the meeting concludes, they reflect on their mistake in attending and make adjustments accordingly. If it's a one-time workshop, they simply go on to more interesting things, glad not to repeat the experience. If they've signed up for a series, they either withdraw or find a more appropriate class.

No one would consider it unnatural or risky for an adult to seek alternatives to an obvious mismatch between his or her level of mastery and the level of a class. Yet, children with similar challenges are expected to endure not just one or a series of mismatches, but often 12 long years of them. At some point, we have to ask, "Should children be forced to endure for years a situation that most adults would find intolerable even for a limited period of time?" If an adult with a gift for language and a basic understanding of French decided to try an advanced class, would any of us say, "Why are you in such a hurry?" or "You might feel out of sync with the students in Advanced French"?

These questions lead to a more important question: Doesn't the term "acceleration" reflect an outsider view—the perspective of an establishment that must defend standardized education as the norm? Those of us who've been listening to gifted children and what *they* say about acceleration know that any advancement in their learning situation makes them feel more normal and freer to be themselves. A central theme of this book is that acceleration restores gifted children to *their* normal state. As such, acceleration embraces all aspects of gifted students' lives—their intellect, creativity, idiosyncrasies, learning styles, social and emotional well-being, sensibilities, and moral and spiritual development. For example, a gifted child who joins a cluster group may be timid and withdrawn, may have a special interest in architecture, may worry about the fate of stray dogs and cats in her town, and may enjoy writing political satire in her spare time. What special needs will an accelerated learning option address for this child? How can her passion for architecture and writing be appropriately challenged? How can her love for animals be channeled through a study of the humane movement in America? How can an accelerated learning option help her to take risks and emerge out of her shell?

We have written *Acceleration for Gifted Learners, K–5* in response to a growing recognition in the field that the educational system in the United States has disastrously shortchanged our schools' brightest students. In October of 2004, the publication of The Templeton Report on Acceleration (Colangelo et al., 2004) alerted the field to the urgent need for nationwide change. In partial response to the No Child Left Behind policy, this acclaimed compilation of research on the widely documented need for acceleration in our schools and the entrenched attitudes and policies that resist it has stirred a healthy debate, in both the gifted and general education communities. The findings of this report have laid a solid foundation for new thinking on accelerated learning and have opened the door to a wide variety of ways and means to accomplish its aims.

HOW THIS BOOK APPROACHES ACCELERATION

Acceleration for Gifted Learners, K–5 has two goals. First, it aims to broaden ideas about what acceleration is, what forms it can take, and how it can best serve the intellectual, social, and emotional needs of gifted students. As *A Nation Deceived* (Colangelo et al., 2004) makes clear, dispelling false assumptions about acceleration is critical to reversing the trend of neglect that has hindered the growth of thousands of gifted children in this country. A key misconception addressed by this book is the tendency to equate acceleration with grade-skipping. In practice, the form that acceleration takes depends on variables unique to each student. A young gifted child may read at an eighth-grade level and talk like a high schooler, but lack the skill to organize his thoughts on paper. An advanced bilingual student may be eligible to skip a grade academically, but may feel a deep cultural bond with her bilingual friends. Some gifted students are academically, emotionally, and socially ready (and eager) to skip a grade; others are not. But *all* require acceleration in some form.

By broadening the concept of acceleration, *Acceleration for Gifted Learners, K–5* casts a wider net over a larger population of gifted students, including underserved populations (e.g., multicultural, multiracial, young, highly gifted, highly creative). This book aims to show that (1) accelerated learning within classrooms should always be available to any student able to meet the challenge (grade-skipping is another matter); (2) accelerated learning options should always address the whole child—abilities, problem areas, culture, learning preferences, social-emotional life, and so forth. In practice, this means that a child who appears average on the basis of testing or some other criteria should not be excluded from acceleration in the class if he proves his ability and mastery in other ways. On the other end of the spectrum, a child who has already skipped a grade should likewise not be barred from acceleration in the new class if she shows by her performance that she is ready for a larger challenge.

Through examples of real classrooms, children, teachers, and parents, this book provides a rich journey through the larger landscape of acceleration. As authors and practitioners, we have focused our attention on the fundamental question of how our gifted students—*all* our gifted students in all their variety—can receive the benefits of acceleration in ways that meet their needs. This question has led us to a consideration of many topics, from the larger meanings and implications of acceleration to an in-depth focus on appropriate content; to learning standards, assessment, differentiation, creativity; and to the vast territory of the social-emotional world of the gifted. What readers gain in this journey is an understanding of the complexity of acceleration but also the potential for variety and flexibility in its design and application.

Second, *Acceleration for Gifted Learners, K–5* is meant to be a kind of guidebook on acceleration, offering a wealth of information and suggestions on what teachers, administrators, counselors, and families can do, in practical terms, to make accelerated learning a reality for gifted students. In its pages, readers will find children they recognize and scenarios they've encountered in their own homes and districts. We have made every effort to look at sound practices and principles using examples of different children so that readers can see how acceleration constantly shifts and adjusts from one circumstance to the next. In keeping with the book's emphasis on the whole child, we have attempted to explore acceleration from the *inside out*—that is, from an understanding of the child's nature (abilities, interests, personal qualities) and needs.

The emotional, social, and spiritual life of gifted children assumes a critical role in this volume, with an entire third Part devoted to the subject. The reason for this is simple. Acceleration, when applied appropriately and sensitively, accomplishes far more than a change in the pace and level at which a child learns. It is a restoration to wholeness, an ability not just to do but to *thrive*. Without emotional and spiritual well-being, accelerated learning is an empty shell of meaningless work.

HOW THE BOOK IS ORGANIZED

Divided into three Parts, the book addresses the practical concerns of teachers, administrators, counselors, and families and explores such questions as "Can I provide advanced instruction for a gifted bilingual child who doesn't meet the criteria for grade advancement this year? How do I know whether my gifted child is working at the right level when he tends to overachieve and pressure himself? How will acceleration affect a gifted child struggling against perfectionism and low self-esteem? What kind of acceleration works for a very young child whose development is uneven and unpredictable? How do I ensure that the kind of acceleration I provide for my gifted students is working for each one of them?"

Part I (Acceleration: Issues and Applications for Gifted Learners by Joan Franklin Smutny) sets the stage for the book by introducing the subject in broad, conceptual terms. Eschewing the popular, rather narrow view of acceleration as a process of hurrying bright children, the first section considers a more fundamental, more human sense of the word as simply referring to the freedom children need to grow, learn, and be themselves. The purpose of this section is to expand readers' ideas on how acceleration can be applied to the classroom and to a wide variety of gifted learners. It is a departure from the lock-step idea of acceleration, where a child advances at a faster pace and higher level but still remains in a linear mode of learning. To be effective, acceleration needs to be "differentiated," needs to incorporate creativity in essential ways, and needs to allow teachers the freedom to discover the strategies that work best for their particular students. The section concludes with the critical role that assessment plays in determining how gifted learners are benefiting from acceleration and what changes are needed for the future.

Part II (Appropriate Academic-Classroom Acceleration by Sally Y. Walker) is an in-depth focus on the "meat" of learning. The section creates a clear picture of what a fully implemented acceleration program might look like, in which all the key elements (curriculum content, thinking processes, student products, learning standards, and district policies) cohere in such a way as to continually reinforce learning goals. The chapters describe in detail how to build higher levels of complexity and a faster pace into units of study, how to identify and incorporate essential concepts and questions that ignite the imaginations of gifted children, and how to stimulate discovery and creative invention. Through examples, this section clearly demonstrates how teachers can plan activities and assigned work that conforms to the goals of accelerated learning. The concluding chapter takes up the subject of district learning standards and policies that seem to run counter to the objectives of accelerated instruction. It provides practical guidance on how teachers can integrate these standards into their accelerated programs and also discusses the urgent need for advocacy as the only way that districts will support a strong policy in support of acceleration for gifted children.

Part III (Social and Emotional Aspects of Effective Acceleration by Elizabeth A. Meckstroth) clearly shows that once placed in an accelerated program, gifted students require specific kinds of support in the emotional, social, and even spiritual realms. Cut loose from the restrictions that used to keep them down in the regular classroom, gifted students in an accelerated program are sometimes at a loss about how to set reasonable goals for themselves; cope with anxiety and sensitivity to evaluation (their own as well as others'); address perfectionism, over-achievement, and low self-esteem; and manage the pressure or tension they may feel in a more challenging academic setting. The chapters are full of penetrating insights into the vast internal landscape of gifted students and how accelerated learning affects and is affected by perfectionism, intensity, difficulties with peers and friends, acute sensitivities, profound intuitive awareness, and complex moral and spiritual sensibilities.

The Part's (and book's) concluding focus on parent and teacher advocacy is particularly apt, given that accelerating gifted children often involves chipping away at the internal and external barriers to their freedom. This demands becoming more acutely aware of biases about giftedness and acceleration and taking a more active role in creating viable alternatives for high-ability learners. It is in advocating for a child that the child herself learns to take up the work and seek, as she must do later in life, the freedom to grow and learn in her own way. Perhaps the most critical aspect of advocacy is nurturing and honoring a child's moral and spiritual development, for in that domain lies the possibility of strength and resiliency in the face of disappointment as well as kindness and compassion toward one's fellow beings.

It is our hope that *Acceleration for Gifted Learners, K–5* will raise the bar on accelerated learning and inspire action that goes beyond minimum proficiency to the joy of discovery and an awakening to new possibilities. The three Parts of this book demonstrate the necessity for acceleration in all areas of a gifted child's life. The aim of the book is to offer a richer definition of accelerated learning and address how children process and apply new concepts when they're engaged and inspired. It is our hope that it has succeeded in offering the guidance that teachers, administrators, and families need to find workable solutions for the gifted children before them.

By sharing the lives of so many gifted children, readers cannot help but be struck by the fact that perhaps the most compelling reason for acceleration is that it is simply the most humane thing to do. And being humane surely must rank among the most important qualities of any educational system. Without acceleration, gifted children live like caged birds, imprisoned by attitudes, policies, and practices that won't allow them to be themselves. Emerson's statement, "No bird flies too high if he soars with his own wings," captures the spirit and substance of this book and its cherished desire to release the potential within every child.

In the poem below, a gifted student from Chicago cries for the freedom that so many children like him fear may not be, but hope will some day come:

Standing, standing
is where I stand.
Sitting, sitting,
I think I'm lost.
There, there
is far away.
Walking, walking,
toward my goal.
My life, life,
I grasp, I hold.
Running, running,
far away.
I've got to get
away from here.
Hoping, hoping,
for a new day.
I always want, want,
what I can't have.
Asking, asking,
for what will never come.
I cry, cry,
to my pillow at night.
Choke, choking.
I'm sorry.
I got nervous.
Finally, finally,
windows have to show me
that the sky is still clear.

—Jarrel, Grade 7

PART I

Acceleration

Issues and Applications
for Gifted Learners (K–5)

Acceleration and the K–5 Gifted Child

WHAT IS REALLY MEANT BY ACCELERATION?

The word *acceleration* conjures up images of velocity: a prize-winning horse gathering his strength to fly across the finish line, or the hands of a concert pianist executing arpeggios in a blur of breathtaking speed. In the context of school districts, acceleration is generally thought of as the process of moving gifted students through a curriculum at rates faster than are typical for their grade or age level. This concept is at the root of concerns among some administrators and teachers that acceleration tends to *hurry* children, potentially harming their natural development (Southern, Jones, & Fiscus, 1989).

Yet to the gifted children themselves, the experience feels less like hurrying and more like the curriculum has caught up with them. A second grader who reads the Harry Potter books and asks her teacher about multiplying fractions could not possibly be advancing at her natural pace if she has to do the work of peers who can hardly read, add, or subtract. A third grader investigating the impact of an invasive plant species on the local ecosystem will undoubtedly struggle in a class where he must submit to much more basic science instruction.

Consider these comments made by three gifted students recently moved into accelerated programs.

"I feel like what I do in school is more like what I do at home."

—third grader

"I'm in my stride now."

—fifth grader

"I don't have to 'sneak read' anymore. There's something for me to learn all day!"
—second grader

So what is actually being accelerated? Not the children themselves, by their own account, but the curriculum. Author David Elkind, noted for his book *The Hurried Child* (2001), made this clear distinction with regard to accelerating the gifted.

In fact, acceleration is really the wrong word here. If it were correct we would have to say that a child who was retained was "decelerated." When an intellectually gifted child is promoted one or several grades, what has been accelerated? Surely not the child's level of intellectual development—that, after all, is the reason for his or her promotion! What has been accelerated is the child's progress through the school curriculum. But this can be looked at a different way, not so much as acceleration as *tailoring*. What promotion does for intellectually gifted children is to make a better fit between the child's level of intellectual development and the curriculum. . . . Promotion of intellectually gifted children is simply another way of attempting to match the curriculum to the child's abilities, not to accelerate those abilities. (Elkind, 1988a, p. 2)

John Feldhusen (1989) made a similar point: "Acceleration is a misnomer; the process is really one of bringing gifted and talented youth up to a suitable level of instruction commensurate with their achievement levels and readiness so that they are properly challenged to learn the new material" (p. 8). Acceleration, therefore, is not as much a process of applying pressure as it is one of removing restraints, restoring *their natural pace and level of learning*. The goal is to tailor the level and complexity of the curriculum to the ability and academic readiness of individual children (Colangelo et al., 2004, p. 53).

The meaning of acceleration, then, has more to do with *tailoring* and *matching* than speeding or hurrying. This includes responding to the smaller tempos and rhythms of gifted learners as they shift and change within and across activities and subject areas. A student's pace may quicken while reading a story, slow down while designing an art project, and leap and halt while exploring the ecological features of a local river. Teachers should assume that the learning needs of accelerated students will change as they advance and require either an adjustment in pace or a break in the routine of a class (by doing an in-depth project, for example). Staying focused on the evolving abilities, interests, difficulties, and learning styles of the child prevents teachers from slipping into a lock-step approach to acceleration.

IS ACCELERATION NEEDED AMONG YOUNG GIFTED CHILDREN?

Is acceleration needed among young gifted children? Yes, it is. Research has long established acceleration as the most effective way to educate gifted students of all ages (Benbow, 1991; Gallagher, 1969; Kulik & Kulik, 1984; Reynolds, Birch, & Tuseth, 1962; Southern & Jones, 1991a; VanTassel-Baska, 1986). Some educators in the field resist acceleration for younger students because they associate it with the pushed-down curriculum of the mid-1980s, when an increasing number of students were failing to assimilate content previously taught at higher grades (Morrison, 1995, p. 303). The position papers on *developmentally appropriate instruction* (disseminated by the National Association for the Education of Young Children [NAEYC] to address this problem) have led some teachers to question the wisdom of acceleration, particularly in the primary grades. In addition, constructivist theory, which emphasizes the need for young students to discover and structure concepts in their own way, can sometimes prevent gifted children from acquiring new content more quickly in a teacher-directed format (Agne, 2001).

Yet, as Bredekamp (1987) points out, the NAEYC documents clearly show that developmentally appropriate instruction means both *age-appropriate* and *individually appropriate*. Hence, even in the youngest grades, teachers need to recognize giftedness when they see it and not generalize about a child's cognitive development because of preconceptions based on age.

Despite studies clearly showing the detrimental effects of holding gifted students back (Colangelo et al., 2004; Southern & Jones, 1991a; Stanley, 1979), few teachers understand the real harm of a weak or nonexistent policy on accelerated instruction. Young gifted students, so impressionable and responsive to outside influences, experience repeated obstacles to their *natural* impulse to inquire, investigate, and explore. Meeting a wall of resistance for the first four or five years of school causes many of these children to settle into a pattern of underachievement.

The following is the true story of a remarkable young man who faced considerable difficulties later in life as a result of early neglect.

> At the time Steve was attending school, his town was focusing most of its attention on providing special services to impoverished and new immigrant

children. Steve was a quiet boy, fascinated by science and in love with creative writing. By third grade, his mother said, he had written a novel and filled two notebooks with journal notes on botany and astronomy. In school, he scored at the top of his class and teachers placed him in the fast group in a few subjects, where he quickly mastered more advanced material. On the surface, he seemed a happy, well-adjusted child.

Later in his life, however, things fell apart. Before the end of his first year at Columbia, he dropped out. His mother said he was shocked by the demands of his coursework and the abilities of his high-achieving peers. He felt inadequate for the first time in his life. He eventually earned a B.A. but had to attend the university part time and required a great deal of assistance to get through.

Although Steve is now pursuing advanced degrees in science, his parents often express regret that they didn't realize how easy achievement for all those years was damaging their highly gifted son. "He had incredibly unrealistic expectations—that if a task was even slightly difficult, there must be something wrong with *him.* He just never seemed like a kid who would ever have a problem like this." Steve needed better organizational skills and research skills in addition to counseling and emotional support. He didn't learn much of this in school because he slacked off and ignored whatever bored him. Since he could still pull an "A" out of his hat with little effort, there was no incentive to learn anything that didn't interest him.

What Steve's parents learned is that *not* intervening in the life of a gifted child from the earliest years is an intervention in itself. Steve did join the most advanced groups in reading, math, and science when these were offered and relished an after-school scholars' program for students interested in science. But these opportunities provided only minimal challenges. Steve quickly assimilated the more advanced content and, as before, settled into a familiar routine of letting his mind wander while the other students caught up. Ultimately, Steve learned to adjust to the slow pace. For him, boredom became a cue to return to imagining a new cast of characters for stories he would write later.

"I just assumed this was how school was, and so it never occurred to me to talk to anyone about it. So I would just bring stuff from home to work on during those times I knew I'd have nothing to do. I had a notebook for writing, a sketch pad to draw characters, monsters and aliens, environments, plot ideas, and so on."

When asked if this really fulfilled him, he replied, "Not really. I remember wanting to learn trigonometry in fourth grade, and my older cousin taught me some, and I couldn't get enough of it. I can remember being sad that I would have to wait for years to really study it. What I think now is that if I'd been challenged in any of my classes, I could've been more prepared later. Columbia had a lot of kids from private schools, and they were really advanced and I just freaked."

Gifted children from underserved populations often suffer the same neglect, but for other reasons. A gifted bilingual student wants to do more advanced work, but her broken English and the fear of losing a treasured connectedness with her own community holds her back. An exceptional child from a broken home yearns to be noticed, but life hardships and weak skills in some content areas make him a "diamond in the rough" (Baldwin, 2003, p. 90). A third-grade gifted child with a disability can explain the chemical properties of different soils and the physics of flight, yet she struggles to write a paragraph. It is unlikely that these gifted children will be accelerated because most schools feel pressured to address perceived deficits in their students and improve skills.

> Darrel changed schools three times from the beginning of kindergarten to the end of first grade. With little exposure to reading or to books in general, Darrel refuses to try reading at all.

> Sandi, a fourth grader, moved to Chicago from a rural area. Though considered gifted in her former school, Sandi has trouble concentrating in class and tells her mother that "everyone's mean in this school."

> Debra lives with her father, a shopkeeper, in a low-income neighborhood. A third grader, she frequently worries about her father and the shop. Sometimes her teacher finds her dozing off in class.

Will these children be accelerated, given more advanced learning opportunities, and strengthened in the areas in which they are weak or vulnerable? Or will their gifts be swallowed up by a relentless focus on deficits and difficulties? Will their teachers discover that Darrel has created 25 original stories in rap, that Sandi has a sketchbook identifying dozens of native plants in Illinois, or that Debra helps her aunt do the accounts for her father's shop? Consider the life of Tammy Debbins, a gifted first grader from the projects, whose school never saw her ability and whose greatest frustration in high school and beyond was that she wasn't "very smart" (Torrance, 1980, p. 152). If acceleration doesn't begin early in the life of gifted children—whatever their ethnic, socioeconomic, or cultural backgrounds—they are at risk of losing their way before they've had a chance to start.

Common difficulties that young gifted children have when *not* accelerated include the following:

- **Early underachievement.** Locked into a curriculum where they must repeat what they already know, gifted children can only underachieve. While they appear like achievers on the surface, inside they are stifling their gifts.

- **Loss of interest and joy.** It is in the critical early primary years that gifted children feel their natural curiosity and energy for learning ebb away as the walls of the curriculum close in.

- **Low self-esteem.** Sensitive and impressionable, they begin to look upon their gifts as "wrong" and to doubt their worth in deeper, more fundamental ways.

- **Social isolation.** Kept apart from other young gifted children, high-ability students often feel isolated and alone. Seeing no others like them, they assume the role of class oddities.

- **Behavior problems.** Some young children feel so disgusted with school that they channel their abilities toward disrupting the class or withdrawing into their own world.

- **Poor coping skills.** Prolonged underachievement in young gifted learners almost guarantees diminished expectations and an inability to cope with new academic or creative challenges, especially later in their lives.

- **Avoidance of opportunity.** One of the saddest results of an early education that doesn't accelerate the gifted is the tendency among some children to avoid more challenging or risky work in order to secure their customary "A" grade.

Contrary to popular belief, holding gifted students to the regular curriculum *is* an intervention; it acts on their lives, confining and inhibiting natural development. The greatest danger for gifted children with no opportunity to learn is that they will accommodate themselves to a lifetime of waiting. An act of self-sabotage, prolonged underachievement has a soul-numbing effect on their growth as human beings.

WHAT LEARNING OPTIONS EXIST FOR ACCELERATING K–5 GIFTED STUDENTS?

In kindergarten through the fifth grade, schools may offer a number of strategies within two general categories: grade skipping (one or more grades) and changes within specific subjects to create a better match for a child's ability and needs. It's important to note that these are not mutually exclusive. Two second-grade students may move up to the fourth grade and halfway through the year may need more advanced instruction in language arts and mathematics. Similarly, students who attend schools that don't grade skip or those who might be harmed by such a radical move also need alternatives—for example, a cluster group with a more accelerated curriculum, a mentorship that provides challenging projects within specific subjects, or a series of Internet courses.

Options for accelerating gifted students have existed for a long time (Davis & Rimm, 1988; Gallagher, 1985; Kitano & Kirby, 1986; Passow, Goldberg, Tannenbaum, & French, 1955; Southern & Jones, 1991a). What follows is a list of the more common practices in kindergarten through fifth grade.

Skipping Grades

- **Early admission to kindergarten.** Children who are academically and emotionally ready can begin their formal schooling at a chronological age younger than the minimum age stipulated by district or state policy. It is designed for the four-year-old who would benefit from entering school up to one year earlier than normal.

- **Early admission to first grade.** This option allows qualified children to skip kindergarten and enter first grade. Parents are frequently the ones who put this option in motion due to concerns that their child will be misplaced in kindergarten. Their advocacy—in the form of standardized testing (through an independent psychologist), a portfolio of their child's work from home, and the possible use of the Iowa Acceleration Scale (see page 12, How Is the Appropriate Form of Acceleration Determined?) in their communications with the school—will often determine whether their child can attend first grade.

- **Further grade skips.** Some gifted students—particularly highly gifted—require more than one grade skip. Though these students are a minority within the gifted population, it is as important for teachers to be aware of their unique needs as it is to understand those of children with severe disabilities. As exceptionally gifted children acclimate to the new grade, they often surpass that level quickly and then struggle with the slow pace that they experienced before. Teachers, parents, and administrators need to maintain a watchful eye on these students to ensure that they're learning at an appropriate pace.

Content Acceleration

Providing content that matches the abilities and unique learning needs of young gifted students is critical both for those children who've skipped grades and those who have not. Content acceleration ensures that (1) all gifted students can advance at their own pace and level, particularly in the areas in which they have special abilities, and (2) underserved gifted populations have equal opportunities to experience and develop their special abilities. For gifted students who do not test well, content acceleration is a lifeline.

- **Continuous progress.** As she or he masters content, the child advances to new content. Continuous progress does not automatically result in accelerated study, but the format allows gifted children who learn more quickly than peers to advance at a faster pace.

- **Self-paced instruction.** With self-paced instruction, the child essentially determines the pace of learning in an assignment or project. Gifted children need some opportunities for learning situations in which they are not adjusting themselves to the pace requirements of a teacher or an assignment. This encourages them to own the learning process. At the same time, gifted students require some kind of contract and guidelines (mutually agreed upon) to support them in determining how much time they should spend on each facet of their work.

- **Subject matter acceleration.** This may take a number of forms. A third grader may leave his classroom for math and language arts in a fifth-grade classroom. Or he may use fifth-grade-level materials and assignments (determined by the teacher with some input from him) to pursue advanced study in a "continuous progress" format or do an independent study with a mentor. He may also undertake higher-grade content in an afterschool or summer intensive program. Fast-paced math and science classes in the model pioneered by Julian Stanley (1979) are an example of this.

- **Combined classes.** Like "continuous progress," combined classes do not automatically translate into acceleration, but they provide the environment for it to happen. For example, a third/fourth-grade split room allows gifted third graders to work with fourth graders both academically and socially. This option can, in some instances, result in a grade skip later.

- **Curriculum compacting.** A now-familiar strategy for differentiating the curriculum, curriculum compacting often begins with preassessment to determine the child's level of mastery in a subject or unit (assessment may mean a simple pretest in a skill area or a more extensive evaluation of the child's abilities through observation, consultation with parents, and review of a child's portfolio). In curriculum compacting, gifted children essentially buy back time for themselves by learning the "required" content more quickly and eliminating what they already know. With the time they gain, they either advance to more challenging content sequentially or divert from the path to investigate a related issue or idea. The teacher works with the students to establish specific goals, a timeline, and conditions for satisfactory completion of their work.

• **Accelerated grouping.** Grouping gifted students together results in clear benefits in both the social/emotional and academic areas (Kulik & Kulik, 1987). This may take the form of a cluster group that pools advanced students from more than one class in a grade. Or it may involve a smaller group of gifted and/or highly motivated students who come together to study a particular subject, culminating in a project.

• **Telescoping curriculum.** Telescoping has the same principle as curriculum compacting except that this option results in an advanced grade placement. For example, a child or a group of children complete three years of primary school in two. The time saved does not lead to more advanced work in a subject or alternative projects determined by the teacher and student, but to placement in a higher grade. At the college level, a similar principle is operating in summer intensive language programs where students learn the first year of French in 10 weeks.

• **Mentoring.** A gifted child works with a mentor, ideally someone with special expertise, who can provide a much more advanced and rapid pace of instruction in a particular area of interest. This option has proven helpful for highly gifted students who cannot always gain the stimulation they need from the school's accelerated program options. A fourth grader who writes like a high school or college student can advance his ability far more by working one-on-one with an author who can give him the expert feedback and support he needs. A fifth grader with a passion for South American reptiles will blossom under the tutelage of a researcher who has spent time in the rainforests of Costa Rica. Mentors lift the ceiling off a child's achievement and can afford to be more responsive to the child's learning styles and needs. (See Chapter 2 for more information.)

• **Extracurricular programs.** Students can enroll in courses or workshops that take place in afterschool or summer programs. These programs offer advanced level content and, possibly, intensive telescoped curriculum. Offerings vary considerably. A highly gifted fifth grader may take a language class at a university extension program. An enterprising second grader may participate in an ecology summer workshop for older students.

• **Correspondence/Internet courses.** A gifted child enrolls in a course either through the mail (which could include videotapes or audiotapes) or, more commonly today, through the Internet. A number of sites offer advanced course work for gifted students (Kanuka, 2005). Sometimes, a small group of gifted students can work together in an online course.

HOW IS THE APPROPRIATE FORM OF ACCELERATION DETERMINED?

Finding the right fit for accelerating a student can only come from *knowing the child*. In some instances, testing presents the best approach. Julian Stanley's (1978) DT-PI approach (Diagnostic Testing followed by Prescriptive Instruction) has benefited mathematically gifted children (Benbow & Stanley, 1983; VanTassel-Baska, 1996). Variations have developed from Stanley's approach, but in essence it follows this sequence: (1) assess a student to determine the extent of the student's knowledge and understanding; (2) design a program to meet specific learning needs, as revealed in the assessment (preferably in the context of a cluster group); and (3) reassess the student to evaluate growth and mastery. The child moves on to a more advanced level as she masters new content.

Though evaluations often involve some form of testing, they should include other sources of information on a child's academic growth, learning preferences, interests, and special talents. In the early primary grades, testing presents special problems. In the first place, young gifted students often develop in uneven ways. A first-grade child may read books at a fifth-grade level but have poor hand-eye coordination; a kindergartner may demonstrate advanced ability and knowledge in math but become fatigued and distracted in an accelerated second-grade math group. Young gifted children who lack experience with tests may score poorly or at least signifi-cantly below their real potential. This happened to a five-year-old named Mario.

> At age five, Mario was a complex thinker. . . . However, he didn't perform well on standardized tests. . . . In many instances, the choices on the paper seemed too simplistic. At other times, Mario read more into the question than the test maker had intended, so his responses were frequently "wrong." One test question asked, "What is the color of coal?" The choices were black, pur-ple, or gray. Mario marked all three. When the examiner asked him why, he responded, "It's black when I see it inside, it's purple when I see it in the sun, and after it's burned it's gray." (Smutny, Walker, & Meckstroth, 1997, p. 124)

Most educators today understand that even though standardized tests provide useful insight in a number of cases, they are usually an underestimation of what young gifted children can do. For this reason, more schools today seek additional sources of information (work samples, observations, informal talks with the child, parent anecdotes, portfolios of the child's work, etc.) to create a more complete picture of strengths and needs. In this regard, the Kingore Observation Inventory (Kingore, 1990) is an excellent tool for structuring classroom observations of children through analyzing categories of gifted behaviors. For early primary children, con-sultations with parents are also key to discovering hidden abilities, as families have not only stories to tell but evidence in the form of writing, sketching, inventions, books they read, experiments they conducted, and so forth.

Consider how these schools determined the appropriate responses to the fol-lowing gifted children.

> When Lira entered kindergarten, she was reading at the third-grade level and knew how to add, subtract, multiply, and divide. At the same time, Lira felt shaky about being away from home because her family had moved twice in the last two years. Reviewing Lira's test scores, projects, teacher observa-tions, and parental anecdotes and consulting with Lira herself, the school decided to postpone skipping her to a higher grade. However, after several months, Lira was able to leave her kindergarten class for advanced lan-guage arts and math instruction (with a group of gifted children in first

grade). She began to make friends with the older students. During the summer, preparations began to grade-skip Lira to the second grade.

Third-grade Keesha moved from a low-income urban environment to live with her aunt and uncle in a small town. She was significantly behind her grade because of conditions in her former school. Based on achievement tests and assessment of skill level, the school decided that she should repeat her grade. Since Keesha had been the smartest child in her former school, this was a serious blow to her self-esteem. The aunt campaigned for the possibility of the child skipping to the next grade halfway through the year based on evidence of her quick rate of learning. The teacher observed and documented Keesha's exceptional progress during the first month and made plans to telescope the third-grade curriculum. The possibility of this has greatly motivated the child.

Jaime is a highly gifted and highly creative fourth grader who wants to become a poet. His teacher said he routinely reads high school-level books, but his test scores don't show this ability. Both his parents and teacher believe he needs some kind of acceleration, but Jaime is nervous about being in a program with "serious brainy types." Jaime has agreed to try doing language arts with a cluster of gifted children in the sixth grade and is overjoyed that this will involve creative writing. At the same time, his teacher is compacting the math and science curriculum to give him more time to research specific topics in ecology. At present, Jaime feels comfortable with this arrangement.

In all three of these cases, the schools drew from the rich tapestry of the children's lives—their feelings, thoughts about proposed changes, feedback from family members, and demonstrated rate of achievement—to create a better match between ability and learning program. While the schools may or may not grade-skip these gifted students, they can still adjust the children's educational program to accommodate their learning pace. They can implement an assess-teach-reassess approach (similar to Julian Stanley's DT-PI) to guide advanced instruction in math or science and use portfolios of a child's writing to arrange for a gifted child to join a cluster group in a higher grade for language arts.

Obviously, the most radical form of acceleration (advancement to another grade) requires the most thorough assessment of the whole child. When a fourth-grade teacher looks at his enthusiastic inventor with an IQ of 140 and wonders how well she or he would fare in fifth or sixth grade, he needs to consider a number of factors:

- High intellectual ability
- Academic skill levels above the mean of the new grade
- Social and emotional maturity
- High motivation and task commitment
- Good physical health and a physical size that fits in with the new grade
- Supportive parents
- Enthusiastic and willing teacher
- Open-ended, trial basis for the change
- Availability of monitoring and counseling during transition (Benbow, 1991; VanTassel-Baska, 1986)

Parents, teachers, and administrators who need a counseling tool for evaluating the feasibility of a particular learning option can use the Iowa Acceleration Scale

(IAS; Assouline, Colangelo, Lupkowski-Shoplik, Lipscomb, & Forstadt, 2003). The IAS is designed to aid educators and parents in making informed decisions about grade skipping and content acceleration. It includes a comprehensive summary of all of the relevant research on acceleration and information on appropriate aptitude and achievement tests for gifted children in different age groups.

Items receive a numeric value, making scoring easy. These scores result in categories that serve as rational guidelines for decision making, discussion, and planning. The form includes several sections for gathering information that will help determine whether whole-grade acceleration or other accommodations are most appropriate for a particular student. The sections include general information, critical items, school history, prior ability and achievement test results, prior professional evaluations, academic ability and achievement, school and academic factors, developmental factors, interpersonal skills, attitude and support, and a summary and planning sheet.

The IAS is an excellent tool for facilitating communication between parents and educators. The scale addresses the most critical aspects of the child's life and translates the data into numbers that teachers and administrators can understand and appreciate. In cases reported by parents to us, the IAS has been a deciding factor. Schools that might have been closed to moving a child to another grade now have an instrument that considers all aspects of the child in a responsible and systematic way.

An enduring question for the future is how schools can provide advanced coursework for gifted children who do not test well or who may have special challenges, including underserved gifted students (e.g., bilingual students, urban/rural poor, multicultural, twice-exceptional, highly creative). How do teachers and administrators respond to a request from a parent whose fourth-grade child is timid and excessively nervous in testing situations and therefore never scores well, despite her exceptional gift in mathematics? What can be done for a precocious kindergartner who reads *Wind in the Willows* and writes poetry in an Emily Dickinson style but is inconsistent and disorganized in the way she does assigned work?

In most cases, a gifted child who tests at an average or slightly above-average level will not be a candidate for grade skipping. Likewise, questions about the child's emotional maturity, high achievement in knowledge and skill areas, and even concerns about his or her physical size may hinder this process. The opposition to grade skipping is such that without clear evidence and documentation in all of these areas, many school officials feel leery of creating what they see as a drastic change for a young child. A four-year-old child who tells his mother that he "can see the world 100 years from now" and wonders what things people in the future might find from his life on Earth is probably gifted, but he may not need to begin school early. A second-grade painter who immerses herself in books about Van Gogh and comes home from school saying, "The teacher didn't like my painting, but I won't cut off my ear," may benefit more from advancement to a higher grade or from an interdisciplinary language arts program for gifted learners. The point is that many gifted children, regardless of their background, learning styles, and interests, need some form of acceleration. Consider these alternatives.

A Gifted Third-Grade Bilingual Student in an Urban School. At present, the school is reluctant to skip the child to the fourth grade. The third- and fourth-grade teachers work out an arrangement where the latter sends students needing extra help to the third grade and the former sends her gifted students to the fourth grade.

The gifted bilingual student goes to the fourth grade for language arts and math. The fourth-grade teacher uses a curriculum from a gifted academy as a guide for further acceleration.

Highly Gifted First Grader With Exceptional Artistic Talent. The first grader's test results are inconsistent and the school psychologist is concerned about the child's emotional maturity. Her teacher compacts the math curriculum and a gifted coordinator mentors her and two other students in more advanced concepts and skills. For language arts, she joins a cluster group in the second-grade classroom that enables her to read at her ability level, write stories and poems, and create illustrations.

A Gifted Fourth Grader in a Rural Area. With little understanding of acceleration, the school sees no reason to consider advancing the child to fifth grade. Yet his teacher compacts the curriculum in mathematics and also provides advanced instruction in language arts and social studies to several students through courses available on the Internet. The fourth grader also attends a special summer program for gifted math students at a college 20 miles away.

More often than not, the children themselves will tell us—through their achievements, enthusiasm, creative and innovative products, motivation, interests, and so forth—what form of acceleration will best meet their needs, when it should change, and how. Throughout the process, gifted children discover their own learning rhythms, and as they grow, they need new and different opportunities—more interdisciplinary study; course work that focuses on innovation and invention; time to explore the creative, the intuitive, the artistic. Gifted children not only learn more quickly than most students their age, but through a rich variety of ways and means. Accelerated programs, therefore, must address both their rate of learning and the depth and breadth of their thinking.

HOW DO SCHOOLS ENSURE THAT ACCELERATION IS WORKING?

In those instances in which acceleration has failed to benefit a gifted child, most likely the adults did not take all of the steps necessary to ensure an appropriate fit between the child and the acceleration program. From our own experience as well as from the findings of other researchers, we offer the following guidelines for ensuring that accelerative learning options work for the gifted child in question.

- **The child is consulted at each step.** This may seem obvious, but it is remarkable how few schools consider consulting gifted children regarding decisions that involve significant changes to their lives. Input from the students—gathered at different times and in different contexts (for young children this is particularly important)—can be critical in making decisions about which forms of acceleration will best serve their needs and in making ongoing adjustments.

- **The guidelines for acceleration are clear to all parties.** Acceleration requires clear guidelines for its implementation. Children need to know what they should expect and what will be expected of them. All of the adults involved—from parents to teachers to administrators—have to know what their areas of responsibility and accountability are and procedures they should follow when any problems arise. Obviously, guidelines emerge from the form of acceleration adopted. They should include underlying principles, goals and objectives, strategies for implementation and ongoing assessment, and strategies for establishing the lines of communication among all parties involved.

- **The guidelines are implemented correctly.** If schools don't implement the guidelines correctly, acceleration will fail to benefit gifted children. For example, if a child skips a grade and guidelines stipulate that the child should receive further content acceleration in his or her new grade, and this doesn't happen, then the grade skip is only a partial success. Or, if a new child joins a cluster group for gifted students but exceeds the level of that group, and the teacher does not assess the new student's level of expertise, the teacher has not followed the guidelines for accelerating that child.

- **The teacher's attitude is positive.** When a team is considering a grade skip for a child, they need to ensure that the receiving teacher is receptive and positive about providing for a gifted child. Likewise, a child qualified for content acceleration requires a teacher willing and able to implement it.

- **The teacher has knowledge in the area of gifted education.** Ideally, the teacher should have some understanding of gifted education. Many educators lack the expertise because teacher certification doesn't require course work in gifted education. However, widespread exposure to differentiation throughout the field has given many teachers experience in identifying students with special needs and making appropriate adjustments to the curriculum. Parents have also played an important role by sharing information from their own research and experience and by collaborating with teachers to create viable learning options for their children.

- **The level of giftedness matches the degree of acceleration.** A common error in acceleration occurs when a school assumes, once a change has been made (whether in the form of a grade skip or content acceleration), that the job is done and requires no further action. All gifted students, particularly highly gifted, require further adjustments as the months pass and they continue to progress at a rapid rate. Otherwise, they begin to face the same frustrations that they had before they began an accelerated program. Too often, schools assume that since a child has joined a cluster group in the fourth grade or has skipped from first to third grade, he or she is learning at his or her own pace and level of difficulty. Parents, teachers, and administrators need policies to ensure that "accelerated" children are, in fact, working at a pace commensurate with their ability, motivation, knowledge, and experience.

- **Proper monitoring and evaluation take place.** Ongoing supervision and assessment are critical in acceleration. Children who have negative experiences or drop out of a program option designed to meet the needs of gifted students were probably showing signs of difficulty all along. Parents and teachers should check in with children regularly, make them feel comfortable communicating their preferences and feelings about the change, monitor their work, and share information with each other on how they feel the program is working.

- **There is comprehensive assessment when a child has problems.** This would involve the child, child's teachers, the school psychologist or counselor, and parents and would also include evidence of his or her growth and progress (tests, assignments, projects, observation forms, anecdotes, etc.). Evaluation should focus on academic achievement, social/emotional well-being, and the development of passions and interests.

- **The acceleration process remains open and flexible.** This is one of the most important points. Despite all of the planning and preparation, a child should never feel locked into an accelerated learning program. Sometimes a gifted child, seeing all of the work that adults are doing on his behalf, will feel reluctant to speak up if he's dissatisfied or feels out of place. There is a balance to be maintained here. Once the adults and child make the best decision they can, given the circumstances, it's important to adopt a relaxed, "try and see" attitude. The child needs time to test the waters, breathe the air in his new situation, and participate fully in reaching a final decision.

Young children experience extraordinary cognitive growth, particularly from kindergarten to third grade, and acceleration must respond to this in a sensitive manner in order to be effective. A child whose grasp of mathematics seems to have suddenly advanced by a leap so that she or he wants nothing more than to focus on the wondrous world of numbers, ratios, and patterns will thrive most in the hands of a teacher who recognizes the change and responds accordingly. Teachers should assess the child's work continuously (whether through observation, testing, or work samples) in order to tailor instruction to the developing child.

WHY AREN'T THE SCHOOLS ACCELERATING YOUNG GIFTED STUDENTS?

Lack of information and philosophical bias are the main reasons why decades of research on acceleration as an effective practice for gifted students have not fostered new initiatives in the schools (Colangelo et al., 2004, pp. 6–9). Specifically, a teacher or parent who recognizes the need and wants to take action often faces the following hurdles:

- **Limited familiarity with the research on acceleration.** In other words, despite a plethora of research studies documenting the benefits and effectiveness of acceleration for the gifted, the schools have little understanding of how to translate it and little concern about the need to do so. Undoubtedly, this is due to a deeper resistance against any practice that would appear to disrupt the orderly progress of students from grade to grade and from one curriculum to the next.

- **Educational philosophy that students should be with their own age group.** Grade placement is a relatively recent phenomenon. Before World War II, it was not uncommon to have a mixture of ages in a single classroom. But schools today tend to hold to rigid views of child development and fail to recognize those whose development is out of synch with the "norm."

- **Concern that acceleration hurries students out of childhood.** This is the classic argument against the practice whenever a parent or teacher investigates the possibility. As mentioned previously, David Elkind's (1988a) comments on acceleration for the gifted are a useful rejoinder here, as he was the most eloquent voice against any practice that would hurry a child.

- **Fear that acceleration hurts children socially.** This is related to the previous concern. The argument goes that if the child skips a grade or attends a class with a higher grade, she or he will feel out of place and have problems making friends. Again, in the majority of cases, the accelerated child has an easier time socially and feels far more comfortable than with his or her own age group.

- **Political concerns about equity.** Equity is really about *equal access* to education, not about being equal in ability. A gifted child forced to twiddle thumbs while classmates learn is not getting equal access to education.

James Gallagher (2004) asserts that "it may be that what has to be changed is not written policy, but merely the attitudes of policy makers" (p. 40). In part, the problem may rest on a superficial sense of acceleration as the very frantic pace that drives us all to distraction. The very word *acceleration* presents, to many minds, images of haste and chaos. Changing the attitudes of policy makers, then, must entail a new way of conceptualizing acceleration—not as a frenzied, reckless pace but as a freedom to learn at a rate and level *natural for the child.*

In whatever form it takes, acceleration should be a *quickening* of the spirit as well as a challenge to the mind. To quicken is "to make alive, vitalize, excite, and stimulate" (American Heritage Dictionary, 1985). For students given a telescoped, hands-on math curriculum or advanced to a higher grade, the experience has an element of exhilaration and even joy. A mother once reported that after her kindergarten daughter was sent to second grade, she jumped into the car saying, "I'm free! I'm free!" A fourth-grade child who spent the year begging his father to teach him algebra finally gained admittance to a special math program and told his parents, "It's a blast sitting with a group of kids like me and figuring math stuff out together." Acceleration should be a "quickening," a vital call to life. It must honor the concepts of thriving, wholeness, and aliveness in the child.

That these students come to life in classrooms where they can move at their own speed and level is a compelling reason for all schools to champion the cause of acceleration. Undertaken responsibly and wisely, acceleration is an act of compassion. It is like taking a large animal confined to a small cage and letting it run with beasts its size and strength. If the creature has not become crippled or weakened by its confinement, it immediately moves—flies, charges, hops, leaps, whatever is in its nature to do.

As both Elkind (1988a) and Feldhusen (1989) have said, "acceleration" is a misnomer. Bearing in mind that a gifted child in the regular classroom is "decelerated," an accelerated option merely allows this child an opportunity to move at her own pace. What to some may appear a pressured, breakneck speed is completely normal to the child. The danger in losing sight of this fact is that we fail to recognize the child in our own classrooms who asks not to be "accelerated" but only for the opportunity to learn without hindrance. This is what the whole move to accelerate gifted children is about: the freedom to learn; freedom to move; freedom for children to be themselves, use their abilities, grow. And it always begins with the individual child whose wishes, aspirations, feelings, abilities, and sensibilities must be honored at each step.

2

Acceleration in a Differentiated Classroom

Let us consider a population of gifted children in a school district. Several have recently skipped a grade, a handful are bilingual and multicultural, one has a reading disability, some have kinetic learning styles, and all feel bored in school. One of the grade-skipped students pops out of her seat every 15 minutes with suggestions for other projects the students could do in an ecology unit. A gifted bilingual student shows his teacher a poem he wrote in Russian (during math class), accompanied by an English translation and delicately etched drawings in ink. A quick learner who struggles to write a coherent paragraph wins a scholarship to attend a special summer program in architectural design at a local college. All of these children attend regular classrooms, and all would benefit from some form of accelerated learning.

Undoubtedly, teachers who differentiate—who respond to the differences between students by adjusting the curriculum—can best manage this unique constellation of abilities (Gregory & Chapman, 2002; Smutny & von Fremd, 2004; Tomlinson, 1999). However, for gifted students, two key problems remain. The first is that a number of teachers who lack experience or training in gifted education tend to lump all gifted children together. Second, students who lack the easy-to-measure academic ability that shows up on tests and in class assignments often receive "enrichment" activities that may or may not include acceleration. A kinetically gifted student, for example, may have the opportunity to do a project on the engineering principles behind skyscrapers and relish building models, explaining them to peers, and going online to learn more, but on closer examination, this student may not be doing particularly advanced work. His interest and engagement are misleading. Though enjoying himself, he's more engaged than challenged. The fact that he needs to process ideas kinetically seems to bar him from the kind of intellectual rigor that his peers, who are linguistic learners, enjoy.

Despite these problems, differentiated instruction does provide the ideal context for accelerated learning to take place for all kinds of gifted students. *First, differentiation always begins with a careful consideration of the children—their unique abilities, talents, learning styles, experiences, and problems.* Who are these children *as people?* What special strengths do they bring to the learning table? What experiences and skills do they possess from the lives they've lived so far? What interests and passions urge them to seek new discoveries? Many teachers create useful profiles of their students that document not only ability, skill, and knowledge levels (as seen in tests, assignments, etc.), but also the likes, dislikes, interests, and special life experiences expressed in the classroom.

Second, in a differentiated curriculum, acceleration takes into account students' learning styles and strengths in various subject areas. It adapts to each student's unique ability, background, and level and depth of understanding. As explained in the previous chapter, the student himself doesn't accelerate his pace; rather, the curriculum responds to his natural pace. Ideally, the flexibility of a differentiated classroom ensures that a gifted child receives the appropriate kind of acceleration in all subject areas.

An energetic student ready for the complexities of advanced geometry may also be a highly kinetic learner, impatient with visual or verbal modes of instruction. How does acceleration work for this child if he takes math in a higher grade or participates in a cluster group of visual/spatial learners? In a differentiated classroom, a teacher can accommodate not only the student's high ability, but also his kinetic learning style. For example, this teacher can give the student sufficient opportunity to work with a variety of materials while digesting advanced math content, talking with other gifted students about his process, or exploring a problem through drama or mime. Such a child is able to move forward at a faster rate not only because the teacher responds to the child's hunger for more challenging mathematics, but because she offers it in the form the child needs.

Finally, teachers who differentiate assess students continuously and use a wide range of methods to do so. They attend to students' observations, discoveries, and descriptions of their own mental processes as they tackle an assignment. They examine students' tests—including behaviors, thinking ability, and answers. They note students' wry sense of humor, quick grasp of new information, penetrating questions, and rich and subtle expression of thought; they feel moved by students' philosophical musings in poems, stories, essays, and art compositions. The importance of ongoing assessment can't be overstated. One of the main reasons some gifted students stop learning in "accelerated" programs is that their teachers don't assess their growth and development regularly. A child who enters fourth grade from second grade may feel that she has found her niche for the first few months, but later in the year she is, once again, stuck in a slow pace. Students in a cluster group may be progressing significantly below their actual potential; the teacher doesn't notice the signs because the cluster appears accelerated in comparison to the rest of the class. A child from Tanzania may read several years ahead of his grade but write compositions full of colloquialisms from his native language. This child later may make significant strides in his writing, but if his teacher doesn't assess his progress, he may remain stuck in a learning program that doesn't respond to this change.

Because differentiation accommodates so many kinds of needs, it's difficult to gauge the extent to which it provides, in a systematic way, a higher pace and level of instruction for all students who need it. Do gifted students consistently advance at the level of their ability? Do high-ability children with unique learning styles and those from underserved populations have access to accelerated learning opportunities? Do those who achieve a new level of difficulty and challenge advance to the next level? Are creatively oriented students seen as candidates for "enrichment" rather than acceleration? Do children with special learning difficulties (due to poor work habits, cultural differences, disabilities, etc.) spend more time addressing their challenges than their strengths? The only way for teachers to know the answer to these questions is by evaluating—on an ongoing basis—the match between a particular gifted student and his program of learning.

Knowing the learning preferences of gifted students certainly helps teachers to tailor accelerated content to each individual's needs and abilities. Howard Gardner's (1993) work on multiple intelligences has provided helpful insight into the different modalities of the human intellect and how it processes new concepts. While visiting a class today, one might find an auditorily gifted child who loves to discuss a subject or idea before launching into her essay on the migration of raptors in North America; a more visually gifted student would be less interested in discussion. A kinetic learner researching the course of four planets learns the most when he translates his research by staging their movements over the course of the year.

Other factors, such as cognitive style and group orientation, also influence how gifted children learn and what adjustments they might need. Below are some examples (Smutny & von Fremd, 2004, p. 73).

Creative/Conforming

1. Ali is academically and creatively gifted. When he listens to an assignment from his teacher, he cannot help thinking of alternative ways of thinking about and executing it.

2. Nika is more academically gifted and feels uncomfortable taking risks and dealing with ambiguity; she asks questions to make sure she understands what the teacher wants, and she tries her best to follow directions.

Whole to Part/Part to Whole

1. Like many gifted students, Ben prefers knowing the forest before he learns about the trees. In a class introducing geometry, Ben wants the big concepts first; then he likes to analyze the details on his own.

2. In some subjects, like science, Tanya likes encountering new phenomena—especially among flora and fauna—*without* having the whole picture in her mind and then exploring the larger issues, questions, and patterns on her own.

Nonlinear/Linear

1. Jessica works best in an interdisciplinary mode. She thinks like an impressionist painting. The dots do have an order of their own, although it sometimes appears as if she is leaping from point to point. She finds it difficult to follow one line of thinking exclusively.

2. Harry loves to follow clean, precise sequences and resists stopping his train of thought to explore a relevant idea in another form or subject. He dislikes being interrupted and wants to follow one track to the end before expanding to include alternative fields or perspectives on his subject.

Inductive/Deductive

1. Jerry loves the process of solving a problem by looking at all of the pieces and logically constructing a solution or formula. He loves it when his math teacher gives his cluster group a challenge with numbers, for example, and leaves them to work it out (if they can) with materials they choose. If he knows the principle ahead of time, the mystery is gone.

2. Amanda becomes frustrated when she doesn't know the principle or process first. She has had little experience working inductively, so she prefers understanding a particular formula or process and then exploring through logic how to use it to solve specific problems.

Introvert/Extrovert

1. Neil is an affable, talkative gifted child who *loves* sharing ideas on how to go about doing projects and assignments. He always learns a lot from others in his group and benefits from articulating his approach to others who can question or challenge him.

2. Anna doesn't mind some paired activities, but even then, she prefers minimal interaction when she's working. She enjoys the companionship of other gifted students in the cluster group and has one or two friends in the group, but she prefers not to be in a position where she *has to interact*; she works best uninterrupted and on her own.

Differences in culture, family life, past experiences, and exposure to a variety of fields and knowledge also impinge on a child's orientation to learning in the classroom. Immigrant gifted children from very different schools and cultures come to U.S. classrooms with assumptions about what's expected of them and then discover either lower or quite different standards for achievement. A gifted child from a family of amateur naturalists who spends every summer and many weekends exploring wild places may have an understanding of natural science several years ahead of her class. These are all elements that need careful consideration as teachers weigh the best options for advancing high-ability students.

Differentiated classrooms help teachers provide accelerated learning for the gifted in three domains: *the environment* (which includes a range and variety of advanced resources), *specific teaching strategies and activities,* and *flexible grouping of students.* In this context, acceleration can assume a variety of forms and adjust to the changing needs of individual gifted students.

RESOURCES

Most teachers who differentiate prepare their classrooms to accommodate different levels of ability and styles of learning. They create flexible seating arrangements that ease movement from whole class to small group work, from simpler to more complex processes. They design learning centers that include materials for different learning styles, which are constantly modified, increased, or adjusted according to need; literary subjects that stimulate interest and inspire new ideas; spaces for independent study and quieter processes; and colorful and vivid displays of art, science, nature, and world communities. Teachers try to create an atmosphere in which learning feels like an adventure, all students feel respected and honored, and children can use their strengths and learning styles to advance at their own level and pace.

To Accelerate

In order to make the classroom a place where gifted students can accelerate throughout the year, teachers need to think carefully about resources. Ideally, they should represent both a range of ability and diverse learning styles and interests.

- **Human resources:** parents, teachers, specialists in the community (business leaders, artists, performers, engineers, ecologists)
- **Print:** books, magazines, stories, poems, essays, journals, crossword puzzles
- **Nonprint:** Internet, video, audio, art (paintings, sketches), maps, globes, posters (of historical figures, pioneers, explorers, inventions, discoveries, achievements), graphs

- **Natural:** plants, terrariums, bird nests, pressed flowers, shells, rocks, fossils, nature photography
- **Recycled materials:** cardboard boxes, egg cartons, bottles, bottle caps, newspaper
- **Primary sources:** interviews, firsthand descriptions, original photographs, letters, sketches

Consider these questions.

- Do the materials reflect the broad interests and learning styles of the students?
- Are the materials consistent with a student's advanced developmental level, experience, and knowledge?
- Do they prompt questions, inquiry, and a sense of wonder?
- Do the materials stimulate higher-level thinking in different subject areas?
- Do they inspire divergent production and self-expression?
- Do they enhance research skills and knowledge?
- Do they enhance the development of creativity?
- Do they embrace the qualities valued by gifted learners—beauty, form, shape, quality of material, level of craftsmanship, ingenuity of design?

An ongoing challenge faced by teachers today is the expense involved in acquiring good resources for gifted students. A 2002 marketing study reported that teachers in the United States spend approximately $400 per year from their own pockets on resources for their classrooms (Riley, 2005, p. 676). This figure would undoubtedly increase if they also supplied special resources for accelerating gifted students. However, there are free and inexpensive materials available that support the unique learning needs of the gifted. (See Riley, 2005, for a full treatment of this subject.) They include advanced content, are often interdisciplinary in nature, represent a wide variety of sources, are complex in the mental processes they stimulate, and are relevant to today's world.

TEACHING STRATEGIES

In a differentiated classroom, teachers use a variety of instructional strategies that specifically address the need for accelerated learning. Though not necessarily comprehensive in themselves, they provide the environment and structure for more effective arrangements.

Compacting

Compacting eliminates content children have already mastered and enables them to advance at a faster rate than their peers. The teacher assesses strengths and needs (through tests, assignments, projects) and then provides faster-paced, higher-level content, at the same time addressing gaps in knowledge and understanding shown by their work. What the students then do with the time gained from eliminating unnecessary content depends on many things—the interests of the students, the preferences of the teacher, the availability of resources, and so forth.

Teachers could move on to more advanced content in a curriculum, present a challenging assignment related to the unit, or work on a project of particular interest to the students.

To Accelerate

While compacting prevents a gifted child from having to repeat what he knows, it doesn't necessarily guarantee accelerated learning. After Thomas tests out of a unit, he may work on an art project one day. On another day, he may read a book as part of his research on chameleons, and on another day, pair up with a gifted child to finish an assignment related to number theory. While this kind of flexibility gives advanced learners opportunities for more challenging work and some freedom of choice, which they love, it has its shortcomings when carried too far. "Sometimes you can slip into a pattern," a third-grade teacher confided, "where you create these little side trips for the gifted kids who already know most of the unit, thinking that you're helping them. But all you're really doing is giving them something to do until the other kids catch up."

Certainly, no harm can come to gifted students who occasionally take up a special interest after compacting out of a particular unit in language arts, let us say, yet care needs to be taken not to neglect their accelerated pace of learning in language arts. Teachers need to consider other ways—possibly outside their classroom—for these students to develop their potential. This may include telescoping the year's curriculum, allowing a child to leave the classroom to take language arts at a higher grade, or allowing him to join a small group receiving special tutoring from a mentor. When confronting a child with exceptional ability, teachers need to think creatively about the best arrangement for advancing his or her gifts. This is particularly important for high-ability students from poor, minority, or multicultural backgrounds. Sometimes these children need a program that combines accelerated instruction with a plan to strengthen skill and knowledge areas.

Tiered Instruction

In tiered instruction, gifted students work within the same unit of study but at a level and pace appropriate for them. In a unit on the ecology of local forest preserves, for example, gifted students could research the introduction of the Asian Longhorned Beetle into the United States, analyze its impact on local flora and fauna, or evaluate current plans to eradicate it.

To Accelerate

Tiered instruction can accelerate learning through more advanced reading material and a greater academic demand (in terms of skill, thinking processes, and new concepts to be learned). Though frequently used in mixed ability classrooms, tiered instruction also applies to different academic levels within a group of gifted students. Advanced students working on a biography unit may read texts at different levels of difficulty and apply research techniques at different levels of sophistication. A highly gifted fourth grader may be able to create a multimedia display about William Shakespeare based upon her investigation of the great Bard's work and synthesis of her research and insight into some of his plays. Other gifted students could not do that. Tiered instruction is an excellent strategy for providing different learning pathways within a group of gifted students.

Mentorships

Because gifted students master content so quickly, they often develop particular interests that are either far in advance of the curriculum or diverge significantly from it. Mentorships can be ideal for these children, enabling them to accelerate their learning in subjects that mean the most to them (Nash, 2001). Highly gifted, culturally diverse, disadvantaged, gifted girls and other underserved populations experience noticeable growth from mentorships (Siegle & McCoach, 2005), which allow greater flexibility in adapting the pace, level, and type of content to individual strengths and interests.

To Accelerate

The key is to find mentors who enjoy working with gifted students; are sensitive to their special needs; and know how to provide appropriate content, activities, and resources to help them reach specific learning goals. A gifted fifth grader with links to a herpetologist at the local zoo may develop a series of projects that he pursues in the time he's gained by compacting the science curriculum. A gifted third grader may have a mentor relationship with an adjunct teacher in the school who telescopes the math curriculum, enabling her to take Algebra I in fourth grade. In both cases, accelerated learning is at work, though the former example is more divergent.

Teachers sometimes express misgivings about the difficulty of finding mentors capable of advancing gifted learners. If no one in the school district can assume the role, many find that they have to search in universities, businesses, art schools, and studios to discover individuals who can meet the demand and give a mentee the right kind and level of challenge. In this respect, *telementoring*—otherwise known as virtual mentoring or e-mentoring—has become a useful and more convenient alternative (Nash, 2001). Teachers can consult The National Mentoring Partnership (http://www.mentoring.org) for guidance on finding appropriate mentors and developing advanced course content. Telementoring as a strategy for acceleration has distinct advantages (Siegle & McCoach, 2005, pp. 483–484). A highly gifted fourth grader in a rural area can be matched with an appropriate mentor despite geographical distance and scheduling difficulties. Third-grade students at the sixth-grade level in language arts and social studies can gain access to the skills and knowledge of professionals and to resources they might never have otherwise.

Independent Study

Researchers recommend independent study as one of the most effective strategies for providing an individualized education for gifted students (Clark, 2002b; Colangelo & Davis, 2003; Johnsen & Goree, 2005; Treffinger, 1986). Common approaches to independent study include the Renzulli Enrichment Triad Model (1977), Feldhusen and Kolloff's Purdue Three-Stage Enrichment Model (1986), Treffinger's Self-Initiated Learning Model (1986), and Betts's Autonomous Learner Model (1986), with the Renzulli model being the best known. Most gifted children prefer independent study as part of their program because of the flexibility and independence it affords and the skills they gain in designing and implementing a course of study. The child and teacher together determine realistic goals, learning objectives, a timeline, and conditions for satisfaction. Frequently, a learning contract is involved that explains the student's responsibilities precisely.

To Accelerate

Independent study is often paired with compacting as a strategy that provides advanced knowledge and skill at the pace and level of individual children and enhances their independence as learners. It provides ways to accelerate students in a wide range of circumstances. A child who surpasses his cluster group in some areas or wants to tackle an assignment in a different way can do an independent study. A high-ability student who has problems sitting down for long periods of time can work quickly in shorter spurts with the freedom to occasionally move around while he's thinking. Independent studies are ideal for gifted children with special challenges because they can draw on their greatest strengths to accelerate learning. They don't have to endure remedial work in reading, for example, before they can use their advanced analytical abilities in math and science.

Planning for independent studies should be undertaken with this goal in mind: to remove all barriers to a child's gifts. A metamorphosis occurs when children can explore and exercise their strengths. Not only do they grow exponentially in their talent areas, but those who struggle with low skills often find in their newly discovered strengths a resource for tackling them.

GROUPING FOR ACCELERATION

Grouping gifted students for accelerated instruction is not simply an organizational strategy, but provides the means for them to receive a differentiated curriculum with real peers (Kulik & Kulik, 1987; VanTassel-Baska, 1992). Teachers who differentiate often place gifted students in a *cluster group* where they are free to master concepts and skills much more quickly. Generally speaking, cluster groups stay together for the year and work on alternative, more advanced content. Many teachers find they can provide for the gifted more efficiently if they combine their high-ability students into one cluster and share the responsibility for developing more accelerated content.

When individual differences in ability, skill, or learning style arise, teachers can make adjustments. Solutions vary from case to case. For one child, the teacher may need to provide some independent work related to what the cluster is doing. Another child may be so advanced in a subject that the teacher sends the student to another grade for a certain period in the day. The same principle applies for significant differences in learning style. Jason can't begin to compose a story without making sketches and flipping through books with images because, as he says, "I just have to see pictures of the kind of places where I put my story first." Kira, the extrovert in the group, likes to talk to peers about her ideas first ("When I talk about it I figure out what I want to change"). If one or more students in a cluster group struggles with an assignment, teachers need to consider learning style and adjust procedures and materials accordingly.

Becca always comes to class with something from the natural world. Yesterday, it was a large pinecone. This morning it was an entire collection of hickory nuts that she used to make a "family" of small figures, using part of the nut as a hat and several twigs as arms and legs. She painted the faces artfully, called them the Hickory family, and composed stories about them. She's in a cluster group in the fourth grade. With her extraordinary imagination and artistic gifts, Becca often gets bored with higher-level work that seems "dry, dry, oh so dry," as she says. Recognizing this, the teacher often integrates creative elements into the assigned work of the group.

Students can also accelerate through other grouping techniques. A fourth-grade student learns advanced geometry in a fast-paced *instructional group* in mathematics and follows other arrangements in language arts and science. A kindergarten child joins a *cross-grade group* of students from two or more grades for accelerated instruction in language arts and mathematics. Gifted students also benefit from *special interest grouping* in which all participants share a high level of motivation and interest. Interest groups usually form for short-term assignments, and children who join them often have areas of expertise that they can share while working on separate projects.

ACCELERATION AS A LEARNING JOURNEY

Is it feasible to accelerate different kinds of gifted students in a mixed ability, differentiated classroom? Yes, it is, provided that teachers can create units that allow students to progress at different paces within a cluster group. To aid the planning process, it helps to conceptualize the curriculum as a journey (Smutny & von Fremd, 2004). Since the word *curriculum* comes from the Latin verb meaning "to run" (*currere*), pace is always an appropriate consideration.

If the curriculum is a journey, then the learners will include a wide range of "travelers." Some are brimming with energy and want to zoom straight to the destination; they've spent their lives sprinting and love the exhilaration of the view, the freedom of moving at their own speed, the spring in their feet as they run. Others are dreamers. They prefer little side streets and stops along the way and ask for time to contemplate the road from a hill or tussock, breathe in the country air, note the unique markings of a migrating flock of birds. A number of travelers need support on their journey. Some forget their walking shoes and ask whether their jacket will keep them warm. Some need periodic stops for snacks and special maps that help them see where they are and how they should proceed to their goal. Some show amazing strengths in their journey but still need help in other areas. Several have a navigational ability that outstrips their peers, but they miscalculate the time it will take them to accomplish each phase of the trip. A few can't read a map to save their lives but can use their compasses expertly, talk to people along the way, and make notes about landmarks.

So how does a teacher accelerate the "travelers" who want to move quickly to the destination as well as those who may want to do so by another route, or those who want to reach the destination more slowly but double the distance by taking side trips? What should be the "destination" of accelerated learners, and what resources and strategies will these travelers need? How does the teacher structure more than one kind of acceleration? What strategies, resources, and materials in the differentiated classroom would most apply to the needs of these high-ability travelers?

A helpful guide to selecting appropriate learning goals in a way that allows teachers to accommodate different kinds of gifted students is to consider the following criteria (Wiggins & McTighe, 1998, pp. 10–11):

The idea, topic, or process represents a "Big Idea" having enduring value beyond the classroom. [This might be the multiple levels of meaning in written and oral language, a subject appropriate for gifted students.]

The idea, topic, or process resides at the heart of the discipline. [A unit on reading and writing poetry does lie at the heart of the discipline because it demands an understanding of how to decipher and interpret meanings from different kinds of texts.]

The idea, topic, or process requires uncoverage. [Tools for understanding and using poetic forms need to be learned and explored so that gifted students can engage in the exploration of different meanings.]

The idea, topic, or process offers potential for engaging students. [Poetry involves rhythm, rhyme, and metaphoric language—all of which lend themselves to stimulating ideas for engagement.]

Gifted students often contribute ideas that expand on curriculum topics. A third-grade teacher once asked a group of gifted children to write down how they would define poetry and what they would like to learn about it. Here are some of their answers.

"Poems are paintings that you read and then paint in your mind."

"Poetry is mysterious. It comes from the clouds and disappears in the sun."

"Why do some poems rhyme and others don't?"

"Is there a special school for becoming a poet?"

"What is the difference between a poem and a fancy paragraph?"

"Why do people write poems?"

"How can I write one?"

The following pages offer a useful process and examples for accelerating instruction for gifted students. Drawn in part from the "backward design process" of Wiggins and McTighe (1998, p. 9), it helps teachers to plan instruction by beginning with the learning "destination" or outcome. Teachers start by asking, "Given who these students are and what their unique strengths, problem areas, and learning styles are, what should they understand and be able to do as a result of this unit?"

Process for Accelerating the Gifted in a Differentiated Classroom

1. Who are my gifted students?

Determine student readiness and preparedness for accelerated learning by assessing the following characteristics:

- Abilities
- Cultural traditions and strengths
- Learning preferences
- Special challenges

2. What is the appropriate content?

Identify what gifted students should understand and master by considering the following:

- Children's abilities, achievement, and mastery thus far
- Essential concepts, knowledge, and skills
- Curriculum goals
- Curriculum standards

3. How will I know that they've mastered content?

Identify evidence of understanding:

- Behaviors
- Comments and discussions
- Observed processes
- Products
- Tests

4. How do I determine appropriate accelerated instruction for gifted students?

Design teaching strategies, learning activities, and resources using the following:

- Learning environment
- Resources
- Adjustments in content, process, products
- Subject-skipping
- Self-paced instruction in independent study
- Mentorship
- Internet courses

5. How do I monitor their progress?

Assess students using the following measures:

- Ongoing observations
- Conferences with students
- Lists of criteria for peer evaluations
- Rubrics

Examples of Acceleration in a Differentiated Classroom

Science—Second Grade

Study of Trees

Learning "Destination" (for the class): All of the children will understand that every part of the tree has a special purpose that helps it to grow and adapt to its environment.

Strategies for Acceleration: Reading and researching advanced materials (books, charts, Internet sites), complex content, self-paced learning, higher-level thinking strategies.

Curriculum Standard: (a) Know and apply concepts that explain how living things function, adapt, and change. (b) Know and apply concepts that describe how living things interact with each other and with their environment.

Zawadi and Nika are two gifted students in two second-grade classrooms that are focusing on a study of trees. Zawadi is a recent arrival from East Africa and has a superior knowledge of science due to the academically rigorous boarding school he attended. Despite Zawadi's high abilities, he's been underachieving and, according to his mother, cries every day before school. At the urging of his mother and teacher, he joins a cluster group forming in one of the regular second grades. Zawadi is quiet and withdrawn a lot of the time, although he enjoys the cluster group of kids who share some of his interests. He confides in his teacher that what he misses most is the "music of the way we talk and my uncle telling old stories." But Zawadi's eyes brighten at the idea of studying trees. He wants to focus on the baobab tree and why it has a huge barrel-shaped trunk. He's a highly visual learner and immediately begins sketching the baobab and labeling its parts.

Nika, who's from the other second-grade class but joins in the same cluster group with Zawadi, is a highly gifted child. She reads at a fifth-grade level and enjoys integrating subjects and sources and finding a creative way to do her work. When the teacher first introduces the subject of trees, Nika asks whether she can include poems and paintings by famous artists. She selects the maple tree for her project ("I want to press some leaves from my own maple tree and write the story of it from the absolute beginning!"). She wants to learn as much as she can about maple trees so she can bring them vividly to life. The teacher often has to think of a wider range of resources for Nika, who has proved to be more advanced than the other gifted students in terms of knowledge, skill, and conceptual understanding (see Table 2.1, page 32).

Table 2.1

LEARNER • **Abilities** • **Cultural traditions and strengths** • **Learning preferences** • **Special challenges**	**Zawadi:** Advanced reader; writes well, but uses colloquialisms from native language. Zawadi's exceptional ability in science means that he can explore the baobab tree in far more detail. He loves the Internet and wants to log onto a science site on the tree. He's a visual learner and needs opportunities to diagram, and to create maps and sketches. Zawadi also needs to connect with his own culture; he could also include cultural traditions and lore around the baobab.	**Nika:** Exceptional ability in all areas! She has an inquiring mind and curiosity about many things. Nika isn't satisfied with anything less than multidimensional projects. In her maple tree study, she wants to research texts, online sources as well as cultural sources (e.g., *The Sky Tree Portfolio* by painter Thomas Locker). Despite her high academic gift, Nika also craves creative work.
LEARNING DESTINATION • **Children's strengths, passions, and backgrounds** • **Essential concepts, knowledge, and skills** • **Curriculum goals** • **Curriculum standards**	Zawadi can embrace the learning destination for the class, but since he brings to this unit a lot of firsthand experience and knowledge about the baobab and is an advanced reader, he and his teacher make adjustments: to use the baobab as a way of understanding how flora survive in the dry desert climate, how flora acquire enough water and preserve themselves during the dry seasons.	Nika can benefit from the same "learning destination" but with her interest in integrated and multifaceted work, she would like to expand the study. The teacher and Nika adjust the focus of her assignment: to understand how a tree species (in this case, the maple) affects and is affected by other forms of life—animals, insects, and humans.
EVIDENCE OF UNDERSTANDING • **Behaviors** • **Comments and discussions** • **Observed processes** • **Products** • **Tests**	Examples: Zawadi's outline or plan of action shows that he understands what to do and is grappling with the material. He can explain what the baobab shows about the environment generally and how flora conserve moisture. His final assignment (writing, diagrams, etc.) shows that he understands the process of water acquisition and conservation in the dry areas of his country of origin.	Examples: Nika can explain how the maple tree sustains itself as well as a whole range of creatures around it. She can demonstrate, through writing and sketches, the interrelationships. Her story about the life of her maple tree shows a detailed understanding of the ecology involved.
JOURNEY (CONTENT, PROCESS, PRODUCT) • **Catalysts for introductory activities** • **Learning environment**	Zawadi is shy and would benefit from interacting with a research partner. Recommendations: brainstorm all of the sources he wants to consult; have advanced level books with pictures to feed his imagination and evoke	Nika wants to spend time with her maple tree—draw it, study it closely, figure out its approximate age. She knows a family in Vermont where she goes with her family every summer. They make maple

• **Adjustments in content** • **Adjustments in process** • **Adjustments in products**	memories of his experiences; work with partner to generate questions for his focus on water and the baobab (he can sketch the tree while he's thinking of questions); include his personal experiences with it—what it felt like, how it smelled, what lore surrounds it, and so on. To help organize his thoughts, he can use index cards with different ideas both from science and his own cultural sources.	syrup. She will create a list of questions and talk to the father in that family (by phone). Internet searches and books will help her understand the specific needs of the maple (its ideal environmental conditions) and how it functions in the local ecology—particularly in how it relates to animals.
ASSESSMENT • **Ongoing observations** • **Conferences with students** • **Lists of criteria for peer evaluations** • **Rubrics**	Zawadi needs encouragement and special care. Periodic observations of how he is progressing with a study partner can determine benefit. The teacher meets with Zawadi to help guide the process and provide steps and criteria. Weaving together the science of the baobab with personal and cultural stories is a complex process. The teacher can use periodic conferences to explore with Zawadi any need he might have for further adjustment.	Nika is an independent and self-sufficient worker. The teacher works with Nika to design a structure that accommodates both her need for accelerated learning and her desire to do creative work. Short conferences help her to review progress and reassess her process. She has a tendency to be a perfectionist and this causes her to spend too much time on less significant steps of a process. The teacher encourages her to keep referring to the list of criteria and the steps of the assignment so that she can see the relative importance of the different parts of her project.

Language Arts—Fourth Grade

Study of Biography

Learning "Destination" (for the class): All of the children will understand the difference between primary and secondary sources in biographies and the value of both in biographies.

Strategies for Acceleration: Reading and researching advanced materials (books, charts, video and audio sources, Internet sites), complex content, self-paced learning, divergent and analytical thinking.

Curriculum Standard: (a) Locate, organize, and use information from various sources to answer questions, solve problems, and communicate ideas. (b) Apply acquired information, concepts, and ideas to communicate in a variety of formats.

Tammi and James are two fourth-grade gifted students. Tammi reads constantly and loves to write. She immediately selects several challenging books and magazines, as well as some online sources, and plunges into a study of the life of

Emily Dickinson. She prefers working independently and quietly and likes to imagine being in the time and place of her "person." She focuses on questions that she most wants to know: How did Dickinson become interested in poetry? What were the most important experiences in her life as a poet? What impact did her poetry have on the world? Tammi usually writes long essays because she keeps finding more material from which to draw.

James gets nervous about anything to do with research. He lacks confidence and skill in reading because he comes from a home where people don't read much; his father never attended college. Yet James learns quickly and enjoys challenging assignments. He wants to focus on Triple Crown winner Secretariat. The teacher has James begin by focusing on the world of horse racing. He finds out what he can about the three race tracks—when they began, how large they are, and so forth. He makes sketches of the tracks and outlines the whole process (what rules govern jockeys and horses, how to read the daily racing form, what happens at each stage of the race, etc.). As James learns more about the world of Secretariat, he begins to stretch himself—tackling books he never thought he could read, asking peers about Internet searches. His final project evolves into a combination of writing, sketches, a model of the three race tracks, and a rap about Secretariat—all of which demonstrate what he's learned.

Table 2.2 summarizes how two gifted students with different learning styles and needs can experience accelerated learning.

Table 2.2

LEARNERS • **Abilities** • **Cultural traditions and strengths** • **Learning preferences** • **Special challenges**	**Tammi:** Fast reader and gifted writer; loves to investigate topics, especially on the Internet; introverted; likes to work alone quietly; can generate complex and probing questions for topics.	**James:** Advanced thinker but has weak reading and writing skills; however, is growing since he came to the school. Loves to talk! Picks up information almost by osmosis; full of interesting information on many subjects; loves the Internet but inexperienced; gifted sketcher; needs to work with hands.
LEARNING DESTINATION • **Children's strengths, passions, and backgrounds** • **Essential concepts, knowledge, and skills** • **Curriculum goals** • **Curriculum standards**	Tammi has read a number of biographies and understands the genre well. Therefore, her learning "destination" will include an ability to analyze the point of view of the biographer. 　She will focus on the biographer's primary and secondary sources and investigate the question of how one evaluates the reliability of a source.	James has an ability to spontaneously invent raps that sum up, poetically, the most significant elements of a subject. His "destination" will include a creative interpretation of his chosen subject and an exploration of how to identify important elements of Secretariat's life and how to communicate this in a symbolic form.

EVIDENCE OF UNDERSTANDING • **Behaviors** • **Comments and discussions** • **Observed processes** • **Products**	Examples: Tammi generates questions for her own study that reveal her understanding of the process of researching and writing biography. Her research process is thorough and well organized. Her essay shows a depth of insight and understanding of the biographical genre.	Examples: James performs a dramatic reenactment of a reporter describing one or more important "moments" or "turning points" in Secretariat's life that shows James's understanding of the horse's unique gift. Display on Secretariat (incorporating reports, stories, a model of a track, rap, and so on) shows James's understanding of the biographical process.
JOURNEY (CONTENT, PROCESS, PRODUCT) • **Catalysts for introductory activities** • **Learning environment** • **Adjustments in content** • **Adjustments in process** • **Adjustments in products**	Tammi doesn't need an introductory activity. She will work independently in her favorite corner with her books. She will provide the teacher with a list of potential primary sources and secondary sources (all of the books, journals, and Web sites she'll draw from). She likes to organizes her thoughts and information from different sources on index cards and shuffle them around. She will generate questions that interest her, things she wants to know about Emily Dickinson, and so on.	James needs to focus on the "big picture" first. He will start off by watching footage on races, sketching the tracks where Secretariat ran, and recreating the "world" of Secretariat. What are the main questions he has about this horse and his world? James will combine footage and firsthand accounts of the horse (primary sources) with reviews of races, genealogy, charts of the horse's record, and talks with trainers or jockeys. To explore main themes and ideas, he can use collage to represent primary and secondary sources.
ASSESSMENT • **Ongoing observations** • **Conferences with students** • **Lists of criteria for peer evaluations** • **Rubrics**	Teacher periodically reviews Tammi's progress, examining Tammi's work with the criteria that she shares with Tammi at the beginning of the assignment. A rubric helps Tammi see where she excels and where she may need to make changes or adjustments. On the basis of all of these, the teacher determines whether Tammi is working at the pace and level that she needs.	Teacher monitors James frequently until he gets his rhythm. Periodic conferences determine what support he may require. James needs clear-cut criteria to refer to; he tends to spend too much time on one aspect of an assignment.

When planning alternatives for (and with) gifted students, teachers need to bear two key points in mind. The first is that *most gifted students benefit from some form of acceleration regardless of their learning style, culture, first language, or whatever special challenges they may have.* James's artistic ability and lower skill in reading and writing should not prohibit him from accelerated learning. As he continues to develop his gifts through more advanced content and activity, he will become increasingly more confident in tackling his own limitations.

The second is a corollary to the first: *Acceleration for gifted students should have a built-in flexibility to assume different forms based on student need, learning style, cultural background, and areas of strength and difficulty.* Zawadi's homesickness for his culture and homeland awakens in his teacher an awareness of his need for connection and relationship. She guides him to personal stories and cultural lore around the baobab tree that he can then integrate with his science study. She helps him select challenging resources for his high ability in science and nurtures his cultural relationship to the tree as a way of creating a bridge from his past life to his present school experience.

A differentiated approach to acceleration attempts to tailor advanced content to the specific strengths and needs of highly able students. It adjusts under careful observation and evaluation of each child's performance and behavior. This process may include measures that provide acceleration beyond the confines of the classroom (e.g., subject acceleration, cross-grade grouping, mentorships). Restoring a gifted child's pace and level of learning often involves continuous tuning in order to result in real and lasting benefits for the individual student. More like an orchestrated dance than a fast-moving machine, acceleration has the flexibility to partner the child's natural movements—including all of the leaps, pauses, spins, and runs that occur in the learning process.

3

Acceleration and Creativity

Closing the Gap

n a keynote speech to the National Curriculum Networking Conference, Michael Thompson (2000) said,

> In too many classrooms, children sit endlessly in a kind of Orwellian isolation, filling out meaningless forms, and repeating things again and again. Already, they have lost the world, and the educational instructions they obey lead them farther and farther from the world as the looming walls of the classroom close in. Like the drones in Plato's cave whose backs are to the daylight, they only get to see dim shadows on the classroom walls. (p. 2)

Perhaps more than any other students, gifted children understand that "Orwellian isolation" and its monotonous repetition. Certainly, acceleration, with its offering of a more advanced curriculum, lets in the fresh air—new terrains of knowledge, mysterious problems to solve, complex ideas just beyond one's grasp. But does acceleration, by itself, give them back the world they have lost? It is more than likely that the "dim shadows on the classroom walls" remain dim without the imagination to bring them fully to life.

Creativity offers the means to lead gifted students *back to the world*. Even the most advanced content remains shallow if it doesn't inspire students with the sense of some real phenomenon at their fingertips. As this chapter shows, creativity enables gifted students to step into the real world of their curriculum and advance—through their imagination, intuition, and creative talents—to heights and depths they never knew while they sat silently in "Orwellian isolation."

THE NEED FOR CREATIVITY

For a number of gifted students, the urge to create is as strong as the urge to accelerate. The tendency of our educational system to separate "academics" and creativity ignores the fact that gifted students often do both simultaneously. Creativity feeds on an abundance of knowledge, concepts, and skills to realize its potential—an abundance achieved through *accelerated learning*. At the same time, accelerated learning needs a reason for being—the *creative response* that acts upon this knowledge and transforms it. "Individuals need knowledge in order to be creative; finding problems of increasing sophistication demands increased understanding of the domains in which the problems are found" (Starko, 1995, p. 126). As anyone who works in this field knows, the brightest minds in our schools will never be content to simply follow the tracks laid by others. They will want to lay track of their own through a new insight or realization, an artistic response, or imaginative proposition.

> When the teacher gave Jerry double-digit numbers to add, she included ones that required him to "carry over." After some time, she found him scribbling all over the page. He had invented four different ways of adding the figures together and then said, "There's a way to add from left to right instead of right to left. Here's 97 + 88. I put down 170 first because it's 90 plus 80 (in the tens column). Then I add up the ones, which is 15, and I put that under the 170 (he lined it up). Then I can tell it's 185 . . . really quick!" Jerry just started first grade.

During a snowstorm, fourth grader Jasmine walked with her mother to the train station. While her mother grumbled about the slippery slush and cold, Jasmine said that the snow didn't bother her so much; she was imagining that she'd been stuck for years in a labor camp in Siberia, that she'd just been released, and that this was the last train out of Siberia. Her mother said that Jasmine was always surprising her with "out-in-left-field" comments. Wondering how she'd heard about Siberian labor camps, she discovered that Jasmine had thumbed through a copy of Alexander Solzhenitsyn's *One Day in the Life of Ivan Denisovich* at a relative's house during the Thanksgiving holiday. With images from the book in her mind, trudging in the snow to the train assumed a new meaning.

Third grader Amanda asked her teacher one day whether anyone had ever made a special device that would enable people to see in two separate directions at the same time. "I know how they could do it," she said when her teacher replied in the negative. "They could use reptiles as models."

Without any art lessons, fifth grader Javier taught himself how to draw and paint at the level of a college art student. His ability in visual art is not just one of execution, but of perception. Standing in front of a series of paintings on the wall, he waved the teacher to come closer, declaring that he knew how the paintings "worked." Looking at a Van Gogh print, he explained in halting English what was obviously a new thought about the design, light, and color of these paintings. During the weeks that followed, his teacher would often find him, early in the morning before school started, studying each painting from different angles.

Jerry's flexible reasoning, Jasmine's imaginative fictional worlds, Amanda's inventive mind, and Javier's artistry are all part of the creative dimension that can significantly extend and expand what gifted students learn in an accelerated curriculum. Certainly, we've seen enough in the field to know that the separation between academics and creativity ultimately leaves gifted students—and *all* students for that matter—with an impoverished education. Alfred North Whitehead put it nicely: "Fools act on imagination without knowledge; pedants act on knowledge without imagination" (Parnes, 1967, p. 7). The creative potential of a gifted child is often only realized in accelerated learning because creativity thrives on advanced mastery within a field and is significantly hampered without it. At the same time, acceleration needs a step beyond expert knowledge, understanding, and skill. Gifted children naturally feel impelled to take what they've learned and step out into the unknown.

The importance of creativity becomes apparent when we look closely at the circumstances in which gifted students thrive intellectually and emotionally. Almost always, they involve situations where high intellectual demand and creativity work together and where students apply their mastery of a subject (gained through accelerated learning) to the creative dimension. This "dimension" may entail different kinds of mental processes—divergent thinking, invention, and intuition, or the "sensing" abilities that guide the earliest discoveries of gifted children.

It might be helpful here to list some of the most important benefits of creativity as seen in our experience with high-ability learners.

- **Through creativity and the arts, gifted children make strong, personal connections with the subjects they're learning.** Gifted students experience a shift from passive receiving to active engagement because of its demand on individual thinking, intuiting, reasoning, analyzing, and imagining.

- **Students make discoveries.** Whether a teacher designs an open-ended inductive reasoning process or uses art media to inspire a poetic composition, the creative dimension stimulates completely new ways of thinking and enables gifted students to innovate and originate.

- **Students with different learning styles can engage in higher-level thinking.** Because of the wide range of processes involved and materials used, creativity can more fully address a wider range of learning styles and also differences related to socioeconomic and cultural backgrounds.

- **Students can develop a sense of artistry and depth of feeling.** Through regular exposure to the arts and the creative process, gifted children focus and revel in their keen sensibilities, exploring such phenomena as the beauty of numbers, the dazzling array of intricate patterns in nature, or the richness of imagery and meaning in stories or poems.

It should be pointed out that gifted students can only experience these benefits if the classroom environment fosters the creative process. Research has proved that classroom environment—particularly in its influence on motivation and creative expression—plays a central role in the degree to which high-ability students can become independent, innovative, imaginative thinkers (Amabile, 1996; Hennessey, 2004). When extrinsic pressures such as competition, evaluation, and external reward outweigh all other concerns, students tend to approach the learning process as a means to an end, undermining creativity and self-determination (Hennessey, 2004).

In an accelerated program of study, gifted students with advanced skills and knowledge are accustomed to assessments of various kinds and to a natural competition with other high-ability learners. They need to periodically distance themselves from these coercive forces and gain practice and experience in *making their own contribution* to the subjects they're learning. This can only happen if the climate of the classroom nurtures the intrinsic motivations of children: inner curiosity, imagination, and passion. Incorporating the creative dimension fosters the development of this inner spirit—the inventor, the mad scientist, the storyteller, the artist.

Guiding Creative Learners

Preparing the Soil

- Openly share your own creative passions with your students.
- Fill the classroom with art, music, and a rich variety of enticing supplies.
- Design work spaces that beckon the creative muse in your students.
- Applaud originality, whenever and wherever expressed.
- Protect students from saboteurs: criticism, censure, premature judgment.
- Celebrate risk-taking and bold endeavor.

Planting the Seeds

- Awaken imagination and artistic sensibilities through example and exposure to creative people and their works.
- Create open time for creative exploration.
- Share jewels of wisdom about the creative process.
- Point out the hidden, less traveled paths; warn against set patterns.
- Celebrate the beginning steps of children's own creative process.

Watering and Feeding

- Design activities that engage the whole child: touching, feeling, imagining, listening, sensing, composing, combining, writing, improvising, constructing, molding, shaping.
- Provide for advanced learning in a variety of fields.
- Assign work that requires creative and imaginative thinking.
- Nurture boldness in vision and endeavor.

Weeding and Growing

- Teach strategies for *constructive* criticism and evaluation.
- Impart coping skills to deal with peer judgment, crippling perfectionism, and frustration with the creative process.
- Support students' trust in their own creative power.
- Give them opportunities to correct errors, refine visions, rewrite, re-create, improve, elaborate.
- Find venues for students to show/demonstrate/perform/exhibit for real audiences in the community.

EXPANDING THE DOMAINS OF CREATIVITY

Clearly, how educators regard and employ creativity depends largely on how they understand intelligence itself. Those who define intelligence as rational thinking manifested primarily through high IQ or academic performance will see creativity as a separate construct. Reviewing scholarship on creativity over the past five decades, Clark (2002b) has pointed out that the "cognitive, rational view of creativity" has been the one most researched in the literature, with a great deal of focus placed on cognitive processing models such as problem solving (p. 78). There are advantages and disadvantages to this, as Clark observes: "Limiting creativity to a cognitive view allows it to be more easily measured, researched, and taught; however, it does not capture the complexity or bring understanding to the other dimensions of creativity" (p. 77).

Perhaps the reason for this is that the creative process still remains an enigma. How do artists, inventors, and writers discover their ideas? What guides their unconventional meanderings, sudden leaps of faith, and risky experiments? Researchers can describe a series of stages that take place when a new discovery occurs or changes in perception lead to a flash of insight, but they cannot account for the means by which a completely novel approach to a problem emerges. For example, the eminent French mathematician Poincaré noticed that behaviors leading up to discovery typically involve a period of labor, a period of rest, and an illumination, followed by additional labor (to solidify illumination). But how this illumination comes or why it does was a mystery to him.

Poincaré's (1913) famous story about how he discovered Fuchsian groups follows this pattern. After many days of working on a solution to his problem, he let the matter rest, drank a cup of black coffee, and then discovered what he termed "Fuchsian functions." Later, Poincaré was stepping into a bus when another idea occurred to him with no conscious effort at all. He realized that the transformations he "had used to define the Fuchsian functions were identical with those of non-Euclidian geometry" (p. 37). He later verified this discovery, which made a significant advance in mathematics.

What actually happened in that moment? We can trace the process that led up to it, but conscious thought did not originate Poincaré's discovery. Arieti (1976) suggests, "Certainly it is plausible to view the creative process as going through the stages of preparation, incubation, inspiration, and verification, but it is also so for the solution of any problem" (p. 18). The illumination stage in creative thinking is the only one that actually creates. On the other hand, conscious thought prepares for this "magic moment." It stretches everything known to the limit and then waits. From there, the process eludes us.

Some have argued that creativity, at its core, is a *way of being*. We can refer to the creative attitude or the creative experience, for example, without requiring a product of any kind. Maslow (1968) saw creativity in terms of "self-actualization." Self-actualized human beings live lives of spontaneity and freedom. Their "peak experiences" (Maslow, 1968) and "encounters" (May, 1975) imply a creative consciousness distinct from either talent or training. Unhampered by concerns over others' opinions, they give themselves license to be original. They distinguish themselves not by membership in an artistic elite but by their keen sense of wonder (Carson, 1965) about the world around them—seagulls clamoring over a fish, the intricate patterns of science, the breathtaking scope of an indigenous storyteller's repertoire.

May (1975), Maslow (1968), Carson (1965), and Rogers (1962) noticed several primary characteristics of creative people:

- Total immersion in the moment (experiencing a temporary suspension of time, past and present)
- Openness to experience as an original event (leaving the past behind and treating the present as new)
- Complete self-acceptance (judging one's self independently of others and validating one's individuality without reservation)

Charles Kettering once commented that an inventor is a "fellow who doesn't take his education too seriously" (Guilford, 1968, pp. 84–85). This doesn't refer to all that one learns within a field, but rather to the conventions and closed mindset that can sometimes accompany academic study. Pasteur expressed this idea best in the famous quotation, "Chance favors the prepared mind." In other words, possessing an advanced understanding of a field and an openness to the unconventional are the best ways to discover something new. The disappointment felt by some gifted children is that the learning of academic content rarely leads them to the perplexing mysteries that most inspire them.

When creative teaching does occur in schools, it tends to focus more on the cognitive domain instead of imagination, intuition, or artistry. Even with Howard Gardner's

(1993) multiple intelligences and the recognition among educators of a wider range of creative strengths (e.g., visual, linguistic, kinetic, intrapersonal), there is still a disinclination to regard the arts or imagination as seriously as cognitive processes.

It's important to note in this regard that among real inventors and pioneers, no such disinclination exists.

> James Watson and Francis Crick worked feverishly to solve the structure of the DNA molecule, but guided their work with the unproven intuition that the molecule of life would be beautiful, and so they only considered beautiful molecules like spirals, not ugly, amorphous molecules. (Thompson, 2000, p. 12)

Lured on by "unproven intuition," the Nobel Prize winners succeeded in their endeavor. Certainly, examples such as this have implications for the way we teach gifted students. In Table 3.1, we consider three other dimensions of creativity (besides cognitive) that have an equally important role to play in the classroom. Though not comprehensive by any means, Table 3.1 can stimulate new ideas on how to integrate creativity into the curriculum for advanced learners. It's important to bear in mind, of course, that these different aspects of creativity rarely occur in isolation. For example, a painter (artistic) may have a creative problem to solve (cognitive) and a world to invent on a canvas (imaginative).

In an accelerated curriculum where children move through course content quickly, teachers need to identify specific times when a creative process will work best. For example, an early primary math class might require students to invent several methods for adding double-digit numbers rather than have them advance to the next task in a unit. In another case, an artistic or creative activity may serve gifted students in preparation for an accelerated unit in language arts. In yet another case,

Table 3.1

Cognitive	Sensing/Intuiting	Imaginative	Artistic

Divergent reasoning
Flexible thinking
Experimenting
Improvising
Fluency
	Depth of feeling
	Keen sensing
	Intuiting
	Heightened
	  sensibilities
		Visualizing processes
		  and possibilities
		  (not in evidence
		  currently)
		Vivid imaginings
		Daydreaming
		Otherworldliness
			Responsiveness
			  to visual and
			  performing arts
			Originality in
			  artistic expression

Examples
 	
– Creative Problem
  Solving (CPS)
– Brainstorming
– Synectics
– Idea checklists
– Attribute listing
	Examples
	
	– Responses to nature
	– Sensory exercises
	– Free association
	– Imaginative
	  processes using arts
		Examples
		
		– Composing
		  stories and poems
		– "What if?"
		  questioning
		– Role playing
		– Divergent
		  production (e.g.,
		  fractured fairytales)
			Examples
			
			– Chamber theater
			  adaptations
			– Paintings and
			  drawings
			– Collage that combines
			  visual media with text
			– Arts as catalysts for
			  creative writing

a child with a different learning style may perform best if she or he can use artistic and creative resources to synthesize what she or he has learned in an accelerated science class.

Teachers who provide accelerated instruction can design creativity charts (such as Table 3.1) to guide their planning. As a reference to different creative domains and activities, visual displays can help teachers quickly identify the best application for specific units or lessons. The combinations and choices are endless. In a science class, for example, a teacher could use brainstorming techniques to introduce a new unit in ecology. Other classes could draw upon visual art objects as catalysts for interpreting poetry or engage students in an imaginative "What if?" exercise in order to analyze a work of fiction from multiple points of view. Creative teaching gives students more independence in the learning process and gives them practical tools that they can use for the rest of their lives. When they get stuck or run out of options, instead of going over the same ground repeatedly, they can apply techniques to stimulate new ideas or explore different resources for inspiration.

The remainder of this chapter explores the four domains of creativity in Table 3.1.

The Cognitive Domain

Over the past 80 or more years, a number of models supporting the creative process have evolved, based largely on observation and study of those who invent and create. *The Wallas Model,* for example, patterned itself on the process that Poincaré followed—preparation, incubation, illumination, and verification (Wallas, 1925). In the preparation stage, a person defines a problem and explores relevant information and sources. Incubation involves letting the problem and information "simmer" for a while; this could entail free writing in a notebook and experimentation or improvisation. During illumination, as Poincaré describes in his own experience, a solution—hopefully a novel one—emerges. In the final verification stage, the creative person works out the details of her discovery or invention, demonstrating its workability.

Many researchers have focused on processes or steps that aim to stimulate divergent thinking. The extent to which divergent thinking is actually creative is debatable. Suffice it to say, however, that certain "creative" processes have become widely known in the schools as a result of Guilford's (1968) scholarship and Torrance's (1974, 1979) research and testing instruments. Teachers often associate the following processes with creative production:

- *Fluency* (generating many ideas)
- *Flexibility* (creating different thought patterns)
- *Originality* (producing unique, unexpected ideas)
- *Elaboration* (extending ideas, embellishing, implementing ideas)
- *Transformation* (changing/adapting an idea or solution into a different one)
- *Evaluation* (assessing the viability and usefulness of an idea)

In the classroom, creative questioning is the most common means for guiding children to deeper inquiry. "What else might be affected by this? What other ways might you solve this problem? How do you know that this is the cause of that? Are there any other sources you can think of that might tell you more about this?"

Here is how a mathematics teacher uses leading questions to help gifted children discover math principles:

> A clear directive to me about the need for inductive thinking came from an offhand remark made by my professor. . . . He pointed out that for 12 or even 16 years of mathematics instruction, students are judged by their ability to apprehend mathematics that has already been formulated by others. Then, when they begin work on their Ph.D., they are expected to discover something new—and they sometimes have no idea how to proceed. When I heard this, I thought to myself, Why not give students the opportunity to formulate mathematical principles while they are young? Over many years, I have developed activities that do just that. I present a situation of some mathematical interest, let the students explore it, and encourage them, through leading questions, to formulate the fundamental mathematical principles that govern it. (Freeman, 2003, p. 73)

In mathematics, as in other subjects, an accelerated level of work often needs to shift pace to allow for a creative process. Understandably, teachers of the gifted have to ensure that they cover advanced content at a quick pace. But the understanding and level of mastery the children gain through such a program carries little significance without the opportunity to formulate mathematical principles or discover unique methods for solving specific sorts of problems. In this math teacher's class, inductive thinking can only result in new insights if the children have sufficient time to mull over the different possibilities and test their hypotheses. To facilitate this, he has his students confront real problems, manipulate and/or construct objects, and collaborate with each other when appropriate. This takes more time than just memorizing math formulas and practicing them. He includes the following suggestions for teachers who wish to open up the math curriculum in this way:

> **Avoid compressing content into a short time.** The less time that is available, the more the instructor must resort to telling the theorems and relying on the students to learn them. Many students become highly adept at memorizing the results of great mathematicians' studies, but the joy of discovery is lost.

> **Allow students time to explore and make their own mathematical discoveries.** Several class management styles work well for inductive thinking activities. Almost always, I begin by presenting an idea to the entire group and then set up a challenge for them to investigate . . . . Then, I allow students to come to me with their discoveries. I respond, either by pointing out an aspect they hadn't considered, by helping them to refine their conjecture, or by approving their work and suggesting a new course of investigation.

> **Keep the activities open-ended.** Encourage unexpected responses. Follow up on students' ideas. Rejoice in new ideas. I enjoy announcing to the class, "It just happened! I've taught this topic to hundreds of students for the past 20 years, and every time I teach it, some student comes up with an idea I've never seen before." (Freeman, 2003, pp. 74–75)

Strategies for increasing a child's ability to generate and apply new ideas have given teachers a repertoire of techniques to use at specific points in a unit or lesson. In brief, here are examples of the more common strategies:

Brainstorming. A strong proponent of what he called "deferred judgment" in brainstorming, Alex Osborn (1963) created four basic ground rules for brainstorming: (1) criticism is ruled out; (2) freewheeling is welcomed; (3) quantity is wanted; (4) combination and improvement are sought. A fourth grader used brainstorming in a class where students were writing biographies:

I thought of all of these different ways of doing a biography and then I came up with this idea of beginning at the end and working backwards. I chose Rachel Carson. I started by thinking about what I wanted my report to be like. And I thought, well, I want it to be about the changes that her book *Silent Spring* created. And then I thought that maybe I should start by finding out more about the environmental problems back then. After that, I read up on Rachel's life. I learned about her discovery about chemicals like DDT and I thought about everything in her life that led her to that point. And then I got this flash. I asked this question: What about Rachel Carson made her the one who could discover this? So, instead of writing this boring paper on someone's life, it became like a mystery search to find clues that would show why and how Rachel Carson became this awesome scientist. What were the seeds in her life that made her follow this line of thinking and eventually change the world?

Attribute Listing. This strategy by Crawford (1964) assumes that any step taken in a creative process depends on changing an attribute of something ("attribute modifying") or applying that same attribute to something else ("attribute transferring"). For example, engineering the airplane obviously involved modifying and transferring the attributes and principles of bird flight.

A community of young boys in an urban slum in Kenya fashioned toy cars and trucks out of tin scraps, wheels, and wire. Over time, they designed elaborate structures with moveable wheels, brakes, and other attachments. Called "child engineers," most had never sat in a car or truck or even stood close enough to examine how they work. The local schoolmaster said that because of their advanced, creative thinking abilities, they surpassed their classmates in academic achievement. (wa Gacheru, 1985)

Idea Checklists. Osborn's (1963) idea-spurring questions have proven effective as catalysts for generating ideas on how to improve on or transform an object, idea, or solution. The checklist strategy for teaching creative thinking has been termed the SCAMPER method: Substitute, Combine, Adopt, Modify-Magnify-Minify, Put to other uses, Eliminate, Reverse-Rearrange (Stanish, 1988).

Synectics Methods. Based on the theory that creative people often combine elements that, on the surface, do not appear related, Gordon (1961, 1974) established guidelines to stimulate this process. An example of synectics: relating the concept of the spine of invertebrates to the skeletal structure that supports skyscrapers.

A pioneer in creative problem solving, Osborn (1963) also founded a five-step model. Briefly, the steps in his Creative Problem Solving Model involved the following activities:

- *Fact finding*. List all known facts about the problem.
- *Problem finding*. Consider different ways of defining the problem.
- *Idea finding*. Generate ideas through divergent thinking and brainstorming.
- *Solution finding*. Establish criteria for evaluating ideas.
- *Acceptance finding*. Apply the solution to individuals/organizations involved in decision making.

Updated by Parnes (1981) as well as by Treffinger and Firestien (1989), this model emphasizes both divergent thinking (generating many different ideas) and convergent thinking (choosing the most promising or inspired possibilities). A further model (Isaksen, Puccio, & Treffinger, 1993) sought to address criticisms that the process was too linear and failed to address the artistic dimension.

Several gifted students in a cluster group did a project on the sharp declines in migratory bird populations in the United States. They asked themselves, "What do birds need?" Each student chose a specific focus to research (which they shared with the others). One chose scarcity of food sources, another habitat loss, another habitat degradation, and another flight patterns that bring them in contact with buildings. When they pooled their research, they wrote down on index cards the most important data that they felt accounted for why the birds' numbers are in decline. The teacher posed questions: Is there a main reason why these birds are declining? The students couldn't agree on a main cause; it seemed, as they talked, that there were many causes. One student asked, "Is it possible for humans to share the world with birds?" This question opened the field to new ways of thinking. Another student said that, perhaps, what was needed was to look at bird habitat needs and human habitat needs. Another student suggested that there should be a distinction made between needs and wants. And so on.

The project became exciting because instead of simply mastering a great deal of information and accepting the analyses of others, the children were actively inquiring into the problem—studying data and analyses of experts, but not stopping there. In the process, some students selected interesting lines of inquiry—one of which is currently being considered by like-minded researchers in Chicago. In response to reports that one billion birds a year die from collisions with buildings in North America, architects for the first time are considering ways to design special windows that don't look invisible to migratory birds. One student became excited about this and wanted to go further and explore how architects could design interesting eco-buildings with greenery around them.

While problem-solving strategies help teachers structure the creative process, many feel constrained by the sequence. Teachers should feel free to pick and choose the pieces of a model or strategy that best serve the interests and needs of gifted children. Embracing more flexibility and variety, a creative process can also draw freely from the arts rather than remain strictly in an academic mode. Problem solving, divergent thinking, brainstorming, and other processes invariably work better when they involve art media (visual materials related to the topic at hand, music, drama, video, etc.). Gifted children have extraordinary imaginations that are, for the most part, undernourished. They crave opportunities to immerse themselves imaginatively in the questions they pose and paradoxes they discover and to draw on a rich combination of sources and materials.

In a creative process, gifted children often work differently from each other, and this poses another problem with models that emphasize sequential steps and group work. One child wants to work alone; another enjoys group brainstorming sessions. One prefers to research something first and then see what questions it raises; another decides to use visual media and free association to think about his project before he starts. Yet in any subject, teachers can expand the range of possible ways gifted students can approach a topic or problem. Any strategies that develop their flexibility as thinkers will help them probe into subjects and formulate questions to an extent they would not do otherwise. Is this creative? Perhaps it isn't, in the strictest sense of the word. The strategies described in this section may not result in anything startlingly original, but gifted children can nevertheless make significant and meaningful discoveries.

The Domains of Sensation and Intuition

Keen sensibility is often the first recognizable sign of giftedness in children. The world bombards their eyes, ears, nose, and taste buds with multiple and complex sensations. The beauty of Canada geese flying south at dusk awes them; the pounding beat of the bass from a passing car radio shakes them to their bones; the gentle breeze that sends fallen leaves into a half-hearted spin makes them want to leap into the air; the pelting rain against their skin feels like the whipping of an angry sky. Young gifted children notice little things—mud squishing through their toes, the spicy smell of dinner cooking, the warmth of the radiator against their feet on a cold evening.

The sensing/intuiting facility can surface in a variety of contexts and combines with other domains.

A second grader fixes a classroom clock that has not worked for several months. When asked by his teacher how he did it, he replied, "I just fiddled with it for a while and then figured out how to make it work." The child couldn't explain his process since he used no systematic approach, but simply drew on the little he knew, felt around, experimented with the pieces, and then acted on a hunch.

A fifth grader says that when she dances to Vivaldi, she feels every note flow through her body like water. "I no longer have bones or anything and there is no space between the music and me." This kinesthetic sensibility has not only fed her interest in the arts but in science concepts related to force, lift, momentum, gravity, and so forth.

A first grader exhibits an extraordinary ability to identify species of plants and birds. When questioned, the child clearly draws on keen visual, tactile, and aural cues. She verifies her identification by remembering minute differences between the beaks of finches and those of warblers, by the shape and "feel" of leaves or by subtle variations in bird song.

Creating a work of art or preparing for a theatrical role engages all of the senses of an eager gifted child and may result in startling new insights. A third grader inhabits the life of a historical figure, an endangered species, or a fictional character and makes an interesting discovery. Class clowns who entertain their peers with spontaneous and satiric monologues (about school, politics, pop culture, etc.) often include imitations that are uncannily accurate in accent, tone quality, gestures, and facial expressions. Other children manifest this same responsiveness and intuitive understanding of the people around them in a different way. They pick up subtle cues from the behaviors of adults, children, and even animals. These students tend to be the ones who do something kind for a family member who's been struggling silently (and who wonders how the child knew) or explains the bizarre behavior of a dog or cat that no one else can understand.

In gifted education, the sensing/intuiting aspect of creativity rarely has as much merit as other aspects. In Western culture, we tend to think of feeling and sensing as somehow unintellectual or unworthy of serious attention. However, nature study is an area in which teachers have been able to draw on these sensibilities in the classroom. A third-grade teacher in an urban area once discovered the benefits of integrating nature study into science, social studies, language arts, and art. She wrote,

> My kids live in a world of concrete, and even though they visit the lake and go to the park, they have little meaningful connection to it. Several of the gifted students in my class have taken a strong interest in the nature part of our classroom. At the beginning of the year, I always start a nature exhibit, which, as the year progresses, the students add to. I have several bird nests that I brought in during the winter, pine cones, branches with interesting bits of lichen growing on them, prairie grasses of different kinds, pressed leaves, and video footage of some of my own bird sightings. The nature corner of our room has classification books for birds, butterflies, bugs, trees, and so on. We have posters where kids can add their species of plant or bird or bug and any observations they have. Children learn to keep nature journals with specific instructions from me on what they should focus on and what details to include in their descriptions (sights, sounds, textures, and so on). The nature center has become an integral part of many units and it has inspired genuinely original work, especially from my gifted students.

Engaging the senses in something tangible—the natural world, visual art, music, rhythm, or sculpture—sharpens the insights and intuitive understandings of gifted students. The ones who spend too much time under the spell of electronic stimuli (television, computers, videogames) will discover a whole new world by reawakening their senses. Some will find that they have an extraordinary auditory memory or that visual patterns, colors, and shapes provide clues they missed before or that the smell and texture of things have the power to instantly transport them to other places and times. As one fourth grader put it, "My nose never forgets anything."

Putting gifted children in touch with their senses and sensibilities has an immediate calming effect. Many of them have to steel themselves against the onslaught of the world—the aggressive blasting of televisions, radios, computers, CDs; the harshness they occasionally see in the behavior of their peers; the disturbing and incomprehensible instances of cruelty, indifference, or ignorance that they pick up from the media. To navigate their daily lives, many of them have to pull back from this sensibility.

The presence of beauty (in a painting, the natural world, a mathematical formula)—the depth, breadth, richness, and variety of texture and pattern—is a gift for the gifted. When the sensing/intuiting aspect of creativity is restored, children notice the difference. A gifted fourth grader who took a summer ecology class wrote the following passage in his journal:

The silence. That is what I notice first. But then, not so silent, for the cicadas are united in a chorus and I feel like I've snuck into their rehearsal. The grasshoppers leap over my shoes as I sit here in my field, wondering why I've wasted so much time not sitting here. Tree swallows on a bug hunt swoop and soar, swoop and soar and I watch in silence. There is, after all, a silence. It is I who am silent, who have nothing to say, but so much to hear and see and feel, here in my field.

The Imaginative Domain

Gifted students in accelerated programs desperately need opportunities to use their imaginations. The imagination presents a realm beyond the known facts, concepts, and theories where children can visualize new possibilities, invent fictional worlds. Often seen as the domain of fantasy or the unreal, in a broader sense, imagination is merely the power to form an image or concept of something that isn't present. Leonardo da Vinci used imagination when he designed his extraordinary flying machines from what he knew about the science of bird flight. Most inventions, scientific discoveries, poems, paintings, musical compositions, and choreographed dances involve the imagination in one way or another.

A third-grade teacher wants her cluster group to understand how literary elements and techniques such as metaphor, simile, imagery, and rhythm convey meaning in poetry and decides to have them compose poems of their own. She provides not only poems for them to read but also posters, prints, paintings, musical recordings, sound effects, and other sources as a way of stimulating ideas. She poses questions about what they observe/hear/feel about the painting or recording, what they imagine is happening, how they would feel, and what they would do if they could put themselves in the painting/print/musical recording, or what figures of speech they might use to communicate the images in their minds.

The students soon become immersed. They explore the sensations, textures, smells, sights, and sounds in as specific language as they can. They try their hands at similes and metaphors (e.g., the night as Earth's "cape of troubles"; the thunder on the plains "rolling like waves of buffalo herds long past"). They discover the power of imagery to communicate deeper meanings.

Aurora

When we scream,
We scream from the realm
Of the unimaginable.
Visible to all, tangible to none.
I live beyond the physical,
Not yet the metaphysical.
What am I?

A combination of forces,
A miracle to the masses
An equation to the few.
Beware, I am omnipresent!

—William, Grade 7

Freedom

A crystal lake, surface smooth as glass,
Suffocated by the foreshadowing mountains.
White strips of clouds, claw marks, tear tracks, decorate the sky.
Shadows reflect on the desolate lake.
Stones at the bottom of the pit look longingly,
Wishing for the mountain to shift, for an open road.
Wishing for freedom.

—Alexandra, Grade 6

SOURCE: Creative writing class at The Project program (2004), sponsored by The Center for Gifted, National-Louis University.

In language arts, social studies, and science, the visual and performing arts often play a major role in stimulating the imagination. High-ability children, with their acute sensibilities and interpretive gifts, should have daily contact with the arts in some form. Art films, prints, photographs, paintings, theatrical exercises, and creative movement (dance and mime) all provide excellent catalysts for the imagination, as will be discussed in the next section. A common strategy for inspiring the imagination is to have students identify with another person, an animal, a phenomenon (such as a thunderstorm), or even an object. Exploring the movement of the solar system as one of the planets, seeing the world through the eyes of different characters in a story, or composing a poem from the standpoint of a thunderstorm in a land stricken by drought—all of these processes stimulate rich and often profound responses from gifted students.

The Artistic Domain

The artistic domain offers the largest creative bounty for a teacher in terms of the wide applicability of the arts to an accelerated curriculum, the extraordinary results for gifted children achieved by this, and in terms of the different learning styles brought to life by an arts-conscious classroom. Not only can "accelerated" students explore talent areas that might otherwise lie dormant, but many gifted children with strong leanings in the kinetic, auditory, and visual areas begin to discover strengths they never knew they had. A child in the third grade wrote a tongue-in-cheek story called "Where's My Tea?" about a small band of colonists furious over the Boston Tea Party. He imagined a secret tea party by devoted tea lovers bent on stopping the revolt in order to save their tea! The piece showed tremendous sophistication and greater historical understanding than the teacher had previously seen in this child. This was the first time the child ever felt excited about a school assignment.

The arts are a powerful resource for creative work, enhancing sensitivity, self-expression, and creative responses to complex problems (Seeley, 1989). Goertz (2001) observes that artists sharpen observation, abstract thinking, and problem analysis when they work. "The artist visualizes and sets goals to find and define the problem, chooses techniques to collect data, and then evaluates and revises the problem solution with imagination in order to create" (2001, p. 476). Students with theatrical gifts examine and improvise situations and problems from multiple points of view, often considering "What if?" scenarios. Musical students express their sensitivity to sound and rhythm in creative writing (both poetry and prose); they perceive patterns and sequences in bird song and analyze hidden structures in the relationships between species.

The arts link the world of sensibility, feeling, and creating to the world of inquiry, reason, and higher-level thinking. To use the arts effectively, teachers need to consider their learning goals—the nature and level of the subjects to be taught, the concepts and skills to be acquired, and the processes involved. Here are some useful questions to consider when preparing to integrate the arts into specific units or lessons.

- What are the students' learning styles, interests, and special talents?
- What should the children understand as a result of this class or unit?
- What kind of learning experience should they have (inductive thinking, sensing/intuiting, imagining/feeling)?
- Given the above, what *kind* of adjustment is needed in terms of the level of difficulty, the actual process they engage in, the materials and sources they use?
- How can the arts support a creative activity already in place? For example, would a problem-solving activity benefit from a theatrical technique? Would a study of U.S. writers in nineteenth-century New England become more vivid with prints, photographs, and paintings of that time and place?
- Do the students enjoy moving? Doing things with their hands? Imagining they are someone else? Something else? Somewhere else?
- Which of the arts would best serve the aims and purpose of this specific lesson? What materials?
- In what way would the arts be most effective—as a catalyst in the beginning? As a process throughout the assignment? As a final project?

Table 3.2 provides some ideas for integrating the arts into the curriculum for gifted students (Smutny & von Fremd, 2004, pp. 91–92).

Creativity and the arts are indispensable for instilling the joy of discovery that many gifted students brought with them during their earliest years of school. To most of these promising children, numbers, words, and growing things are not "subjects" isolated from the world, but part of their daily lives. The arts enable this vivid personal connection to continue. Gifted students with agile and hungry minds need a rich and varied medium for learning across the disciplines. Their growth and engagement depend on experiences that enable them to discover, for example, that the shapes and patterns they see in math also occur in art, in movement, in architecture, and in the countless phenomena of nature. One has only to look at a child excitedly explain how the array of shapes and patterns on a plant determines its species to realize how significant the arts are. Without this creative and artistic dimension, accelerated learning cannot accommodate the unique sensibilities and talents of our most able students.

There is a great need to include the creative dimension in accelerated learning. Even in classrooms where gifted students can learn at the pace and level of their ability, children long for something more. While some scholars may question the extent to which an imaginative or creative problem-solving process is truly creative, the

Table 3.2

Arts as Process	Arts as Product
Language Arts 1. Paintings used as story starters or as catalysts for poems 2. Music played to create mood for a speech or presentation; music played to generate ideas for stories, poems 3. Dramatic role-playing to understand point of view in stories 4. Mime of a story or poem as teacher reads it out loud	**Language Arts** 1. Create paintings/drawings of a story plot; collage of a poem. 2. Invent a rap biography of famous person; create soundtrack for a story. 3. Adapt a popular story to create a chamber theater piece. 4. Choreograph a dance to interpret story or poem.
Social Studies 1. Prints of historical period as source of ideas and concepts 2. Role-playing of different cultural views of an issue; impersonations of a key historical/political figure 3. Investigation of dances of another culture or another historical period to gain insight into the people 4. Use of music from another culture/time period to explore characteristics of that culture/time period	**Social Studies** 1. Incorporate ideas from history, politics, and culture into a visual art piece. 2. Compose a song, rap, or melody around two key concepts in a historical event. 3. Perform a chamber theater adaptation based on a story about immigrants at Ellis Island. 4. Create a dance or mime history of an event.
Science 1. Paintings/prints to explore light, shadow, gravity, and perspective 2. Music and sound as sources for identifying different science phenomena 3. Movement used to learn actions and rotations of planets in solar system 4. Documentary of a scientist to generate a discussion of his or her discovery	**Science** 1. Create a diagram, painting, or drawing that illustrates two scientific facts about the rain forest. 2. Create a surrealist-type painting about time, space, light, or gravity. 3. Impersonate a scientist and explain what she or he most valued about a discovery. 4. Create a dance or mime project around several science themes (e.g., gravity, time, light).
Mathematics 1. Prints/photographs to identify geometric shapes; use of cubism to explore properties of cubes and other shapes 2. Use of rhythms to explore idea of fractions (whole notes, half notes, etc.) 3. Dramatization of math problems to understand process and find solutions 4. Use of jumping to work out the results of an addition problem; creation of physical movements to express different operations—addition, subtraction, and so on	**Mathematics** 1. Create a geometric painting that illustrates properties of geometric shapes. 2. Create a drawing or diagram to show a mathematical operation. 3. Impersonate a number or a mathematical symbol and write or list what is most valuable about it; provide examples. 4. Choreograph a dance or mime piece that expresses at least three key math facts; improvise new mathematical situations by extending the dance or mime piece.

SOURCE: Smutny, J. F. and von Fremd, S. E. (2004). *Differentiating for the young child: Teaching strategies across the content areas K–3*, pp. 91–92. Thousand Oaks, CA: Corwin Press. Reprinted with permission.

students themselves are in little doubt about the value of the experience. Perhaps the clearest change that children sense by embarking on a creative adventure is the shift from a mode of receiving to that of giving. They find themselves no longer in the position of just responding to external demands, looking for finite solutions, and being lost in "Orwellian isolation." They discover, instead, the possibility of a "profound engagement," the lure of new paths yet to explore, and a journey out to some distant horizon where they can recapture the world.

4

Assessment for Accelerated Learners

Clarissa skipped from second to fourth grade and is adjusting well to her new situation. By January, however, she found herself surpassing most of her classmates in mathematics.

Robby is new to the district and joined a cluster group in fifth grade. While he enjoys the academic challenge, which he lacked in his previous school, he's behind in some skill areas.

Marisol attends second grade and is exceptionally gifted in language arts. She excels in a fast-paced instructional group for reading and writing in the third grade, but longs for opportunities to compose stories and poems.

As mentioned in Chapter 1, acceleration may not serve the students who need it if teachers don't attend to their changing needs. The appearance of a new interest, the achievement of a skill that once eluded them, a sudden leap in cognitive growth, a struggle resulting from uneven ability—all of these influence how gifted children advance through an accelerated program. This chapter attempts to build on the assessments teachers routinely do in their own classrooms by focusing on areas in which "accelerated" students may need more careful attention. Are they progressing in an advanced curriculum at the level of their gifts or still moving along at a level significantly below what they can do? Are weaknesses in skill or knowledge areas curtailing their progress? Are differences in culture and learning style adequately addressed in the program? What about social and emotional well-being?

To examine these and other questions in the context of the classroom, we will consider two gifted students and how teachers assessed their growth to determine the appropriate pace and level of learning.

Noah is a highly gifted child who skipped from the first to the third grade halfway through his first year. At first, the novelty of more difficult content and new, older kids reawakened his love of learning. He enjoys reading and writing, although he struggles with his penmanship. Because he's a perfectionist, this can sometimes be a problem as he writes and rewrites. He says that he doesn't want to pass in papers that look "like a little kid's." He also adores science, spending every spare minute in his back yard investigating insect life and pulling up the purple loosestrife that, he has learned, is an invasive species in his area.

Desiree, fourth grade, is a gifted student who loves poetry and storytelling. She attends a summer program every year for gifted writers and has already published a couple of poems in a children's magazine. Recently, her teacher placed her in a cluster group (combined with the other fourth grade) that is currently working on poetry and story composition. Desiree also has an exceptional artistic ability and spends her lunch period sketching a wide range of subjects—kids in the class, the corner of the window where plaster is crumbling, the head of an inquisitive pigeon staring into the window. Desiree sometimes needs help creating reasonable goals for herself. She gets enthused about so many ideas that she tends to expand her project, bite off more than she can chew, become overwhelmed, and then quit. She also loses interest in a project when it's almost completed and hastily concludes it in order to move on to the next thing.

In most cases, a gifted child who's unhappy in an "accelerated" learning program is not advancing at a pace or level appropriate for him, or is in a classroom setting that doesn't accommodate his learning styles. This happens for a number of reasons. For example, a teacher may see a child like Noah as already "accelerated" and therefore may not notice when he surpasses his new peers in some areas. Most highly gifted students will require further acceleration after they've adjusted to the new grade and, in some circumstances, may need to skip an additional grade. Then there is a child like Desiree, an intensely visual learner who sees writing poems as paintings and stories as "routes on a map" that she first draws and then composes in language. Desiree sees patterns that no one else does and is capable of complex thinking far greater than her peers. Some teachers may not recognize how the powers of an artist and writer apply to other subject areas. Again, a more careful observation and recognition of her abilities would correct this and provide accelerated content in the areas where she clearly needs it.

Understanding how well a child is doing in an accelerated program also means attending to the *whole child.* Assessment does not merely involve figuring out whether a student's ability matches the pace and level of a child's assigned work, but understanding her sensibilities, interests, creative strengths, and so on (Fisher, 1998). Does this accelerated learning program respond to the child's hunger and readiness for a faster-paced, more advanced curriculum with more challenging concepts and questions? Does it feed his imagination, stimulate his curiosity, and nurture the inventor in him? Does it respond to her learning styles, her interests, and her emotional needs (e.g., a need for safety, a need for time alone, a need for encouragement)? Does it also enable her to strengthen a particular skill or knowledge base?

At its best, assessment ensures that an educational program stays current with a gifted student, serving her academic, creative, social, and emotional needs as they change and develop. For younger children—particularly in the early primary grades—the most beneficial assessment focuses on students' natural activities and behaviors in the classroom, uses a range of tools and processes, and recognizes individual diversity in learning styles, rates, and needs (Bredekamp & Rosegrant, 1992, pp. 22–24). Pre- and post-testing and the rating of student products are rarely sufficient to determine how well a particular program is working for a gifted student. Instead, observations, portfolios, and rubrics of a gifted child's work go much further in helping teachers evaluate progress and pinpoint specific areas in which she requires more challenge or support. Here is a summary of how they aid teachers' assessments.

- **Observation.** In order to be effective, observations need direction and focus. The Kingore Observation Inventory (Kingore, 1990), for example, provides a range of specific categories that teachers can analyze (advanced language, analytical thinking, meaning motivated, perspective, sense of humor, sensitivity, accelerated learning). With guidelines for their observations (Coil & Merritt, 2001, p. 84), teachers can target areas in which gifted students need further adjustment. Observations should include the following:

  1. The main learning outcomes for a child

  2. Criteria for achieving them

  3. A rating scale for judging the criteria

- **Portfolios.** In the case of younger students, portfolios of student work are the most reliable evidence of ability and learning styles (Kingore, 1998).

They validate hunches and observations and enable teachers to talk with students and their parents, to evaluate progress and change, and to broaden ideas and choices for future programming (Kingore, 1993). Ideally, portfolios should include these elements:

1. A clearly stated purpose
2. Evidence of links between course content and materials selected
3. A variety of products that demonstrate competency and growth in different areas
4. Direct correspondence between concepts learned and classroom instruction
5. Evidence of cognitive and creative growth in the learner through selected work (not just student's best work)
6. Student's selections based on his or her self-evaluation and understanding of himself or herself as a learner with unique academic and emotional needs (Clark, 2002a, p. 31)

- **Rubrics.** Rubrics are scoring guides that help teachers keep track of learning goals and expectations and assess students' progress at each phase of a unit or activity (Coil & Merritt, 2001). Teachers can design two kinds of rubrics: developmental and summative. A developmental rubric provides immediate feedback and helps guide the learning process. A summative rubric assesses student work at the end of an assignment, and the purpose is to evaluate a process that is difficult to quantify. Rubrics should include the following:
  1. Criteria
  2. Rating scale of stages for different degrees of mastery
  3. Descriptors that assess each aspect of the assigned process and where it belongs on the scale

Portfolios and rubrics also nurture the capacity for gifted students to evaluate their own work and progress. Self-assessment is essential to any child's progress as a learner (Black & William, 1998). Gifted children have a tendency to be severe critics of their own work, especially when they don't understand the larger rationale for an assignment or the criteria for successful achievement *before they begin.* Accelerated students need to become more knowledgeable about themselves *as learners* and gain practice assessing their work based on clearly articulated goals and criteria. Lacking the tools to evaluate their own progress or achievement, they can't improve their learning. The kind of formative assessment explored in this chapter enables students to grasp their learning goal in an assignment, their position in achieving that goal (based on evidence gleaned from rubrics, self-observation, teacher observations, etc.), and the way to reach that goal (Black & William, 1998).

Though most teachers are familiar with the different ways to assess students, Table 4.1 depicts a range of commonly used strategies for gauging the progress of gifted learners in an accelerated learning program.

The remainder of this chapter will use Noah and Desiree as examples to demonstrate how students can progress through an accelerated unit and what their teachers can do to determine whether their program actually serves their needs. This is not a formula for assessing gifted students, but rather a spotlight on the issues and

Table 4.1 Strategies for Assessing Gifted Students in Accelerated Programs

Techniques	*Goals*	*Contexts (examples)*	*Methods (examples)*
Informal observation	To note behavior as a method of gaining informal impressions of key aspects of student work	Group discussions Oral reading Reporting back from group discussions Journal writing	Checklists Anecdotal records Notes on student work
In-depth analysis	To analyze specific aspects of student work, reflecting upon what it reveals of a student's strengths and weaknesses	Responses to direct questions Tests Drafts Role-plays Note-taking and summarizing Portfolios Artistic/creative work	Rubrics Criteria checklists Anecdotal records Lists of grades or marks Tables linking activities with specific learning outcomes
Consultations and discussions	To gain understanding about aspects of student work (such as thinking strategies, feelings, intuitions, sensibilities) that are difficult to obtain through other techniques	Casual conversations Interviews Questionnaires Conferences	Conference logs Rubrics Checklists Anecdotal records Consultations with parents on specific learning issues
Self-assessment/Peer review	*For teachers:* To understand students' ideas on task or process, what they understand and what confuses them, and how they perceive their peers' work *For students:* To develop self-awareness and self-regulation	Journals Criteria lists Structured peer assessment formats Records of completed work Portfolios of "best work"	Anecdotal records Tables linking activities with learning outcomes Rubrics Peer assessment forms

questions that teachers need to address in order to make accelerated instruction more responsive to individual needs.

NOAH

As mentioned previously, Noah skipped second grade and now attends third. He can read and understand texts at the young adult level and even, in some subjects, college level. His mother says that she's always finding him buried in the family encyclopedias and the many books they have on identifying birds, insects, plants, and trees. It was he who found the purple loosestrife and informed her of its danger to the local environment. When his teacher introduced a new unit on locomotion, he practically exploded out of his seat, waving his arm in the air and asking to do his on flight. He wanted to integrate what he had observed in birds and link it to the science of flight in airplanes. Here is what the teacher and Noah planned together within a unit on locomotion.

Learning destination: To understand how the science of flight observed and studied in birds (and visible in Leonardo da Vinci's wonderful flying machines) applies to the development of airplanes. (See Learning Destinations in Chapter 2.)

Assignment for Noah: To create a display/report that shows how principles such as weight, lift, thrust, and drag apply to bird flight and how scientists and engineers used these principles to design airplanes.

Sources: Noah is a voracious reader and therefore had free reign to consult a collection of books from the classroom and library as well as his own home to explore how the shape of birds' wings affects air flow and enables them to lift off from Earth. Noah also wanted to examine pictures of birds, designs of airplanes, and watch birds in his yard. He asked, "How do different shaped wings determine the kind of fliers these birds are?" Noah also had materials (construction paper, cardboard, string, wire, etc.) to construct an airplane and/or bird as part of his display and demonstration. From the beginning of his project, he became intrigued by da Vinci's flight designs, including his drawings of a propeller, a helicopter, and a parachute.

Noah had a number of tasks.

- Read a book or combination of books on bird flight, and diagram and explain the science behind it. What is it that enables birds to lift off the Earth and maneuver through space?
- From materials you choose, construct a model of a bird or birdlike contraption with a head, body, wings, tail, and legs that will help you show someone else how the principles of flight work.
- Do research (on Internet and library) on a past inventor/designer who drew from bird aerodynamics to create an airplane design. Did these designs become planes in the inventor's lifetime? What are the limitations? Note your conclusions.
- Create a design (or model) for a flying machine based on what you've learned. Apply the concepts of *weight, lift, thrust,* and *drag* to your design.

The teacher provided acceleration for Noah using the following resources and assignment criteria:

- The number and level of the texts he used
- The application of his understanding to a model and diagram
- Research on the Internet and library that integrated historical information
- His ability to synthesize and analyze concepts and innovate by creating his own flying machine

Assessing Noah

From prior experiences, parental feedback, and records, the teacher knew Noah's strengths and weaknesses and planned for them. She gave him a large index card that listed the criteria for his project. This helped him stay on track and aided him in making decisions about how to proceed.

My Project: To show how people created airplanes from what they learned about bird flight.

Criteria:

- The display/project comes from at least two books and two Web sites (approved by my teacher).
- My model or sketch of a bird shows what makes a bird "aerodynamic," and I can use it to explain how flying works.
- The display/project shows at least one of the da Vinci designs and both its strengths and weaknesses (e.g., what made it aerodynamic and what were its limitations as a flying machine).
- My own airplane design addresses the concepts of weight, lift, thrust, and drag and includes explanations of why I think it would work as a flying machine.

Because of Noah's advanced reading ability and young age, the teacher didn't require too much writing. He could write notes from his research and sketch designs to document what he was discovering from books and Internet research. From these, he was later able to write several short paragraphs explaining his sketches and the science of flight in both birds and airplanes. His teacher had him start his project with Scholastic's *The Story of Flight* as an introduction to basic scientific concepts and the inventors and pilots who contributed to the evolution of airplanes and other flying machines. He then selected two other books on flight (in consultation with his teacher). He also went to the library and online to learn more about the da Vinci designs and made a list of materials he would need to make a basic model of a bird (or birdlike contraption).

Making the model was an excellent way to support Noah's fine motor skills, which were lagging, and to give him a way to apply what he was learning. He wanted the wings, tail, and legs to have some maneuverability in order to illustrate how birds change direction, land, or take off. Because da Vinci was a bird watcher and based his ideas on what he saw in birds, Noah felt that he, too, could discover things from observing the birds in his back yard fly to and from the feeder. He made notes such as, "The sparrows move their tails to change direction. The legs of birds are stretched way back when they fly." The teacher could see that Noah relished studying the science behind flight and loved explaining the formula for level, steady flight: Lift = Weight and Drag = Thrust.

The teacher used a number of strategies to assess Noah's learning. Before beginning the unit, she drew on past experiences with Noah as well as tests, work samples, and anecdotal evidence to determine the appropriate level and pace. Knowing that he needed help structuring his projects, she sat down with him to work out what steps he should take to begin the process. The teacher knew, from the start, where he would require more support and where he could tackle difficulties on his own. He worked in a cluster group, which also allowed him to share and test his ideas. One of the other students also focused on aviation within the unit. Periodically, the teacher checked in with Noah and what struck her most was how much he relished his project. He surprised her at one point by stating emphatically, "The problem with da Vinci's machines was that they were powered by people, not motors. Birds are different. Did you know that a sparrow's heart beats 800 times a minute when it flies?" Noah exhibited an extraordinary gift for synthesizing and analyzing a lot of information from different sources simultaneously.

After the project ended, the teacher sat down with Noah to discuss his experience with the project. She used the questions below as a general guide and noted his responses for her records. The goal was to support Noah's metacognitive awareness by asking him to reflect on the strengths of his project and weaknesses in skills or understanding.

What did you discover about your own learning?

- Which of the tasks did you enjoy doing the most? Why?
- Which do you think you did best? Why?
- Is there anything you think you could have done better? What could you have done?
- Was there anything you had difficulty with because you didn't know how to do it? If so, could you explain this?
- If you were beginning this project again, what would you change? Why?

In his comments, Noah expressed particular enthusiasm for his discovery that da Vinci's idea of the human body powering his flying machines was a major problem in early thinking about aviation. He practically forgot his challenge with penmanship as he scribbled out what was, for him, a key issue for the flapping wing planes: How do we match the amount of power the aircraft needs to take off with what a human being can provide? Noah easily tackled the process of reading and research, as it is something he does a lot at home, but added that he sometimes forgot what he was looking for while he read. He said that he got so interested in the different shapes and designs of bird species and how this affected their flight that he would lose track of time.

Noah had some trouble sketching out a design because he couldn't master the control he needed to get the proportions right. But at least he could do enough to draw arrows and demonstrate how flight worked. When he got to making a model, he had fun once the teacher helped him get started. Noah doesn't feel confident in tasks that involve making and constructing things; however, a couple of kids from the cluster group were helpful in suggesting how he could approach it. When asked how he would change the assignment to make it more interesting, Noah thought he would include myths and stories about flying—such as Icarus—because "it would show that we've been wanting to fly for a long, long time."

The teacher used the following questions to guide her assessment:

Skills

- Which tasks did Noah do independently? Which required assistance?
- How effective was he in organizing and pacing himself as he selected sources, analyzed the information, theorized about the concepts, and produced a report/display to show what he discovered?

Affect

- Did Noah enjoy the project? How well did he deal with the demands? What kind of assistance did he need?
- Did he enjoy working on his own? Did he interact with his cluster occasionally, and did this aid the process?

Cognition

- Noah's considerable knowledge about science in the natural world and his ability to investigate a subject on his own equipped him to explore aviation; using bird flight as the entrée to this study worked well. To what extent did Noah grapple with the concepts of flight and theorize about design as it relates to weight, lift, thrust, and drag?
- To what extent did experimenting with his own designs contribute to his understanding of the ways in which shape and materials affect the stability of an "airplane"?

This process may appear long and involved, but, in fact, much of it occurs moment by moment as the teacher supervises, consults with the student, and notes down new discoveries and insights about his learning, special needs, and talents. Noah's teacher keeps a file for each student where she can record, briefly, the most important insights or information that will help her plan in the future. The criteria list that Noah kept with him as he worked on his assignment was also useful for his discussions with the teacher and accompanied her own observations in the file. Because of Noah's young age, the teacher also sought the feedback and support of Noah's parents, who offered to aid her in any area in which she needed assistance. Several times, Noah's mother, who has a background in gifted education, came in to work with the cluster and filled in some important gaps in the teacher's understanding of Noah's needs.

Assessing Noah's performance in the aviation project revealed some important insights about the appropriate pace and level at which he needs to advance. These were some of the most important conclusions:

1.   Noah quickly assimilated information from books and Web sites on his topic. He craves assignments that remove the ceiling on how much text he encounters and the level of difficulty. He is a child who needs to acquire a certain amount of knowledge *before* he can analyze more abstract concepts. He feels most at home in inductive reasoning situations where he can discover how, for example, the principles of flight operate with birds, parachutes, balloons, airplanes, and so forth. Care needs to be taken to ensure that Noah continues to advance at this level. The possibility of his taking a couple of subjects—particularly science—at a higher grade should be considered at some point.

2.   Noah needs encouragement in handwriting. He feels self-conscious about it and tries to get out of doing it whenever he can. It has helped him to work on other small motor skills by creating designs, sketches, models, and maps that enable him to practice the skill he needs in handwriting. The problem is mostly psychological and, according to the mother, some family members might have unintentionally reinforced it by telling him that "for most people in our family, writing looks like chicken scratch."

3. Noah worked well on his own during the research, reading, and note-taking segment of his work. But he needed assistance pacing himself—figuring out how much time to give himself for reading, experimenting with models, and so forth. He got panicky at one point when he realized that he spent too much time online checking site after site. The teacher had to sit down with him and go over the criteria list, helping him create priorities for his work. What is most important and why?

4. An area that Noah himself mentioned was integrating other subject areas. Specifically, he would like to have included the imagination and stories and myths around flying. Noah's parents have always supported the creative side of Noah, and this should be included in future assignments when possible. Obviously, designing his own flying machine gave him an opportunity to invent, but he said he would rather delve into the world of story, painting, poetry, and even film (he mentioned flying superheroes such as Superman and the film *Fly Away Home*, about a father and daughter who created a flying contraption to help a flock of geese find their way south for the winter).

DESIREE

Desiree is a highly sensitive, introspective student whose writing has, as her summer teacher described it, "the stillness of a Monet pond and the power of a gathering storm." She scribbles in small notebooks all day long, snatching five-minute breaks, lunch time, or recess time to jot down ideas for stories or poems, to capture an image or find a metaphor for "the thing in my head." In a unit on satire, Desiree's cluster group expressed an interest in composing their own satires or parodies. Desiree asked her teacher if she could take the Cinderella story and compose something that would satirize the "mall culture" of kids her age. She wanted to call the story "Mallarella"—about a girl whom the popular mall crowd treats as a low kid on the totem pole. She had been thinking of this since the teacher first mentioned the possibility of the cluster creating their own parodies and pulled out a notebook full of plot lines and ideas she'd scribbled out the night before.

Desiree couldn't decide what sort of plot would give the most punch. At one point, she asked, "Should I have Mallarella give up on the prince dude as unworthy of her time, or should I have the guy be someone who's deeper and interested in Mallarella not because she's beautiful but because she's a girl who's real and smart?" Desiree created a list of different plots and character descriptions, exploring how they might work in her parody. The teacher created the following structure for her work:

Learning destination: To understand how parody (through a set of specific techniques) can poke fun at something or someone while it simultaneously reveals important ideas or truths.

Assignment for Desiree: To write a parody based on the Cinderella fairytale that makes fun of the enslavement of young people to "mall culture" and criticizes its shallowness and injustice. The assignment will include the study of other satires and/or parodies, a knowledge of strategies for composing satiric works, and analysis of their appropriate use in this story.

Sources: Desiree told her teacher that she knew a lot about parody just from living in her family. Her uncle and mother had long distinguished themselves as the humorists in the family; at special gatherings, they would regale everyone with hilarious stories that parodied someone or something. Sometimes, it was imitations of people they all knew and creative retellings of old family history. Other times, it had to do with a family member's clever response to encounters or situations in which a stereotype or prejudice was in evidence. African American Desiree learned that satirizing social misconceptions about gender and ethnicity can help remove the sting of difficult experiences.

Although Desiree already had many ideas to begin her project, she and the teacher created a list of sources to broaden the possibilities. As Desiree is a visual learner, often "seeing" vivid images of characters, environments, and scenes while she reads and writes and sketching as she thinks, the teacher felt that Desiree should have visual sources as a way of generating ideas. Together, they discussed cartoons, caricatures, and films, including *Shrek,* a movie that parodies "the knight rescues the girl and slays the dragon" story and its assumptions of female helplessness. Desiree understands the difference between satire (which ridicules human behavior with the intent of stimulating or preventing change but may not be funny) and parody (a humorous genre that imitates another work of art in an exaggerated fashion for comic effect).

Desiree also wanted to draw ideas from books she's read, such as *Gulliver's Travels* and Orwell's *Nineteen Eighty-Four,* and a number of satiric news media.

The teacher and Desiree made a list of tasks.

- Focusing on visual stimuli (cartoons, caricatures, films, etc.), books, and stories, consider several of the main techniques of satire and describe how they work. Examine *diminution* (which reduces the size of something so that it may appear ridiculous or be examined closely), *inflation* (which takes a real-life situation and exaggerates it to the point where it looks humorous), and *juxtaposition* (which places things of unequal importance side by side so that things/people/traditions/institutions lose their status and seem frivolous). How do the authors use them?
- Decide on the object of your parody. Is it social behavior, an institution, a cultural tradition, a global problem, or a political situation? What about this topic bothers you and why? Brainstorm which strategies might work the best and why. Share your ideas with peers in the cluster.
- Write out the goal of your parody—what effect you want the piece to have on the reader. Next, write a paragraph each describing what will happen in the first, second, and third parts of your parody. How will you begin? How will you create suspense and tension/conflict? What techniques will you use to build this? How do you foresee the climax of your story and how will it conclude?
- Write the parody. Include sketches (wherever you choose). Share with peers in the cluster.

The teacher provided acceleration for Desiree using the following resources and assignment criteria:

- The cluster group, which functions at a faster pace and more advanced level than the regular fourth-grade class
- The conceptual level of sources provided for the assignment
- Analysis of the techniques of satire and the impressions they create in three or four sources (at least two must be significant written works)
- The sophistication level of the creative process (requiring application from a variety of sources, synthesis of ideas from these sources, and analysis of the effects that satiric techniques have on a specific parody)
- The demand to compose a parody within a relatively short time—including collaborating with other peers, analyzing strengths and weaknesses, and editing/refining the final version

Assessing Desiree

Desiree enjoys working independently and seldom needs direction. However, she does have a tendency to expand on a project until it becomes unwieldy and often needs support completing her work. Her mother says that Desiree gets impatient once she knows how a story's going to conclude and hurries through to the end. Here is a criteria list for Desiree's project.

My Project: To create a parody of Cinderella that uses some of the techniques I've learned about satire and parody.

Criteria:

- The story draws on my analysis of cartoons, caricatures, films, television shows, and at least two books, focusing on the question What strategy is at work here?
- The parody illustrates *diminution, inflation,* and/or *juxtaposition* to create its effect.
- The story has a strong message or point of view about a condition, behavior, or institution.
- The story has a strong beginning, middle, and end; is vivid in imagery; and is suspenseful throughout.
- The story includes a plan for revision based on feedback from a writing partner and conference with the teacher.

After approving the sources for Desiree's parody, the teacher lent the cluster group a variety of "story summaries" (written by gifted students in past years) that they could use as models. As she sifted through caricatures, notes she wrote from films and television shows she'd viewed, and books she read, Desiree considered these questions: "How is the artist/author/filmmaker creating this image? What techniques does she or he use?" After writing a list of the different strategies of satire employed in these sources, she began to consider the technique(s) most suitable for her parody. Desiree enjoyed this process immensely, writing copious notes and creating preliminary sketches of characters in her Mallarella story. She became immersed in sketching and scribbling ideas for new plot twists—testing satiric techniques on her story concept. "What would be the best way to make my cruel mall gang ridiculous? What technique of satire should I use? What kind of characterization? What changes to the original plot?"

From prior experience with Desiree, the teacher knew that she had problems keeping her projects a manageable size; with very little effort, a small assignment could become a month-long project. Therefore, she assigned a writing partner who had worked well with her in the past and this, combined with the teacher's supervision, enabled Desiree to stay on course. The two classmates worked side by side as they investigated the different techniques used in selected sources, brainstormed what would work best in their parodies, and reviewed each other's summaries. Desiree expressed some worry that she wasn't moving as quickly as her partner, primarily because of her sketching (which she felt helped her think) and because she generated so many ideas that she couldn't decide what to do first. But her partner proved supportive in this regard, offering feedback on her ideas for plots. For example, at one point, he told her, "This idea is really funny and kind of cool, but it doesn't really create parody," which helped her stay more focused on the priorities of the assignment.

Despite groaning her way through the "story summary" (She complained, "It's so boring to know the structure in advance!"), Desiree found it an invaluable guide, and she was able to compose a working draft quickly. She employed the technique of *inflation* to make the mall girls look shallow, ridiculous, and outrageously demanding. In her African American culture, in which women are strong, the idea of fawning over and obeying a gang of abusive girls would be considered shameful. So instead, Desiree had Mallarella stand up to their ridicule and teasing (which they often did in the presence of the most popular guy in their group). Desiree re-created the fairy godmother as a befuddled chubby woman who fell into her home through a crowded closet, covered in dust. Instead of a horse-drawn carriage, Mallarella had a Mercedes with a fine looking driver—a man who had many of the same interests as Mallarella and who didn't mind her big feet and less than stylish clothes. She invited him to attend the party. At first, Desiree was going to have Mallarella eventually win the popular guy (whom the mean girls wanted), but later decided to have Mallarella become close to the driver instead.

Once the writing process began, Desiree and her partner each worked alone through the week. After they each completed a working draft, they shared their stories with one another, using the criteria list as a guide for reviewing their parodies and making suggestions. Though initially afraid of this phase of the process, Desiree was inspired by her partner's positive responses and his ideas on how she could strengthen her story. Following the guidelines of the teacher, which stipulated that students were to begin their peer review with what they liked in a student's work, Desiree's partner made her more aware of her strengths. His suggestions were also instructive, showing her several places where he found inconsistencies in the text and where he felt the need for more development. Desiree performed the same service for her partner, and in this way, they became catalysts for the completion of their parodies.

After Desiree completed her parody (with a series of sketches), the teacher studied it carefully and sat down with Desiree the next day. She asked the following questions as a way of focusing her on the central issues related to her learning process.

What did you learn about how you learn?

- What parts of writing the parody did you enjoy most? Why?
- Which do you think you did best? Why?
- Is there anything you think you could have done better? What could you have done?
- Was there anything you had difficulty with because you didn't know how to do it? If so, could you explain this?
- If you were beginning this project again, what would you change? Why?

Helping Desiree focus on specific questions encouraged her to see the value of her experience and to be less fixated on what she thought was wrong. Desiree said that she loved the discovery process, figuring out what would make her parody a powerful indictment of the kind of meanness she often saw in the social scene at the mall. She always enjoys the writing process, but this assignment gave her the opportunity to make a strong social critique. Through composing her own parody and experimenting with satiric techniques and devices, she discovered the possibility of making powerful statements without being "like a preacher no one wants to hear."

Desiree also said that this assignment forced her to be creative and analytical at the same time. "I had to think about my parody and imagine what kind of characters and plots would make it happen." Reading satire and parody and also viewing it in cartoons, films, and television shows gave her ideas on how she could apply the techniques to her subject. "I've learned a lot more by trying to write my own parody than I would have gotten just by reading it."

From there, Desiree and the teacher talked about what she did well. Desiree mentioned the fact that she's a fast reader and gets an abundance of ideas from what she reads. She analyzed different texts (Swift and Molière were her favorites) and viewed visual sources at home (cartoons, movies, and television shows) to help her strategize for her story. Desiree also felt that as a creative person, she had a gift for imagining different options for her story. "It was fun seeing so many different ways to go and figuring out which one worked best for the story." In this respect, the "story summary" helped her to stay on course. She resisted the summary at first because it took some of the fun out of the process, but it saved her time and enabled her to progress much more quickly. Her usual process had her writing spontaneously and then having to do serious reorganizing and rethinking later. "Now I can look at my summary and say, 'Okay, where am I and why am I stuck?' The summary also doesn't force me into anything, but it saves me because I don't have to go back and do a lot of switching around."

When asked further about the writing process, Desiree said that she felt she could compose a first draft quickly, but then she would get bogged down. "A lot of times, when I first read what I wrote, it just looks all wrong." She said that all she could see were the faults, and she didn't want to share the draft with anyone. There were always passages that didn't work, and Desiree couldn't always tell what made them "wrong." Sharing with her partner helped address this problem more than she anticipated. As already described, he was specific about all of the things that worked well and equally specific in explaining where the story, in his opinion, needed development or clarification. Another technique (suggested by the teacher) was to have Desiree read it aloud to herself at home or in a corner where she could hear her own words and see where the story wasn't working. These two strategies enabled Desiree to critique her own writing in a more constructive way.

As they focused on each question, the teacher shared her thoughts about how she saw Desiree's work—her strengths, weak areas, and needs for the future. Primarily, her aim was to find out if the level and pace of the process was a good fit for Desiree's present academic, emotional, and creative needs. She covered the same ground as Noah's teacher.

Skills

- Which tasks did Desiree do independently? Which ones required assistance?
- How effective was she at organizing and pacing herself as she selected sources, analyzed the information, theorized about the concepts, and produced a report/display to show what she discovered?

Affect

- Did Desiree enjoy the project? How well did she deal with the demands? What kind of assistance did she need?
- Did she enjoy working on her own? Did she interact with her cluster occasionally, and did this aid the process?

Cognition

- Desiree's considerable gift in writing and her ability to research a subject on her own enabled her to quickly gather information and insights related to parody and to create a structure (summary) to support her writing process. To what extent did she understand the theory behind parody?
- To what extent was she able to apply techniques of satire in such a way that they communicated the message she intended?

As they worked through Desiree's writing and sketches, the teacher focused on the key obstacle to Desiree's advancement—perfectionism. The teacher shared a quote from an interview of Toni Morrison that essentially said that her first drafts were always terrible and that for her, the draft was simply the raw material from which she would then craft a book. From her perspective, the real writing began *after* the draft—in the revising and editing. Together, the teacher and Desiree discussed the importance of understanding that all of the work Desiree does in the cluster group is, in a sense, a work in progress. They also talked about how it was important to focus her energy on learning as much as she could about the art of satire and parody and on discovering ways to apply the techniques used by satirists through the ages.

The teacher had Desiree create a list of guiding thoughts to help her avoid the tyranny of perfectionism during the revision and editing process. She advised Desiree to write this list on an index card and keep the card taped to her desk or in a place where she could look at it as she revised and improved upon her work. This card aided Desiree considerably as she examined her story again and made several significant adjustments (see Chart 4.1).

MY WORK-IN-PROGRESS

1. My draft is just the beginning. This is where the real writing starts!

2. I will begin with the good in my draft. Even if it looks like a total mess, I can list the things that I like and go from there.

3. The things that don't work point me to the places where I can grow as a writer. I can list these things as well and brainstorm different ways to approach them.

4. I can work on the story from any angle. There's no law telling me what to do first. If I get stuck, I'll just keep moving and come back to it later.

5. If I get really stuck, I'll ask my teacher or a student. Asking doesn't make me stupid. Asking is smart!

Chart 4.1

From informal assessment throughout the project, observations, and discussions with Desiree, the teacher drew the following conclusions:

1. Desiree is a lightning-fast reader and assimilates new concepts quickly. Given her interest in satirists like Swift and Molière, she can tackle sophisticated texts and analyze the techniques employed and the effect they create. As an intensely visual learner, though, Desiree needs to work with sketching pad in hand and relishes prints, cartoons, paintings, and photographs—any visual aids that give her access to her subject. She needs some encouragement in claiming this as her way to learn rather than feeling she shouldn't always need to sketch and diagram things.

2. Desiree is prolific in the ideas department. An endless stream of stories and poems knock at her door. She told the teacher once that when she lies quietly in her room at night, she has to put a small notebook and pen nearby because sometimes characters come and demand to be heard. This abundant quality, however, sometimes overwhelms her in projects. She feels pulled in many directions and hesitates over several ideas at once. What Desiree needs is help structuring assignments. Her teacher and parents are working together to encourage the habit of establishing realistic goals, identifying priorities of the assignment, and identifying the most appropriate steps to reach these goals. This simple process, reinforced at home and at school, will help Desiree avoid slowing down because of an unfocused and muddled approach.

3. Desiree is an exceptionally talented writer and needs no assistance in the actual writing. But, again, she does need to create at least a tentative summary before she starts writing so that she doesn't waste time wandering all over the map. In the past, Desiree would start a writing assignment in four or five different ways before realizing that it didn't really fulfill the requirements of the assignment. Though resistant initially, she realized after creating a summary for her parody that it helped guide her process without limiting her options. She's beginning to recognize that these sorts of tools can really aid her to progress at her ability level.

4. Desiree said that she felt a little constrained in having to write a story rather than a play. She felt that projects like this should allow students to make choices in the form their writing takes. When she began sifting through her material, making sketches, and writing notes to herself, she found herself visualizing a play rather than a story. When the teacher asked her whether she could adapt her story, Desiree said that she could and would like to try a written script as an alternative creative choice for her parody. In the future, projects involving writing should give Desiree more flexibility in selecting an alternative genre.

Assessing students in this way enables teachers to respond to specific needs and to make adjustment from month to month. Gathering information from a wide variety of sources (see Table 4.1) helps teachers to avoid misleading conclusions based on partial information. Recording observations doesn't have to take an inordinate amount of time. Many teachers do it on the fly, jotting down a few notes and placing them in a file or in a special notebook designed for this purpose. These, in combination with test scores, grades, prior anecdotal information, and consultations with parents, can provide clear directions on problem areas and indicate where a child may need more acceleration (or a different kind of acceleration).

Opportunities for gifted children to review and evaluate their learning experiences in this way are critical to their growth and development. Whatever methods teachers use to gauge their students' progress, self-assessment should always be among them. In the first place, many gifted students are deeply in tune with their learning preferences, strengths, problem areas, interests, and idiosyncrasies. It is not unusual to find a young gifted child who can comment astutely about her inner world. A first grader once said, "Sometimes when I'm sitting at the dinner table, I'm thinking, thinking, thinking . . . far off on the other side of the galaxy! And no one can see me there." A third grader wondered why his teacher wouldn't let him do his report backwards. "She freaked out when she saw me writing on the topics at the end of my outline before the beginning and middle. But I always like to start at the end because then I know how to get there."

In the second place, many gifted students can be harsh judges of their own work and ability. Impatient and perfectionistic, they draw conclusions from their experiences that are hasty, inaccurate, and potentially damaging to self-esteem. They may feel that a mistake signals some deeper failing in themselves as students or that their advanced ability in certain subjects makes them freakish and unsuitable as friends.

These promising students need to develop the tools to assess their own work so that they can see its worth while also recognizing where they need more practice, instruction, or mentoring. The "metacognition" that grows over time gives them an understanding of their own learning path—in essence, the key to their own intelligence and its way of discovering, understanding, analyzing, and creating new worlds. For gifted students in accelerated programs, assessment can be the beginning of genuine, independent learning.

PART II

Appropriate Academic-Classroom Acceleration

5

Acceleration
of Content

After graduating from college with my degree in education and psychology, I thought I could teach almost any subject in the classroom. I had a liberal arts background and was armed with teacher manuals that told me what to teach, what assignments to give, and what sequence to follow. You might say that I had an equal measure of youthful arrogance and ignorance. The textbooks and teacher manuals were my holy books; they told me exactly what needed to be taught. Little did I realize that this was not necessarily what my students would need.

How is content determined? What is important for students to know, and how is this decided? Why does content differ from school to school? How can content be accelerated to meet learners' needs? What is the underlying structure of knowledge? How can complexity and depth be added to the basic content to facilitate acceleration? These are the fundamental questions that will be addressed in this chapter.

VARIATIONS IN CONTENT

Content is the *what* in learning; that is, content is a selection from all of the areas of human knowledge, and as such, it reflects the nature of knowledge. Not all of human knowledge has the same value to education, so specialists in a subject area—who follow the "logic" of organized learning—generally determine content or what they perceive to be important to know within their area of expertise. Subject areas that are recognized as essential core subjects are required in the curriculum; these are the areas that must be included in what is taught in public schools and require standardized assessment and evaluation. However, over time, even this required content has changed as our culture has changed. One famous example is the Sputnik-era attempt to improve science and math scores across the United States—in this case, cultural fear of being outdone by another country produced a massive shift in educational content. Another shift in emphasis is resulting from the trend towards career specialization. As areas of specialization increase, so do the number of specific subjects a child must master.

Not all schools are created equal, and the differences across schools clearly affect what is selected as relevant content and how that content must be taught. For example, one school may be in an affluent suburb. The people who reside in this suburb are predominately professionals with advanced degrees who value education and want the best education possible for their children. They are involved in their child's school. Many parents volunteer regularly; one group of parents recently hooked up the network needed for their latest computer purchases. Parents also hold successful fundraisers and bring additional money into the school. School referenda are almost always supported and passed, and most of the educators at the schools are in the process of working on, or have already earned, advanced degrees. Professional conferences on the latest educational trends and methods are attended frequently, and professional development is sustained through follow-up meetings.

Another school is in a remote rural area. The parents in this area are predominately farmers. They are hard working and take pride in their families, but income is limited, so recent school referenda have failed to pass. Increasing taxes to fund schools is not an option for these people. The school is small, and children travel a distance by bus to reach it. It has been increasingly difficult to attract teachers to this area; young graduates would rather be in large cities. Their staff is primarily older, longtime residents. The school board worries about what will happen when these seasoned teachers retire. The school's books are older, the technology is not up-to-date, and there is a daily struggle to make ends meet. The school has an almost family-like atmosphere; the children and families are all known in this community.

Finally, a third school is located in a large urban district in a decaying part of the city. The area around the school is composed largely of housing projects. Students come from a range of cultural backgrounds, but poverty binds them together. Although the staff is dedicated, they frequently spend more time on discipline issues than on content, and thus there is a high staff turnover rate. Many young teachers begin teaching at this school; they get experience and then move on to nicer districts. Some parents work two jobs, so it is impossible for them to participate in school activities. Many parents had undesirable experiences when they were students, and as a result they try to avoid the school. Resources beyond the outdated texts are nonexistent.

From these three examples, it should be clear that not all schools are able to teach the same content in the same ways. The resources, clientele, and organization of a school affect content as well as the way it must be approached. The same child may have a completely different experience in each of these three schools, even when studying the same topic. In addition, the differences across schools create sharp contrasts in how content is taught and, even more, how it is accelerated. For example, one first-grade class is studying farm animals. The students in the rural school have grown up with these animals; many students have the responsibility of helping to care for them. A few students may already be "resident experts" on the topic. For them, the regular textbook work may be redundant and boring. Some young students may be ready to pose questions and find the answers to those questions, thus beginning research. They might look at the differences in farming in different regions of the United States, changes in farming over time, costs of farming, and farming as a life occupation. Students in the affluent suburbs or urban environments may never have come in contact with farm animals; thus, they need some real-life experiences to make their learning meaningful. For them, a trip to a farm would be more appropriate. They might further explore animals of interest, the changes in farming, or the problem of disappearing farmland. Background information is essential for those students who have not been previously exposed to the content. One cannot successfully accelerate without having a solid knowledge base.

Learning rate also plays a part in what is taught and learned. The average learner may take 17 to 25 repetitions to learn basic information, above-average students may learn in about 10 repetitions, and gifted students learn in one to five repetitions (Bloom, 1985; Rogers, 2001). All students do not learn the same way on the same day, and in addition, even one student may not learn the same way from one day to the next. To expect that a class will all do the same work at the same time is to ignore individuals and their needs. Michael, a child described in our previous text, is just such an example (Smutny et al., 1997).

> Michael exudes energy. His black hair and matching eyes sparkle as he enters the class. His knowledge of certain subjects astounds both his classmates and his teacher. His hand is always up, his mouth usually open, and his body gyrating with enthusiasm. When given group work, he consistently is the first person finished.
>
> Exciting as it is to have this bright, ebullient child in her class, the teacher often feels overwhelmed as she tries to keep up with him and keep the rest

of the class on track. Some days it seems as if Michael completes the class assignment before she has even finished explaining it! She finds herself dreading the moment when he will wave his arm and call out, "I'm done— now what can I do?" (p. 41)

CONTENT ACCELERATION

When we hear the word *acceleration,* we might picture a car with the gas pedal pushed to the floor. We think of "gaining speed." However, it is crucial to acknowledge that there are different ways to implement acceleration in the classroom, depending on the student, teacher, and resources. Acceleration should be much more than just speeding through the grade-level content or advancing to the next grade. Knowing the student is key to choosing the form of acceleration most needed. Being able to answer the questions, "What does this student need? What is appropriate for this child to do?" is paramount to the success of the student. Acceleration choices include (but are not limited to) early admission, advanced content, self-paced instruction, partial acceleration, ungraded classes, curriculum compacting, telescoping, mentoring, extracurricular work, service learning, advanced resources, talent search programs, and foreign language learning. All of these choices are described and discussed here.

One of the easiest ways to accommodate the young advanced learner is to *enroll the child in kindergarten early,* prior to the scheduled "cut-off" date prescribed by the school or state. It is simple for the child who needs schooling earlier. The child does not need to readjust to new classmates and surroundings or to learn new routines for a different class, as might be the case in skipping a grade. The process is so easy, practical, and effective it is hard to understand why some districts are reluctant to use early admission. One administrator felt that he needed to "hold the line [date]" for fear of pushy parents who want their child accelerated. Many districts or schools shy away from early admission because there is little hard data to document appropriate placement for the child. A helpful instrument in the decision-making process is *Iowa Acceleration Scale: A Guide for Whole-Grade Acceleration K–8* (Assouline et al., 2003). Testing, observation of the child in the school environment, and/or interviews can provide further helpful information in the decision-making process.

> Jan was a child who read at age three, loved math, and soaked up new information like a sponge. Her mother took her places, did things with her, and enrolled her in a preschool for "socialization." Jan amazed her preschool teachers. She was so far advanced that she preferred talking to her teachers rather than playing with the other four-year-olds. Her birthday was unfortunately just a few days after the cut-off for kindergarten. Her mother was shocked at the school's reluctance to admit a child who so badly needed the kindergarten experience and knew most of the content. Waiting another year would definitely place Jan with the class of preschoolers with whom she had little in common.
>
> After meeting with the school administrators, Jan's mother convinced them that there needed to be a conference with the preschool teachers to discuss Jan's academic needs. Following the meeting, it was agreed that there would be a "conditional" acceptance with a trial period for Jan in the kindergarten class.

At this time Jan is excelling in kindergarten. Her teacher is wondering about having Jan advance to first grade. Jan's transition to kindergarten was easy and effortless. Her knowledge base far surpasses even the students in this class.

For some students who already know the content of the grade that they are entering, *early admission to the next grade level* may be needed. This can occur at the beginning of—or during—the school year. Teachers can determine if grade-level acceleration is appropriate in a number of ways: testing, observing, portfolios, parent input, evidence of work or growth over time. Again, the *Iowa Acceleration Scale* can be helpful in the decision-making process. Once the grade acceleration option has been chosen, it is imperative that the educators work to make the transition smooth for the student. Are there gaps in learning that need patching? The child may be a terrific reader who comprehends at an advanced level but still needs to be introduced to a phonetic analysis skill to aid in decoding new words. Are there pieces of content skipped in the acceleration that need to be taught? Usually these can be learned with ease; they just need to be addressed. It is essential that accelerated students are not left with holes in their learning.

Lori was an example of a child who benefited from early admission to first grade. She had no holes in her learning and was more than ready for the next grade's content.

Lori was reading at age three, doing addition and subtraction problems at age four, and astounding adults with her advanced vocabulary. After her first week in kindergarten, it was apparent that there was no fit for Lori and the kindergarten content. She preferred the company of older children and seemed to have nothing in common with her chronological age peers. First grade welcomed her and she readily moved from kindergarten to first grade within a week. She felt comfortable with the move and did very well with first-grade content.

Students may also be provided with *content that is progressively more advanced* as material is completed and mastered. This is a form of continuous progress. The content becomes accelerated when a student surpasses chronological age peers in the level of content and the rate of learning, and materials are sequenced to correspond with increasing levels of content depth. James was a candidate for continuous progress. By using advanced resources, his level of knowledge was honored and yet he continued to study with his age peers. His teacher made the effort to find the needed resources and to adjust the content to his elevated level.

James was a "dinosaur-ologist" at age five. He knew more about those big, ugly, prehistoric reptiles than most adults knew or even cared to know. When his kindergarten class was studying dinosaurs, his teacher provided him with advanced books and resources so that he could further his study. He looked at the work of paleontologists and the background needed to do such work. He examined other extinct species and made connections to present-day endangered animals. His work enriched the entire class and his love for dinosaurs was honored.

Self-paced instruction is different from continuous progress in that the student has more control over the rate of progress. When the student is a "resident expert" in an area, she or he may wish to pursue this area in depth. This can take the form of a special class during the summer, weekend, or evening. It also can be accommodated in the classroom with the assistance of the classroom teacher. Some teachers are reluctant to let a student advance in a chosen area because the student will not be working with the rest of the class. The benefits clearly outweigh the disadvantages. The student will have the opportunity to have her or his information and interests validated and will be able to share and extend the learning for the entire class. This does mean that the classroom teacher must locate appropriate materials to accelerate the learning. It is much easier with the assistance of technology and the resources available on the Internet. Abby's story demonstrates this technique.

Abby, a fourth grader, was solving math problems at an accelerated rate and level compared with her age peers. In order to make sure that she had the necessary skills, Abby's teacher placed her in a program in which Abby progressed through set activities that increased with difficulty and at a pace with which she was comfortable. When she felt that the work in class was repetitive, she would go to the box of skill cards and work at her own pace through the accelerated skills. She also used a computer program that allows students to accomplish self-paced instruction. Abby's teacher met with Abby on a regular basis to work through problems and to keep up-to-date and accurate information on Abby's progress.

Keith is a perfect example of *subject matter acceleration* or *partial acceleration.* His small school had limited resources, but the teachers were able to adapt the content to meet his needs in his one area of expertise.

Keith's skills in math were outstanding, but in other areas he was very appropriately placed with his chronological age peers. In first grade, Keith far surpassed his peers in math. His first-grade teacher had an agreement with the second-grade teacher. Keith would attend the second-grade math class but return to first grade for his other subjects. When Keith was in second grade, accommodations were made for him to go to third grade for math only. He loved the challenge and excelled in math. In his small school district, the teachers used this strategy to make the best use of subject matter acceleration. The cost was minimal, and the benefits were huge.

A word of caution is needed when working with subject matter acceleration or partial acceleration. There needs to be a clearly defined progression with a scope and sequence for accelerated learning. Teachers at future grade levels must be aware of the acceleration and committed to extending it. When this is missing, a student may spend a year or more waiting for others in class to catch up. It can have devastating effects on the child who has progressed wonderfully and then suddenly encounters a wall of resistance. This can happen easily and without malice when the student moves to another school or changes buildings within the district. Communication and future planning are essential.

Combined classes, and in some cases, *ungraded classes* may allow younger students to become engaged with advanced material and work with older students. While not "planned" acceleration, this model may meet the needs of the younger student who is accelerated beyond her or his chronological age peers. This may or may not lead to advanced grade placement at a later time. For example, one district has a class with ungraded students who excel in the typical first-grade, second-grade, and third-grade reading and math classes. This ungraded class studies broad-based themes with topics that are appropriate. Advanced reading and math resources are utilized as students are taught how to begin and progress with independent study to explore areas of interest. In addition, learning centers are designed with multiple levels of options for students to explore.

A class of this type requires the teacher to have flexibility and content knowledge. The depth, complexity, and pacing of instruction is very different from that of the regular class. Smaller class size is an additional benefit along with advanced resources. Curriculum needs to be planned and written with scope and sequence so that students are not left with holes or missing pieces in their learning, and acceleration can occur naturally.

Curriculum compacting is a strategy used in differentiation in which the teacher reduces the time spent on the standard curriculum. For the student who demonstrates proficiency, drill, skill, and practice exercises are eliminated. Using the time saved, the student may work on enrichment activities or proceed to more advanced content.

When using curriculum compacting, instructional goals are based on assessments that match the content. Mrs. Taylor, a teacher in a standard classroom, uses compacting effectively in her fifth-grade math class. When doing whole-class instruction in math, she gives the students practice problems to complete. If students feel that they can accurately complete the five hardest problems designated by Mrs. Taylor, they do not need to complete the additional practice problems. In this case, they have bought the gift of time to work on enrichment activities or to complete other tasks. Additionally, at the beginning of each math unit, Mrs. Taylor gives a pretest. She works in small groups or independently on accelerated work with those students whose test scores demonstrate that they already know the material. The accelerated students are required to join the other students from time to time in order to strengthen an area of weakness, to share projects, or to participate in group discussions.

Telescoping is much like curriculum compacting, but the result of the time saved in compressing the content is placement at an advanced grade. Curriculum compacting does not ordinarily lead to grade advancement, while telescoping can compact two years of work into one year, thus allowing for grade-level acceleration. For this reason, telescoping may require adjustments in school policy to allow for grade-level acceleration.

For the student who has not yet been exposed to the content but who learns at an amazing rate, the prospect of telescoping can be a needed lifeline. Telescoping may be done on an individual basis or with a small select group. The pacing is rapid and the content is accelerated.

In *mentoring,* a student is placed with a mentor or expert in the content area. The result is that the student advances at a more rapid pace or engages in a deeper level of instruction. The following is an example of one teacher who made mentoring an important part of his class.

> Mr. Waters did an interest survey of his fourth-grade students. Those who expressed advanced knowledge or a deep passion about a topic were candidates to work with high school students who shared the same interest

or passion for the subject. Mr. Waters coordinated this mentoring program with the high school students, who were dismissed earlier than his elementary class. The buddies worked together twice a month under his supervision to explore topics of interest they shared. Close, continuing relationships were formed and the students learned from each other.

In order for mentoring to be successful, educators must develop and maintain a mentoring plan. There needs to be a process of enlisting mentors and matching the mentors to mentees. In this process, collaboration with other teachers is essential. Meeting with the mentors is crucial in order to plan the work and set the stage for both mentors and mentees, as well as explain details of the plan, including a forum for regular feedback. Regular feedback, which ensures a positive mentoring experience, can be provided by responding to journal entries and holding informal group or one-on-one meetings. Evaluation of the work should document leadership skills on the part of the mentor as well as academic growth on the part of the mentee.

Mentoring can work at all grade levels. Intermediate students have worked with students in kindergarten in a tutoring capacity or in sharing a common interest area. Mentoring at the high school level can take the form of having professionals in the field share work with students who aspire to careers in that field. The benefits of mentoring extend far beyond the classroom walls: for example, many mentors become lifelong friends or friendly colleagues in competitive disciplines. The myths that talented individuals are driven to fulfill their gifts, that they are self-sufficient, and that they will make it on their own must be dispelled. Joshua Lederberg, Nobel Laureate, spoke of the frustration felt by those whose abilities surpass those of their classmates and sometimes even their teachers: "My teachers were wonderfully supportive but they didn't know what to do with me. Nobody took me in charge, gave me a sense of what to do. I could have used more guidance on what to read, how to structure what was going on, even an occasional exam now and then could have been offered as a way of pacing what was happening" (Subotnik, 1995, p. 218). A mentor can support, negotiate, and ameliorate the problems confronting the gifted child (Arnold & Subotnik, 1995). The value of mentors for ethnic and gender minorities who choose fields in which they are underrepresented should also not be overlooked. Appropriate exposure and training through mentors in broad areas is essential to attract women, minorities, and members of other underrepresented groups who may not have the advantage of believing what is possible or seeing possibilities (Arnold & Subotnik, 1995).

With *dual enrollment, correspondence courses,* or *extracurricular* work in high school and college, some students can graduate early. Younger students may also benefit from correspondence courses and extracurricular work. For some select young students, correspondence courses may provide the challenge they need. More and more classes are available on the Internet, as well as by mail. However, to be successful, the student must be self-directed. Elementary students who are advanced may also benefit from accelerated content and occasionally may even be encouraged to work at the high school or college level.

Alia is fourteen and now working for a Ph.D. in engineering. She began reading when she was eight months old and now devours 100 pages an hour. By the time Alia was seven her mother realized she could no longer help her daughter. Alia attended elementary school in the morning, high school in the afternoon.

"And the high school students were awful," Alia says. "They tried to steal my answers."

She went from fourth grade to college. "There was really no other option," she says. "I could go to college, do nothing, or rot in fifth grade." (Heller, 2004)

Developing a campaign or working to provide a service in the community is a creative and low-cost method of advancing content. Researching a topic, letter writing, speaking at a public forum, and calling and e-mailing people in positions of power gives the learner authentic tools to apply to the content as well as to life. Accelerated content includes seeing what occupations are involved in the service, learning what the work of those occupations is like, and understanding the skills and knowledge needed to work in those occupations. In addition, learning how the world outside the classroom functions and working on authentic problems is empowering, and community involvement builds self-confidence and self-esteem. When a student learns that he or she can actually make a difference, the impact on the student and the community is huge. Barbara Lewis's (1998) book *The Kid's Guide to Social Action* outlines in detail the steps necessary to make this work in the classroom.

Resources need not be kept at a particular grade level; they can extend far beyond the grade. Dictionaries, thesauri, books at multiple levels on the topic of study, and advanced reference materials are all examples of how resources can be applied in the regular classroom to accelerate learning. Make sure that books that are two grade levels above the reading level of the typical grade-level students are included in classroom resources. Being exposed to advanced resources, Andi (age 10) exclaimed, "It showed me new things to stretch my mind."

Talent search programs are another excellent example of how acceleration can be implemented. Students who perform at the top of their class on standardized tests are given the opportunity to take a test that is generally given to older students and has a higher ceiling. The students who are consistently at the 99th percentile may know the material extremely well, but how much more do they know? How far beyond their grade level are they functioning? Because they have reached the ceiling for the test that they are taking, it is not known how far they can go.

Matt, a fifth grader, was average in language arts, but in math he excelled. Matt's teacher did not know what to do. On every math test he scored at the 99th percentile. Even the advanced math books his teacher supplied provided no challenge for him. It was suggested that he participate in the talent search program with top sixth graders. In this talent search program, the SAT was given to sixth graders to determine how much they knew and how well they could perform above their standard curriculum. Matt willingly took the SAT test. He finished rapidly and told the tester that it was fun! When his scores came back, he had surpassed any of the others taking the test. His score was better than the average eleventh graders taking the SAT. His school allowed him to take advanced algebra, and he was eventually placed in high school math classes. He maintained his place in his regular classroom for other subjects, as that placement was appropriate for him.

The *study of a foreign language* is also a method of accelerating learning for young students. In other countries, students are expected to speak at least one or two additional languages fluently. In the United States, we learn only English in elementary schools. In many districts, the option to study a foreign language is typically not introduced until high school. However, many believe that the optimal time to teach a foreign language is at the primary level. Teaching another language promotes cultural understanding as well as acceleration of content.

> Mrs. W. had the middle school Spanish teacher come to her kindergarten classroom three days a week for half an hour. He introduced her students to their Spanish names, taught students the Spanish terms for the days of the week, months of the year, family member names, and colors. Mrs. W. continued his lessons by introducing other words and concepts. The children sang songs in Spanish and even read some easy books in Spanish. By the end of the year they had a repertoire of sentences that were quite natural and were excited to continue their foreign language experience.

CONTENT AND THE STRUCTURE OF KNOWLEDGE

When attempting to create a successful acceleration experience, looking at how knowledge is organized can aid the way acceleration is provided in the classroom. Knowledge is organized to create meaning, foster accessibility, and support learning at different levels of expertise. To organize knowledge content, we first must look at the learning standards to determine what content we want the students to learn; however, knowledge organization extends this learning beyond facts and skills. At the beginning of a school year, an educator might ask, "What do I want my students to take with them after this year is over?" Usually the answer includes some elements from all levels of knowledge: facts, skills, concepts and their related topics, overarching principles, and essential questions.

At the basic level, teachers and students work with *facts:* specific details or verifiable information. Facts can vary in difficulty, ranging from knowing that $1 + 1 = 2$, to knowing that $68 \times 47 = 3,196$. In order to be meaningful, facts need to be tied to the bigger picture of the discipline and knowledge in general. If facts are presented in isolation, the student memorizes the information but does not see the connections and soon forgets the memorized facts. Isolated, the facts have no importance or connection to anything; they are just bits and pieces of information. Students need to know how to apply facts, and for this they need skills.

Skills are the second level in knowledge organization: They are the techniques, strategies, tools, or methods that enable a learner to use facts rather than just know them. Examples of skills are dribbling a basketball, learning how to print one's name, or decoding a word phonetically. Each of these skills takes basic facts to a higher level, utilizing them in the world. However, skills in isolation do not maintain their usefulness without deeper understandings, or concepts.

Concepts (sometimes referred to as *themes*) are universal, broad, timeless, and abstract. They link content areas by touching on the commonalities between them, and thus they may encompass multiple subjects. Examples of concepts include courage, responsibility, destruction, relationships, justice, fairness, freedom, beauty, discovery, exploration, eternity, infinity, tolerance, revolution, constancy, cycles, myth, culture, identity, voice, perspective, classification, ideas, rituals, migration, cause and effect, persuasion, altruism, and equilibrium. Concepts are sometimes referred to as the "Big Ideas."

Individual disciplines may also have concepts specific to each area, and these must be learned to master the content area. The following are examples of disciplines and their sample concepts:

- **Art:** color, line, shape, space, texture, form
- **Literature:** voice, motivation, perception, heroes, antiheroes
- **Music:** pitch, melody, timbre, harmony
- **Mathematics:** number, ratio, probability, proportion
- **Science:** classification, order, cycle, matter
- **Social Studies:** culture, revolution, conflict, cooperation, governance
- **Health and Physical Development:** space, rules, movement, play, strategy, wellness

Concepts are often linked to a specific topic that is an example of the concept. *Topics* are subject-specific and are selected for focused teaching and learning. As such, topics are more concrete than concepts. A good, representative topic has the following characteristics:

- It reflects the knowledge of the discipline.
- It is interesting to the teacher and to the students.
- It clarifies relationships between the topic and knowledge in the discipline.
- It is familiar to students and grasped in depth by the teacher.
- It lends itself to student materials and available resources.

The highest level of the organization of knowledge is the level of principles. *Principles* state fundamental truths, laws, rules, or doctrines that explain the relationship between two or more concepts. For example, love and peace can both be linked by the underlying principle of the Golden Rule. Principles are what students should know, the agreed-upon truth about the concept; they provide deeper understanding to give meaning to concepts. Table 5.1 contains some examples of concepts with their related principles.

Finally, *essential questions* can be answered using all the levels of knowledge. They direct teaching and learning toward understanding concepts and principles. In

Table 5.1

Concepts	*Principles*
Patterns	Patterns help us predict.
Conflict	Conflict may be natural or human-made.
Community	A community has members.
Systems	Systems are made up of subsystems and parts.
Survival	Living things develop adaptations to their environments, which enable them to survive in the environment.
Power	Power may be used or abused.
Change	Change is necessary for growth and creativity.

a sense, they are the picture frames around a lesson, allowing the students to see the bigger picture. The following are examples of essential questions.

- Why are rules essential?
- Why do rules change?
- How do patterns aid in prediction and problem solving?
- What characteristics does a survivor have?
- When is it good to be different?
- How did environment shape diverse North American peoples?
- What constitutes a contribution?
- What determines whether a contribution will be positive or negative?

Understanding the related facts, performing the necessary skills, and developing an appreciation of the concepts and principles related to an essential question drive successful learning, and thus successful acceleration. When a student is able to ponder the essential questions, knowledge exists within a context of understanding rather than in isolation. When viewed in this way, acceleration can be seen as a natural result of adjusting the content complexity and depth in order to allow learners to move beyond their current understanding. The next sections focus on increasing the complexity and depth of course content.

CONTENT COMPLEXITY

Content complexity can vary within a grade and extend far beyond a particular grade level; some third graders can learn only the four stages of metamorphosis, while others are researching the developmental biology and biochemistry that dictates how each stage evolves into the next. In order to increase content complexity to a level appropriate for accelerated students, educators can choose from several different tools: altering perspectives, focusing on changes in a field or discipline, and highlighting interdisciplinary connections between concepts.

One simple way to increase the complexity of any content area is to see a topic from different *perspectives.* For example, if Cinderella were from Texas, rather than from Germany, how might her story be different? Who would be the desired beau? What would be the event that would attract a crowd? What would be the attire? Footwear? Mode of transportation? What might the Fairy Godmother look like? How would it be different if Cinderella were from New York City? This can be done so easily with literature. As another example, children might take the point of view of different characters in the story and use each character's point of view to rewrite the story. With Goldilocks and the Three Bears, the bears would tell a completely different story than would Goldilocks. The wolf has a different point of view than the Three Little Pigs. Through these manipulations in perspective, the gifted child can further his or her natural tendency to try to understand the subtleties of each story.

A second method that can be used to increase the richness of any content area is to examine how the discipline has *changed over time* as well as its implications for the future. No field of study remains constant; disciplines such as technology and medicine change almost daily.

Seeing things from a historical perspective can change the way students view a discipline, and it can help students get excited about future possibilities for discovery—we didn't have all the answers a decade ago, and we don't have them today. We might ask our students, "What changes in science and medicine have occurred over the past 10 years? What are some recent developments? What do we know now that we didn't know 100 years ago? Are there new illnesses today that were unknown even 50 years ago? Were there illnesses in the past that we no longer fear because advances in science and medicine have eliminated or cured these dreaded diseases? How were these discoveries made? How long did these discoveries take? What was it like to work on this problem, day in and day out? Based on these discoveries, what seems to be next on the horizon?"

Linguistics is another example of a discipline that lends itself to this kind of "change analysis." Students love to explore old ways of saying things as compared to modern-day usage (especially when it makes their teachers feel old!). Educators can help students explore older books that have been rewritten to update the language to be more understandable to current readers. We might ask, "What new words do we use now that didn't exist 50 years ago? What brought about the change? How has technology changed our language? What might happen to the future of language?"

Finally, complexity can be added to any curriculum by introducing students to *interdisciplinary connections.* No content area stands in isolation; all are connected with common threads. For example, reading is infused into all content areas. Math is crucial to science, but it is also essential to almost every other discipline. Its importance in measurement is huge. It also is fundamental in social studies—charts of social and historical trends rely on a good understanding of graphing devices. Health and physical development would be at a loss without math. How could one keep score in a game if math were not involved, or count calories, know cholesterol levels, heart rates, or height and weight? Art and music are both heavily laden with math. Musical notes and rests are based on fractions; measures must add up.

To begin exploring interdisciplinary connections, it is easiest to start with a major concept or theme (the Big Idea) and investigate the generalizations that follow. Generalizations are principles that can be applied across disciplines. For example, if we were to take the concept of "work," some generalizations might look like this:

- Work is continuous.
- Work precipitates more work.
- We're always working, even when we're at school or playing.
- Growth comes from work.
- Work brings material and emotional rewards.
- The future will bring different kinds of work.
- Experience affects your skill at any job.

In each content area, we can examine the concept of work and find connections and implications that increase the complexity of that content area. The concept acts as the rope that holds the bundle of disciplines together.

- Explore **language** and how the changes in the types of work people do (industrial revolution, technology revolution, information age) have altered how books are produced, words and their meanings, forms of communication, careers, foreign languages, and literature.
- **Social science** classes could look at communities and how they work together or have more individualized work patterns; how work has affected

customs, families, celebrations, occupations, education, personal growth, advertisements, media, communications, economics, the world community, and cultural awareness.

- **Biological sciences** can explore how work revolutions have produced and eradicated different diseases, medications, animals, plants, occupations, environmental issues, health issues, and aging.
- **Environmental science** can examine how changes in our work habits (commuting, night shifts) have affected the environment.
- In **fine arts** there have been changes in music, instruments, theaters, plays, movies, musicals, paintings, sculpture, photography, and ceramics that are all due to changes in the way we work. Changes in what is regarded as "art" have occurred, as well as who are considered "artists"—for example, the technology revolution brought animators to the forefront as modern-day artists.
- **Mathematics** has also changed with our work patterns. Although it could be argued that mathematical facts remain the same, the way that they are used and manipulated has changed according to the technology we rely upon. For example, at the grocery store, computers show sale totals, the amount tendered, and the change to be returned. Some sales clerks are hard pressed to know the correct change if it is not computed!
- Changes in our work habits have certainly altered **health and physical development.** For instance, in the United States our recent habit of overeating and getting little exercise can at least partially be traced to the reduction in jobs that require physical effort.

CONTENT DEPTH

Accelerating content relies on increases in content complexity as well as the depth of the content—the quantity of information conveyed. Scratching the surface does not meet the needs of a hungry learner. Have you ever been invited to a meal and expected to be served a huge dinner, and to your surprise you were served an appetizer instead? School can be like that for the gifted child. They want a full meal of the subject but are only given a taste. By going deeper, we allow these students to delve thoroughly into a subject. Again, we can draw on several tools that allow us to deepen any content area for our avid learners: examining the jargon of a field, learning the rules that govern a discipline, discovering ways to apply the content to life outside of school, and determining the underlying issues in any subject area.

One way to deepen course content is to examine the *jargon,* or language, particular to a subject area. Every discipline has its own jargon. For example, there is the jargon of mathematics: At different levels of analysis, we must understand what *denominator, vector,* and *infinity* mean. There is also musical jargon; music students may start out learning the definition of a scale, then learn the features that separate a major scale from a minor, chromatic, or pentatonic scale.

Learning the *rules* that govern a discipline will also allow students to delve deeper in their learning. All disciplines are governed by rules; some of the rules are stated and known (explicit), while others may be unstated or implied (implicit). For example, if you are a musician, there is not only a vocabulary to know and to understand but also rules for playing the music and the instrument. Vocabulary supports these rules but cannot replace them. Some rules, like how to tune an instrument, are explicitly taught. Others, like how to play music so that it sounds "romantic," must be learned implicitly with practice. Similarly, there are rules that govern grammar, spelling, and writing. Primary students learn that sentences begin with capital letters and end with a punctuation mark. As their writing progresses, they learn rules for correctly using commas, quotation marks, colons, and semicolons. All of these rules are learned explicitly. Over time, students can learn implicitly how to use these explicit rules to evoke different emotions with their writing.

Relating knowledge to our daily lives is an essential and engaging method for increasing the depth in which any discipline is learned. As educators and students, we must learn to always ask ourselves, "Why is this important to me? How will I apply it in my life?" Content must have personal value or relevance to each student in order for the learning to be meaningful. In studying history, students learn how European settlers in centuries-ago North America encountered problems and worked to solve them in order to survive and establish their communities. Today, students may face problems in their communities that are not as removed from the new settlers as they once believed: They must forge alliances, save resources such as time and money, and discover the leaders among them. Looking at how others have dealt with similar problems helps students deal with these day-to-day issues; they can learn from history what has worked and what has not. If we want students to be lifelong learners, we must help them make the connections between their coursework and life outside school.

Finally, being able to get to the level of the *"real" underlying problem* in a subject area takes content to a different level. For example, in social sciences, we teach that communities may face issues with crime, finances, leadership, health, planning for growth, and education. Often issues that are discussed are superficial to the real problems, and the precipitating causes are not addressed. Left unsolved, the problems may grow. Getting to the underlying problem takes knowledge of content at an advanced level that extends across disciplines. In a sense, problem solving with deep thinking skills is truly higher-level thinking.

Gifted students need less time to learn content and more time to explore it in depth and in all its complexity. Giving students time to examine new ideas resulted in Emily (fifth grade) saying, "We were encouraged to do unusual projects and things we had not experienced. This challenged me, rather than studying subjects that I already knew." Eva, a nine-year-old accelerated student, put it simply when she said, "I have had the chance to explore learning. My teacher has affected my life because she has expanded my learning and helped me build skills. The hard work has helped me to be able to act as an independent person."

6

The Thinking Process

We all proclaim that we want students to be good thinkers; knowledge alone is not enough. Businesses want employees who know how to generate ideas, solve problems, ask needed questions, determine which sources are reliable, and think creatively. In a popular reality television show, the CEO of a large corporation does not look for a puppet whose strings he can pull. Instead, he looks for a decision maker who can analyze, synthesize, and evaluate information to create a plan of action. He looks for a person who has mastered the higher levels of thinking.

In an educational setting, the thinking process addresses the question, "What do you want students to do with the content they're learning?" By using higher-level thinking skills, learners can construct personal meaning from big ideas, develop self-understanding, engender a deeper understanding of the content, become self-directed and self-motivated, and enjoy wonderment and inquisitiveness about the content. Richard Paul's (1997) *Critical Thinking: What Every Person Needs to Survive in a Rapidly Changing World* provides in-depth information that extends well beyond this chapter.

ACCELERATING LEARNING THROUGH CRITICAL THINKING

Most students who are candidates for acceleration already have excellent thinking skills at the more basic levels, so our acceleration programs must emphasize the development of higher-level thinking processes that extend beyond the grade level. Many students have had the advantage of enrichment. A few others need more than enrichment can provide. Enrichment activities are aimed at grade-level content and thinking skills and provide much novelty and extensions of the content. Acceleration reaches beyond the grade level and stretches students at a faster pace. This can be done with the thinking process as well as within content. Curriculum must contain opportunities for students to advance their learning by providing optimal challenges that transcend the levels of knowledge, comprehension, and application. According to Benjamin Bloom's (1956) thinking hierarchy, one can gauge a student's thinking process by the kind of actions a student can take with the knowledge in a subject area. Each level of the hierarchy includes those beneath it, so working at the top level of "evaluation" necessarily draws on all the preceding levels (see Table 6.1).

Teaching students to identify their own level of reasoning can promote thinking at higher levels. For example, Mrs. K. wanted her students to explore their thinking and to begin asking questions at the higher levels of Bloom's Taxonomy. In order to do this, she posted a chart of the levels of thinking with the key verbs. Before long, the students were familiar with the levels and verbs and even encouraged each other to ask questions at the higher levels.

This section explores the skills that support higher-level thinking, including the use of correlations in reasoning and research as tools that help students access and develop critical thinking skills. In addition, we give a brief introduction to some tools that can be used to facilitate creativity.

SKILLS FOR HIGHER-LEVEL THINKING

Ideas constantly flash through the minds of many gifted learners. Jack explains, "Sometimes my mind feels like it is going to explode with ideas." These students need

Table 6.1   Thinking Skill Hierarchy

Thinking Skill	Description	Key Verbs
Knowledge	Knowledge asks the learner to remember material. It can be as simple as recalling math facts to remembering complex formulas.	Recall, remember, list, recognize, select, memorize, match, define, identify, name, or label
Comprehension	Comprehension addresses the level of learning that asks the learner to show understanding or to translate the information from one form to another. Comprehension involves interpretation of the content.	Explain, restate, paraphrase, translate, give examples, generalize, illustrate, rearrange, transform, demonstrate, infer, summarize, comment, interpret, or clarify
Application	Application requires the learner to use the information in another situation, to summarize, organize, or apply what is known. Application requires a higher level of understanding than both knowledge and comprehension.	Apply, use, choose, restructure, generalize, dramatize, transfer, solve, or organize
Analysis	Analysis examines information in detail in order to distinguish, compare, and contrast or to isolate variables. By breaking down the content into parts, the learner can understand the relationship between the parts and see the organizational plan. The complexity of analyzing information is much more involved than knowing, comprehending, and applying the information.	Compare and contrast, analyze, classify, describe, deduce, categorize, diagram, subdivide, list, or differentiate
Synthesis	Synthesis asks the learner to change or create, forming a new whole. It is putting together a new plan or unique idea. Synthesis stresses creativity.	Hypothesize, imagine, adapt, speculate, originate, formulate, design, develop, modify, construct, produce, formulate, manipulate, or create
Evaluation	Evaluation requires judging the value of information based on specific criteria. The criteria may be one's own, based on the class, or from other outside sources.	Justify, judge, consider, weigh, criticize, rate, appraise, decide, interpret, infer, or conclude

SOURCE: From Benjamin S. Bloom, et al. *Taxonomy of Educational Objectives*. Published by Allyn and Bacon, Boston, MA. Copyright © 1984 by Pearson Education. Adapted by permission of the publisher.

to feel safe to ask probing questions and explore ideas that go beyond their grade and beyond the norm. It is therefore essential to create an environment that exposes gifted students to concepts and experiences that go beyond regular classroom expectations. They need the opportunity to work within a structure that allows them to explore ideas, wherever they lead. Such a structure can be provided by sequencing, classification, comparing and contrasting, correlations in reasoning, and problem solving.

Sequencing

The ability to put objects or events in order encompasses both analytical and evaluative skills and is critical to an organized life. We arrange names in alphabetical order in a phone book so that we can more easily find the desired name; we re-create a chain of events in order of occurrence to make sense of an incident. By breaking tasks into manageable steps, we make the process of completion doable.

Chris is very creative and has excellent ideas. His problem is not that he lacks intelligence—quite the contrary! He just doesn't know how to organize the multitude of ideas brimming from his brain. His writing is so random that it is hard to connect ideas or follow his thoughts; he doesn't have a clue how to clear up his confusion. Chris needs to learn to sequence his thoughts.

Determining the pertinent information or important points in our creative efforts or those of others allows us to reach the higher thinking levels of analysis, synthesis, and evaluation. Without sequencing, our thoughts are disordered at best. To extend and expand the sequencing skills of our gifted students, we can use time ordering, ranking, and prioritizing.

1. Time Ordering

Begin probing and highlighting the temporal order of events by asking questions such as, "What came before this? What's happening now? What will happen as a result?" Encourage children who are on the cusp of advanced thinking to stretch even farther by encouraging "future thinking" as opposed to "now thinking." To achieve this, you might read a story and stop at strategic points, then encourage the students to predict what will happen. What happens after the story ends? Continue after the final page to write a sequel. What happened prior to the story? Write a prequel! Table 6.2 gives more ideas that can help your accelerated students explore temporal ordering.

2. Ranking

When making a purchase, do you ever compare the amounts in bags of potato chips? Or when you select errands that need to be done, do you consider which is easiest or most difficult before you begin? What about when you pack the car for a vacation? Do you look at the size of the items you want to bring before you begin packing? If you do any of these things, you are ranking items. Students can begin to learn how to rank by listing items or people.

- Smallest to largest
- Youngest to oldest
- Easiest to hardest
- Shortest to tallest
- Units of length, area, volume, and weight (use both metric and imperial measures)

3. Prioritizing

When you buy a car, what features are important to you? Gas mileage? Reliability? Ease of handling? Number of passengers? Comfort? Safety? Do you have a list of choices ranging from a top choice to other options if your first choice doesn't work out? If so, you are prioritizing your car purchase. Prioritizing is a

Table 6.2

Events	Methods
Historical events	Arrange by time. Create a timeline, listing events by the date. Then ask how things would be different if a pivotal event happened later than it did.
Events in a story	Sequence events in the order they happened in the story, then tell the story backwards.
Holidays	Determine which holidays happen first, second, and so on. Include holidays from nondominant cultures.
Life events	Ask students to make a lifeline with major events from their life or create a lifeline for their parent(s). At what age did memorable events occur? Correlate life events with important local, state, national, and international events.
Steps in problem solving	Choose a problem and brainstorm about what steps are needed to solve it. List in order.
Steps in completing a task	Write a "how to" list for a task. Have classmates try to accomplish the task by following the written instructions exactly as written. Revisions are accepted. Laughs are expected.
Cycles	Students can order the seasons, reproductive cycles, behavior patterns, life/death cycles, the water cycle, and so on. Then they can reverse the order and explain why the cycle will or will not work in the new order.

special case of rank ordering: When prioritizing, the rank order depends on your subjective measure of what is important to you.

Making choices or organizing time can become easier with prioritization. You can help students prioritize various things.

- The kinds of questions they like to answer
- The most important to least important outside project
- The most interesting to least interesting homework
- The ways they would like to spend their time on a field trip

Classification

Without an ability to classify objects in our environment, we would not be able to evade danger, respond to situations, live in a community, or distinguish explosive from benign chemicals. For example, I am extremely allergic to poison ivy. If I see a plant with three leaves, I keep away from it. Classification also helps me define my next step in any situation. If I have chest pains, I would need to go to a cardiologist, not an orthopedic surgeon. Classifying relationships is also crucial to community life, especially when it comes to the duties involved in the relationship. The president of the United States has certain responsibilities to the people he or she represents. As a registered voter, I have a duty to learn about the candidates, the responsibility of voting, and the right to vote to express my choice of candidate.

Relationships can extend beyond people—classification of plants, animals, and chemical elements helps us understand their characteristics.

Classifying objects is more than just naming them; classification is a level of analysis that also identifies attributes or characteristics that make an object unique. For example, if we were to classify an animal as a bird, we would know that it is a warm-blooded vertebrate who breathes through lungs, lays eggs, and has feathers. Classification adds information to what is already known, and students can use this information to place any item into an appropriate category. Students need to be asked what criteria they can use to help in the classification process so that they take a thorough look at the characteristics of the items they are being asked to classify. The reverse is also true: When observing items that are already classified, students must be able to describe why each fact, topic, concept, or principle fits in a particular category.

The following are categories that students could classify; the degree of acceleration determines the depth and complexity of the classification process.

- Writing (persuasive, descriptive, expository)
- Ecosystems
- Good nutrients
- Living and nonliving things
- Vertebrates/Invertebrates
- Stars
- Forms of locomotion
- Eras of Earth
- Uses for plants
- Chemical and physical changes
- Style of music
- Musical instruments
- How people from different cultures address the need for food, shelter, clothing, love, belonging
- Native American people by the region of the country in which they live
- Occupations and goods or services
- Past and present (transportation, tools, education, dress, medicine, careers, music, art, sports, beliefs, technology)
- Greeting cards by print, graphics, size, color, occasion, handwritten message, animals, scenes, flowers, borders, orientation, price, maker, artist, mood
- Numbers by multiples to determine greatest common factor

Comparing and Contrasting

When I consider which route to take to work, I compare and contrast the various streets and highways, the time it will take, the amount of traffic, road construction, and the distance from my home to my workplace. My decisions about which job to accept, which products to buy, which events to attend, which car to drive, or which house to purchase are made by analyzing features and comparing and contrasting their similarities and differences.

Comparing and contrasting is an evaluative-level thinking skill that requires learners to distinguish similarities and differences between objects, organisms, events, ideas, or people. When students make decisions about similarities and differences they gain a deeper understanding of the content. One type of graphic organizer that works well to visually demonstrate comparisons and contrasts is the Venn diagram (see

Figure 6.1). The two or more overlapping circles demonstrate the differences in the non-intersecting sections and the similarities in the overlapping section.

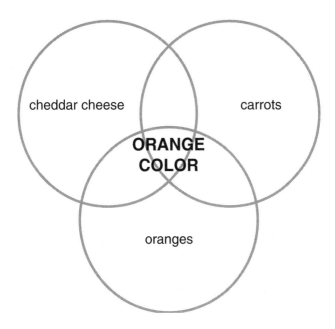

Figure 6.1

Another graphic organizer can place similarities and differences into columns to determine how they each affect the classification of the items (Table 6.3).

Table 6.3

	Item A: *Race Cars*	*Item B:* *Space Ships*	*Affects What* *Category?*
Similarities	Go fast	Go fast	Transportation
	Carry people	Carry people	Transportation
	Fun to watch	Fun to watch	Entertainment
	Mechanical	Mechanical	Technology
	Require a team	Require a team	Community
Differences	Stay on land	Travel in space	Location
	Bright colors	Usually white	Color Scheme
	Very expensive	Wildly expensive	Cost
	Crash a lot	Rarely crash	Danger

Topics for compare and contrast exercises are endless; accelerated thinking occurs by moving the simple, concrete example to more complex and abstract examples that extend beyond the standard grade-level material (Table 6.4).

Table 6.4

Topic	Simple Example	Complex Example
characters in a story	Cinderella vs. Snow White	two biographies of the same person by different authors
nonfiction and fiction about the same topic	a book on dogs vs. *Clifford*	a book on frogs vs. *Wind in the Willows*
communities	school vs. neighborhood	rural vs. urban
occupations	police officer vs. fire fighter	banker vs. stockbroker
transportation	bicycle vs. motorcycle	airplane vs. spacecraft
creation and enforcement of rules and laws	class rules vs. home rules	city laws vs. state laws vs. national laws
maps	map of school vs. map of home	map of state vs. map of the world
animals (footprints, food, locomotion, habitats, skin covering, metamorphosis)	animals with fur vs. animals with scales	carnivorous vs. herbivorous animals
music (types, rhythm, instruments, volume, pitch)	horn vs. drum	trumpet vs. clarinet
city and/or country	your city vs. another city in a different part of the state	Harare, Zimbabwe vs. Mexico City, Mexico—Assess what part geography and resources play in the development of a capital city in a less-developed country
time periods	yesterday vs. today	nineteenth century vs. twentieth century

Problem Solving

Many of the benefits we enjoy today are the result of persistent individuals using their problem-solving skills to cure diseases and advance technology. In problem-based learning, students think through a problem, acquire needed information, and propose a solution. Problem-based learning originated in medical schools, where it has been used to diagnose illnesses and select appropriate treatments.

Problem solving is a higher-order thinking skill that enables students to apply learning from the classroom to their real lives. Accelerated students will already have many outside interests that compete for their time and resources; perhaps one of these interests can be the focus of a problem-solving effort. Another idea is to engage a small group of students in solving a classroomwide problem, such as how to raise money for new computers, or how to manage disagreements among students. Completing a pro/con chart is one method that students can use to clarify their thinking as they solve the problem of their choice (Chart 6.1).

Problem:
Alternatives
1.
2.
3.
4.
Decision:
Why I/we made the decision:

Chart 6.1

Below are some topical issues that teachers can use to incorporate problem solving.

Simple Problems

- A gardener has just planted a vegetable garden. There are birds and rabbits nearby. What problem does she or he need to solve? How might she or he solve it?
- A student pushes in line. Is this a problem? Why? What might we do?
- Suppose you see smoke coming from a closet. No one is around. What is the problem? What might you do?
- What was the problem in a story? How was it overcome? What other solutions might there have been for that problem?
- How might you have handled this situation had you been the character in the story? Rewrite or tell the story using your solution.

Complex Problems

- There are several inexpensive and reliable sources of fuel for cars and trucks that are also environmentally friendly. However, they are not in widespread use. What problems need to be overcome in order to change this situation? How might you solve these problems?
- More and more communities are having problems with air pollution. What are the problems created by air pollution? What are some ways that these could be solved?
- Marie Curie had to find a way to take care of her two children while she was also investigating the root cause of radiation. In what ways could she solve this problem?
- What problems did the Easterners face when they embarked on westward expansion? What would be possible solutions?
- What problems did Native Americans face when Easterners came into their territory? What would be possible solutions?

Correlations in Reasoning

When the tragic bombing of the World Trade Center occurred in New York, the country was shocked and stunned. Nothing like this had ever happened in U.S. history. How could the planning of such terrible acts have gone undetected? Our country began to search for causes. By knowing the causes or correlations, we hope to avert future attempts at terrorism.

Correlations in reasoning involves clustering questions to determine reasonable explanations for the occurrence of an event, carefully asking questions, and considering the resulting evidence. Correlations in reasoning can clarify human motivation and action. It enables one to determine responsibility for actions and to avoid making hasty conclusions. Through correlations in reasoning, students can gain an understanding of topics such as extinction, endangered species, character motivation, causes of war, or actions of historical figures. Beyond the application of such judgments to daily life, correlations in reasoning is essential in the work of lawyers, judges, law enforcement personnel, doctors, nurses, pilots, truckers, school bus drivers, teachers, scientists, accountants, engineers, business owners, reporters, writers, and others. Areas of the curriculum in which correlations in reasoning fits naturally include the spread of disease, the growth of cities, the extinction of species, weather prediction, nutrition and meal planning, behavior motivation, westward expansion, historical events like the Chicago fire, and immigration.

Correlations in reasoning includes the higher-level skills of analysis, synthesis, and evaluation:

- Asking important questions about the event
- Generating ideas about possible causes or correlations
- Considering evidence necessary to show probable cause
- Making a judgment about the cause based on the evidence (adapted from Swartz & Parks, 1994, p. 386)

Each of these steps, as outlined here, can be applied to almost any event or research problem.

1. Developing Questions

Being able to ask good questions may be more important than knowing the answers, and it is the first step to making correlations in reasoning. In order to ask questions, one must have knowledge of a topic as well as a broader understanding of the principles that guide it. Questions can range from simple to complex and from concrete to abstract. Questions that begin with *who, what, where,* and *when* are more simple and concrete than those that begin with *how* or *why.* For example, regarding the World Trade Center bombings, questions such as, "Where did the bombs fall?" or "What tools did the terrorists use?" or "Who trained the terrorists?" are more concrete than "How could the bombings have been prevented?" or "Why would someone want to kill other people?" By examining the questions students ask, the teacher can assess the students' level of comprehension and understanding of the topic. In addition, guiding questions can help students form their own questions.

2. Generating Ideas

Narrowness in thinking limits possibilities and restricts the outcome. For example, when my car did not start, I thought that it needed a new battery. However, shortly after I purchased a new battery the car continued to malfunction. The battery had indeed been worn down, but it was not the basic problem. I had not generated enough ideas to get to the real problem, which was related to a malfunction causing wear on the battery.

The second step in the correlational reasoning process is generating ideas to answer the questions raised in the first step. Some possibilities may come from the ideas of other people, or they may be self-generated. The more ideas we generate, the better the chances for finding the best answer to the question. I gathered ideas about my car from the repair shop, the car dealer, and family members. Quite a long list evolved. Some of the items were quite evidently not at the root of the problem, but then one skilled repairman noted that I had a new directional locator that continually sent a signal that allowed him to determine the vehicle's location. He thought that this might wear the battery down when the car was not being driven. The solution was as simple as calling the directional locator company and having it properly reinstalled.

When I asked friends, relatives, and my mechanic for ideas, I was effectively brainstorming solutions to my problem. Brainstorming in a classroom setting can be done individually, in groups, or with the entire class. There are rules for brainstorming:

- All answers are accepted—write down every suggestion, unless it has already been contributed by someone else.
- You may make only suggestions—no criticisms or affirmations.
- When ideas seem to stop flowing, review what you have listed. Can you piggyback on an idea by adapting one of the ideas already listed?
- Fit the ideas into categories, then look at other categories that may not have arisen and the possibilities those categories bring. For example, I need to get to a meeting tonight. I might focus on driving and the route to take without taking into account that I could car pool, take a taxi, or ride a bus or train. These different suggestions might solve the problem of parking that I could encounter later.
- Ask what information is needed before you can make a decision about which idea would work best in the situation.

Generating ideas can fail if there are not enough possibilities generated, the ideas are all of the same type, or the ideas are all ordinary or all useful. The best brainstorming sessions focus on quantity, originality, and variety.

3. Considering Evidence

How reliable is the information that you have? Where did it come from? What background and experience does the person who gave you the information have? Is the idea reasonable? To think critically is to question and evaluate the information that surrounds us and to not accept blindly all that we hear and see without assessing it. Good critical thinkers act on their own, using their best judgment; they avoid following the crowd. A critical thinker reasons things through and does not accept the word of another without knowing the motives and perceptions of that person. Considering evidence, which depends on our ability to determine the reliability of sources, is the next step in correlations in reasoning. Students need to be able to ask pertinent questions thoughtfully and respectfully and to access information freely. In the classroom, you can begin to discuss the reliability of sources during the following activities:

- Examining television commercials
- Finding information about what is a healthy snack (Breakfast cereal? Bread? How can you tell if the label on a food product is reliable?)
- Reading *Chicken Little* and discussing the reliability, or unreliability, of sources of her information
- Reading multiple accounts of a current events news story and viewing the TV news account of the story
- Examining multiple sources about a historical event or person
- Collecting multiple accounts of what happened on the playground or on the bus
- Interviewing eyewitnesses to an event

Once the reliability of background information is clarified, students can select the most reliable information to apply to their correlations in reasoning project. The final step in the correlations in reasoning process is to make an educated guess about the root cause of the event, based on the most reliable evidence.

4. Making Judgments/Predictions

When I consider the process of making predictions I immediately think of our local weatherman. He must always look toward the future and make an educated guess about what he thinks the weather will be like. Access to the latest technology; communication with other weather centers; and directions, speed, and proximity of the weather fronts all play a part in his prediction. Some days his predictions are better than others. His accuracy depends on the reliability of the information that he receives and how well he uses the information to make an informed guess.

Making a judgment about the cause or conditions of any event is similar to making a prediction: In both cases, we must understand how the state of the world preceding an event relates to the event that occurs. The difference is that judgments are educated guesses about what facts led to past or present events ("The World Trade Center bombings occurred because of religious fanaticism"), and predictions are educated guesses about how past and present facts will lead to future events

("If religious fanaticism becomes more widespread, the United States may experience more violence").

To be proficient in making judgments and predictions, we need to be cautious in how we make connections between events, their causes, and their outcomes. Judgments and predictions, therefore, need to be founded on well-supported, solid information. Exercises in judgment and prediction can be incorporated into classroom lessons in the following ways:

Judgments

- **Weather:** What caused the tsunami of 2005? What evidence do you have to support your belief?
- **Recycling:** Why has recycling not caught on in this country as it has in some European countries? What alternative causes might be at play?
- **Blackouts:** What caused the series of blackouts in the early 2000s in the United States? How could they have been averted?
- **Fire Safety:** What causes panic in a fire situation? What can be done to reduce these causes so panic is not a dominant element?
- **Playground Behavior:** Why do kids bully and taunt one another? What changes in rules, consequences, or tone of the school can result in more friendly playground behavior?

Predictions

- Read only part of a story. What do you think will happen? Why do you think so? Later, compare your prediction with the actual outcome. Rewrite or dramatize the ending to fit your prediction.
- What would your life have been like if you were born in 1800? 1900? 1950?
- How would your life be different if you had been born in a different state? A different country? England? South Africa? Japan? China? Sweden? Italy?
- What would happen if we added another substance (such as sugar, salt, alcohol, food coloring, oil) to water?
- What is likely to happen with the destruction of the rain forests?
- What will Earth be like in 2050? Consider global warming, population growth, energy consumption, and pollution. Tell what facts you are using to determine your prediction.

Research

Aaron was a resident expert on astronomy. He knew all the constellations. His interest was intense and his knowledge far surpassed the recommended grade-level books we used to teach our unit on space. When Aaron was given the option of skipping the required reading and researching an area of astronomy that he'd like to explore further, his eyes danced with anticipation.

Research can be a highly effective tool in promoting both acceleration of content and critical thinking skills for students who need the opportunity to reach beyond what is expected at their grade level. Research encompasses all of the elements of conditional reasoning while fostering creativity and fluidity of thought. The research process can be linked to the process of scientific investigation, as the pathway may be similar or even identical. Just as the scientific process often contains elements that rarely flow in a specific order, the trial and error of the true scientific endeavor applies to research as well.

Once a research project begins, students automatically access their own wealth of knowledge. This activation of background knowledge is a key component of the thought process that occurs as students become re-familiarized with their connection to the topic. What may occur next is the process of formulating a question or problem that needs solving. What have the students observed that will lead them to an educated prediction? Students may then determine a hypothesis or prediction statement that they are interested in testing. The hypothesis is key to the investigation and often is a result of the particular students' background knowledge of the topic, as well as the sources that the student has used to investigate it. Because of the personal nature of background knowledge, the hypotheses of different students can vary greatly, leading to self-guided, differentiated instruction. If students have had access to a great deal of the content, they may choose a higher-level investigative hypothesis and, therefore, accelerate the content to their level.

Once the hypothesis is set, students must determine how to collect the data needed to determine the correctness of the hypothesis. As students analyze the collected data, new hypotheses may emerge, supporting fluidity of thought. The results, in turn, may lead students to further investigation, pulling them to a deeper understanding of the topic or content.

After all of the data is gathered, summarized, and graphed in a way that allows for the creation of knowledge on the part of the student researchers, they can then draw conclusions about their work. Do their data support their hypotheses? What can they infer from the knowledge they have gained? How do their results open the door for further investigation and, therefore, a deeper understanding of the content or acceleration of the content?

FOSTERING CREATIVITY IN ACCELERATED LEARNERS

Students who are highly creative are often viewed as being "out of step" with their age peers, a perception that can sometimes produce a negative image of these students. Imagine having Robin Williams, Jim Carey, Whoopi Goldberg, or Calvin from Calvin and Hobbes in your home or classroom. Their antics may make you laugh, but living with or teaching a highly energetic, creative person has its limitations. Often, highly creative children need an accelerated curriculum that breaks away from the rigor and repetition that stifles them.

Lori was highly creative and her teacher did not see her fitting in with her kindergarten class. When interviewed by the gifted specialist, Lori was asked to draw a picture of her school. Lori asked for a big sheet of paper. She explained that her school had a different view, depending on how you looked at it. "If you came in the front door it would look one way," and she proceeded to draw a picture of the front of the building. "However, if you want to know where my classroom is, I must draw the school as if I am a bird, so that you can see the hall leading to the classroom. And if you want to know where we play, I'll have to draw the back of the school because that is where the playground and playground equipment are located."

Lori saw things creatively, with multiple perspectives. For her there was no simple answer, but multiple answers. Neither her classmates nor her teacher understood her highly creative and complex thinking.

Keeping the creative juices flowing is essential to the acceleration process, and the simplest way to do this is to tie creative thinking to solid content by using any number of methods, including creating alterations, exploring forced relationships, making analogies, and using identification/personification.

Asking students to make *alterations* in a story or project based on new information can result in huge creative leaps that are both fun and thought provoking. For example, a class studying space could break into small groups to work on designing a space suit. Students can be prompted to ask questions such as, "What properties would make the suit comfortable and accommodate human needs? What adaptations need to be considered for survival?" When groups have their space suits designed, each group could be assigned two creative ways to alter their suits from the examples listed below.

- **Magnify:** Make larger. A seven-foot-tall basketball player is traveling into space. What accommodations need to be made for this suit?
- **Minify:** Make smaller. A small child is traveling into space. How would the suit need to be different for this child?
- **Modify:** A person with a physical disability wishes to experience space travel. What would be needed for a person with a spinal cord injury? A hearing or vision impairment?
- **Substitute:** Apes will be going into space instead of humans. What problems and/or solutions would this create?
- **New Use:** How could the space suit be adapted for underwater exploration?
- **Combine:** Combine communication, timekeeping, and record-keeping technology (such as a cell phone, watch, and camera). How could you do this in the smallest possible space?
- **Rearrange:** Design the interior of the space suit. What is essential in the design for safety and human needs? What is desirable for comfort?
- **Eliminate:** What would happen if gravitational pull on Earth were to disappear? How would the space suit have to change? (Adapted from Eberle, 1982)

Another creative technique is that of *forced relationship.* In a forced relationship task, two completely different content areas must be linked and a narrative justifying the link must be developed by the students. For instance, a teacher might have the class list objects associated with space and make a separate list of objects associated with a garage sale. Students would select one object from each list, such as a quasar and a bookshelf. Then they would combine the two to create something new—perhaps a quasar shelf. What would it look like? Students can draw the new, combined item and explain how it works.

Using creative *analogies* is another strategy that stimulates creative thinking. Students link interdisciplinary content that is similar in form or purpose and compare and contrast the elements. In what ways is a spaceship like a submarine? In what ways are they different? In what ways is space litter both similar to and different from highway litter?

Finally, *identification and personification* exercises can be used to create an appreciation for other perspectives, which is a crucial element of creative thinking. One approach that works well with accelerated students is to ask them to write a story about a discipline that piques their interest, then choose the point of view of a tool, a person, or an object about which they are curious. For example, students might describe a moon landing from the point of view of a moon rock. What would the rock say and do if it could speak and act? Or they might try to describe a telecommunication satellite from the perspective of a meteor. What does it feel like to have radiation bouncing off your surface?

Society desperately needs creative thinkers. They are the people who will design and build tomorrow's information technology, find medical cures, design the clothing of the future, and create the transportation and communication tools that will bring us together. The more complex the problem, the more creativity is needed to find the best possible solution. By fostering the creativity that is already budding in our youngest accelerated students, we become, in effect, gardeners of the future.

7

Product Development

As I walk through the halls of an elementary school, I love to look at the student work that is on display. I am always amazed at how the mobiles, turkeys, snowflakes, bunnies, and flowers tell so much about the little artists who made them. It is easy to pick out the neat, orderly, precise worker and the one who didn't quite have all of the pieces together. I especially like the projects that require creativity on the part of the students; they speak volumes about the children who made them.

These creative efforts, along with everything from traditional tests and quizzes to dance performances and student-designed Web sites, are *products*—vehicles that demonstrate to what extent a student has mastered the content and is able to apply it. The success of a gifted program depends crucially on the selection and evaluation of appropriate products by the educators and students. This chapter guides the reader through the art of product selection and evaluation.

PRODUCT DEVELOPMENT IN AN ACCELERATED SETTING

Products chosen for accelerated gifted students need to challenge existing ideas and produce new outcomes. They should encourage the utilization of new materials, techniques, and forms. The chance to work with mentors or experts in a field can also be used to enrich the array of products that can be used in accelerated programs. Products selected for gifted students must engage their learning modalities, support independent study, and allow assessment with rubrics that allow for acceleration. The degree to which the product engages the student to work above grade level is the degree to which the product is accelerated. Many products are appropriate at a particular grade level and provide novel experiences. These products would be classified as enrichment opportunities. Products that model the work of an expert in the field and that examine new ideas, forms, materials, and techniques are accelerated and extend far beyond the norm.

ENGAGING LEARNING MODALITIES

Products that engage students' learning styles allow for a realistic assessment of ability. Unfortunately, it is commonplace for schools to get tied to paper-and-pencil responses when the student is largely verbal or kinesthetic. I recall asking four-year-old Paul, "Who is Christopher Columbus?" Paul wanted to know whether he could act out his answer. "Why not?" I thought. Paul proceeded to the kindergarten climbing bars and started to sing, "Sailing, sailing, over the ocean blue." I asked, "Captain, where are you going?" Paul responded, "Well, where I want to go and where I end up are two different things. Really, Columbus should have had bifocals so he could have read the map and seen where he was going. Ben Franklin invented the bifocal much later, though." Did Paul know the information? Certainly. Did I learn more about Paul than a paper-and-pencil item would have divulged? Absolutely. Do our curricula allow for the diversity of the Pauls in our classrooms? Usually not. If not, we need to make accommodations so that these extremely bright students are not given pablum when they are ready for solid food.

Children are born to touch, feel, move, dance, run, explore. They get into everything! That is the way they learn. They are tactile-kinesthetic, global learners. However, school requires listening, following directions, and analyzing spoken information. Once children enter the school arena, educators expect them to make the switch to become primarily auditory learners. Those students who do well tend to adapt, making the switch rather seamlessly. However, those who are visual or tactile-kinesthetic may have a more difficult time in classrooms that demand predominately written or oral products. As learning modality is completely independent of intelligence or creativity, it is remarkably inappropriate that only a single modality is represented in most product selection.

Visual learners tend to prefer pictures to words and would like to see what the finished product should look like rather than hearing the task explained. They like to work with color and graphic organizers. Charts, pictures, and graphs are second nature to them.

The tactile-kinesthetic learners prefer hands-on activities, concrete examples, moving while learning, learning by doing, investigating manipulatives, and using a word processor rather than writing by hand. They favor products that allow them to become involved physically, to try something out, to move and explore with their bodies and hands. Tactile-kinesthetic learners do not retain or enjoy lectures. They also don't like public speaking; they prefer to be succinct or tend to shy away from speaking before a group.

When you design projects for students, products should be available that allow for the differences in learning styles so that students can be productive and demonstrate what they know and how well they can perform. This applies to *all* students. Unfortunately, accelerated elementary students are many times expected to perform more effectively on written assignments. All too often, some teachers believe that "fun" (loosely defined as anything not written) products should be eliminated and replaced with tests and written reports. Rigor isn't limited to written work. Products that break through the traditional presentations and that go beyond the grade boundaries demonstrate acceleration in another dimension. The car designers who create new models to be more fuel efficient and safer are not held to a particular level of work or a particular learning style modality. Their thinking needs to be creative, pushing what is known, utilizing their current knowledge, and exploring new avenues. The same can apply to elementary students. Products should be loosely defined enough so that any level of knowledge, creativity, or insight can be demonstrated. Allow for acceleration of product development. Table 7.1 is a menu of product options along with the learning modalities they employ.

The degree of complexity, originality, and depth of understanding demonstrate the degree to which acceleration is present.

Supporting Independent Study

For advanced learners, independent study may be a very useful way to accelerate learning. Many gifted learners are "resident experts" or eager to become an expert in a chosen area. They live, breathe, and eat their favorite topic; they are consumed by it. They often know more than their teachers in these areas, so independent study becomes necessary for learners to learn more. Products that support independent study should be created as a joint effort—by both the teacher and the student. The section on research in the previous chapter addressed some of these

Table 7.1   Menu of Product Options and Learning Modalities

Product	Written	Oral/Auditory	Visual	Tactile/ Kinesthetic
Acrostic poem	X			
Advertisement	X		X	
Advice column	X			
Audiotape		X		
Autobiography	X			
Ballad		X		
Banner	X		X	X
Bio poem	X			
Board game			X	X
Book	X		X	
Book jacket			X	
Brochure	X		X	
Bulletin board	X		X	X
Calendar	X		X	
Campaign speech		X		
Candidate platform	X	X		
Card game			X	X
Cartoon	X		X	
Charade				X
Chart	X		X	
Collection			X	X
Column analysis			X	
Comic strip	X		X	
Commercial	X	X	X	
Concept map	X		X	
Costume				X
Critique	X			
Crossword puzzle	X		X	
Dance			X	X
Data sheet	X		X	
Debate	X	X		
Demonstration	X	X	X	X

Product	Written	Oral/Auditory	Visual	Tactile/Kinesthetic
Diagram (with labels)	X		X	
Diary	X			
Dictionary	X			
Diorama			X	X
Directions	X	X		
Display			X	X
Dramatization				X
Drawing			X	
Editorial	X			
Encyclopedia entry	X			
Experiment	X		X	X
Fable	X			
Fact file	X			
Fairy tale	X			
Family tree	X		X	X
Field trip				X
Flannel board presentation		X	X	X
Flow chart	X		X	
Game	X	X	X	X
Game show	X	X	X	X
Glossary	X			
Good-bad story	X		X	
Graph	X		X	
Graphic Organizer	X		X	
Greeting card			X	
Haiku	X			
Help wanted ad	X			
Hidden picture			X	
Illustrations			X	
Infomercial	X	X		
Informative speech		X		

(Continued)

Table 7.1 (Continued)

Product	Written	Oral/Auditory	Visual	Tactile/ Kinesthetic
Interview	X	X		
Invention				X
Invitation	X			
Jigsaw puzzle			X	X
Joke book	X	X		
Journal	X			
Labeled diagram	X		X	
Labels	X		X	
Learning center	X	X	X	X
Learning profile	X		X	X
Lecture	X	X		
Letter	X		X	
List	X			
Magazine	X		X	
Manual (how to)	X		X	
Map (with legend)	X		X	
Maze			X	X
Menu	X		X	
Metaphor	X			
Mobile			X	X
Model			X	X
Mosaic			X	X
Movie	X	X	X	X
Movie review	X			
Mural			X	
Museum exhibit	X		X	X
Musical composition	X			X
Myth	X			
Newspaper	X		X	
News report	X	X		
News story	X			

Product	Written	Oral/Auditory	Visual	Tactile/ Kinesthetic
Nursery rhyme	X			
Observation log	X		X	
Oral report		X		
Outline	X		X	
Overhead transparency			X	
Painting			X	
Pamphlet	X		X	
Pantomime				X
Paragraph	X			
Pattern			X	X
Persuasive Speech		X		
Photo journal	X		X	
Picture			X	
Picture book			X	
Picture dictionary	X		X	
Play	X	X	X	X
Play-Doh characters			X	X
Poem	X			
Pop-up book	X		X	X
Portfolio	X		X	X
Postcards	X		X	
Poster	X		X	X
PowerPoint presentation	X	X	X	
Problem solution	X	X		
Product descriptor	X			
Proverb	X			
Pun	X	X		
Puppet			X	X
Puzzle			X	X
Questionnaire	X	X		
Quiz	X			
Quiz show	X	X		

(Continued)

Table 7.1 (Continued)

Product	Written	Oral/Auditory	Visual	Tactile/ Kinesthetic
Radio show	X	X		
Rap		X		X
Reader's theater	X	X	X	X
Rebus story	X		X	
Recipe	X		X	
Relief map			X	X
Research report	X	X		
Rhyme	X	X		
Rhythmic pattern		X		X
Riddles	X	X		
Role play				X
Rubric	X			
Scrapbook	X		X	X
Sculpture			X	X
Self-portrait			X	
Self description	X			
Sequel	X			
Set design			X	X
Sign			X	
Simulation	X	X		X
Skit				X
Social action	X	X		X
Song	X	X		
Speech	X	X		
Story	X			
Summary	X	X		
Survey	X	X	X	X
Table			X	
Tall tale	X			
Test	X	X		
Thank-you note	X			
Timeline	X		X	

Product	Written	Oral/Auditory	Visual	Tactile/ Kinesthetic
Travelogue	X	X	X	
Travel poster	X		X	X
Trivia game	X	X	X	X
TV commercial	X	X	X	X
TV program	X	X	X	X
Venn diagram	X		X	
Video game			X	X
Videotape		X	X	
Vocabulary list	X			
Wanted poster	X		X	
Weather forecast	X	X	X	
Weather instrument				X
Weather report	X			
Web (concept map)	X		X	
Web site	X		X	X
Wish list	X			
Worksheet	X			
Written report	X			

ideas, but at the bare minimum, an independent study plan should include the following:

- Several topics of interest, settling on one or two for in-depth study
- Questions the student would like to answer about the topic
- Places the student will look for information (e.g., books, people to talk to, places to visit, experts in the field)
- A plan to communicate with parents regarding the status of the project and any special help required
- Space for materials in the classroom
- Realistic goals, including deadlines (see the Independent Study Form, Chart 7.1)
- Planned time for an older student or outside expert to help with the project; have appropriate community members visit the school to view the product, meet the student, and provide helpful feedback.
- Planned daily meetings with the student(s) to assess progress or areas needing help

Self-evaluation is an important component of product development. Students must learn to ask themselves, "How well did I do on the project? What would I do differently if I were to do this again?"

Independent Study Form

Topic:

What I want to know: _____

My question(s) for the topic:

Who _____

What _____

When _____

Where _____

How _____

Why _____

To find out I will read _____

Write _____

Look _____

Listen _____

Draw _____

Need _____

I will share what I learned through (product) _____

I will be done by _____

Signed (student) _____

Signed (teacher) _____

Signed (parent) _____

Chart 7.1   *Independent Study Form*

Self-Evaluation Form for Independent Study

Student Name: _____

Topic: _____

Yes   No

____   ____   I chose a topic that I liked.

____   ____   I had questions about my topic.

____   ____   I found more than one resource about my topic.

____   ____   I took notes on the information that answered my questions.

____   ____   I made something.

____   ____   I shared my project with others.

I learned how to _____

I did a good job at _____

I could have improved my project by _____

_____

Chart 7.1 *Independent Study Form*

Rubric Development

Regardless of whether products originate from the classroom content or independent study, product assessment needs to be built into the curriculum early on. Students need to be clear about the expectations for their work when they start working. A rubric is a guideline of expectations that lists criteria—from unacceptable to excellent—with gradations of what the product could look like. When designed well and with care, rubrics are powerful tools for both teaching and assessment. By having expectations clearly delineated, students often improve the quality of their work. The rubric addresses the questions, "What does quality look like?" and "How can I improve?"

There are two types of rubrics: holistic and analytic. The holistic rubric lists all aspects of the product together; the product is looked at as a whole. If any one criterion is not at the same level as the other criteria, the score is lowered to the level of the weakest criterion. For this reason, its use is limited. An example of a holistic rubric follows (see Chart 7.2). This rubric assesses the product on the basis of the following criteria:

- Accurate information
- Understanding of the content
- Vocabulary supports content
- Creativity

Holistic Rubric Example	
• Information gives many specific examples with clarifying details to show depth of information • Content goes beyond basic understanding with depth and complexity • Vocabulary is advanced • Innovative, unique, new perspective with supporting details	**6 Exceptional**
• Information provided with examples and details • Content is explored at length • Vocabulary demonstrates understanding • Novel content	**5 Great**
• Information accurate • Connection to content is clear • Appropriate vocabulary used • Shows idea new to learner	**4 Good**
• Information missing important details • Connection to content weak • Vocabulary accurate but limited • Standard format, conventional	**3 Fair**
• Information flawed • Connection to content unclear • Vocabulary inaccurate and limited • Copied	**2 Below Standard**
• Little attempt made to give information • No link to content • Vocabulary unrelated • Copied poorly	**1 Unacceptable**

Chart 7.2 *Holistic Rubric Example*

The holistic rubric is helpful if the entirety of work is being examined, rather than each piece individually or each section for its own merit.

An analytic rubric lists each criterion independently. The final score is obtained by adding the scores for each criterion together. Analytic rubrics are especially helpful for students who excel in some areas but not others—perhaps students are tactile/kinesthetic learners and the product calls for a large visual/auditory component. Chart 7.3 is an example of an analytic rubric for a product using the same criteria that were established in the holistic rubric example.

Rubrics allow students to become better evaluators of their own work. With a well-developed rubric, students are able to see at a glance what still needs to be done and what has already been done well. This can cut down on the "Am I done yet?" queries. In addition, rubrics make grading much easier. The teacher does not need to comment on every strength or weakness but instead can refer to the rubric, which

Product Criteria	1 Unacceptable	2 Below Standard	3 Fair	4 Good	5 Great	6 Exceptional
Accurate information	Little attempt made to give information	Information flawed	Information missing important details	Information accurate	Information provided with examples and details	Information gives many specifics with clarifying details to show depth of information
Demonstrates understanding of the content	No link to content	Connection to content unclear	Connection to content weak	Connection to content is clear	Content is explored at length	Content goes beyond basic understanding with depth and complexity
Vocabulary supports content	Vocabulary unrelated	Vocabulary inaccurate and limited	Vocabulary accurate but limited	Appropriate vocabulary used	Vocabulary demonstrates understanding	Vocabulary is advanced
Creativity	Copied poorly	Copied	Standard format, conventional	Shows idea new to learner	Novel content	Innovative, unique, new perspective with supporting details
Scores for each row						

Total of all rows _____

Chart 7.3 *Analytic Rubric*

supplies the standard. Finally, rubrics also help parents know exactly what their child needs to accomplish in order to be successful. This aids in communication about the assigned product. Parents can also use rubrics to assist their children with their homework or products.

> When the principal of her school made the announcement that teachers would use rubrics for the students' products, Miss R. was not exactly enthused. She thought only of the time that was required to put the rubrics together. She had been assigning grades for years; she knew what she was looking for, so why did she have to go through this labor-producing process? After the first rubric was handed out with the initial assignment, the light bulb went on for Miss R. She no longer received parent calls asking her what exactly was expected. The students knew the criteria for grading ahead of time, so many student questions were eliminated. When the products came in with the attached rubrics, they were far superior to those of previous years. They were just what she specified. Miss R. became a rubric advocate.

Analytic Rubric	
Criteria	*Points*
I worked hard and did my very best.	4
I did my work.	3
I did less than I could have.	2
I did not try.	1

Total _____

Chart 7.4   *Effort Rubric for Young Child*

Rubrics have an added value for the gifted student, as they can be stretched like elastic. Instead of stopping at what their project looks like when it is "good," students can choose to explore what is beyond mastery: the work of a professional in the field. This gives accelerated students a sense of choice about their own efforts as well as the feeling that their extra work, should they choose to do it, will be recognized. The elasticity keeps the flexibility of the rubric functioning for a continuum of learners, as well as showing growth in a single learner over a period of time.

Rubrics can also help students learn to self-evaluate, a crucial tool for self-directed learning. Once students can become honest with themselves about how well they've worked, they can move more effectively toward their personal best. For the young child, a sample product rubric may look like Chart 7.4.

Rubrics are meant to be flexible, not cast in concrete; they can be altered for almost any purpose. Asking the students for their feedback will let you know whether adjustments are necessary—remember that gifted students often see the picture with more clarity than the teacher. For fun, students can develop rubrics to "grade" their parents, the president of the United States, or the school principal. Along that vein, it is also fun and very useful to ask our students to create rubrics for our teaching. Our accelerated children can help us brainstorm to discover what elements of teaching style are important to their learning. In the process, we can understand what does and doesn't matter to them. Students can use this "teaching rubric" to anonymously grade the teacher throughout the year, providing us with continuous feedback. The rubric itself can be redesigned as students gain a better understanding of their own needs. In this way, our attempts to reach our personal best and accommodate the needs of our students model persistence, attention to detail, and effort.

8

Standards
and Policy

The education pendulum has a way of swinging against the needs of gifted students. The movement to "leave no child behind" has focused attention on students who have not attained grade-level expectations, without recognizing that students who excel beyond grade level may also have special needs. This shift usually arises from several factors, including incomplete or misleading representations of research, concerns about budget constraints, fears of elitism, and poorly constructed gifted programs. Recently, for example, the movement to eliminate tracking and institute heterogeneous grouping was done in response to research that suggested that tracking-induced labeling was damaging to students' self-esteem (Oakes, 1985). "Fairness" and "equity" were regarded in the United States with awe, while acceleration was regarded with suspicion and classified as elitist. In Fairfax County, VA, seven high schools eliminated class rankings in order to do away with distinctions and honors. In 1993, Los Angeles city schools abolished the grade "Outstanding" in order for more students to achieve high marks. A professor of education at Harvard, Charles Willie, said that the goal of education should not be "excellence" but "adequacy." Excellence was a matter of personal choice and sacrifice (Sykes, 1995). Classroom organization was, in many cases, based on random assignments, and few opportunities for grouping were allowed. This strategy allowed lower-performing students to have more flexibility in learning opportunities and to avoid labels. On the other hand, the elimination of tracking was interpreted by some educators to mean the elimination of *any* grouping. It was perceived as elitist for a school to have a gifted program. Many school districts placed gifted students in regular classrooms, without regard for or awareness of their needs (Kulik, 1992).

In many cases, gifted education has been perceived as an "extra," an easy target for budget cuts. Acceleration is perceived as a frill. As a result of not having their needs met, a significant proportion of capable learners are not utilizing their skills or are even dropping out of school. In fact, when compared to other nations, the United States falls short with the education of its most capable students (National Assessment of Educational Progress, 1992; VanTassel-Baska, 1993). As a nation, we certainly cannot afford to lose the talents of these students. However, without administrative structure and support, gifted programs are doomed to fail. This chapter focuses on strengthening the backbone of gifted programs: the standards and policy structure that permits educators to employ the best practice for all. Acceleration is a need and a right to an appropriate education for some gifted students.

STANDARDS

Improvement in the U.S. educational system is based on standards for student performance. Standards drive the tests that every state administers to its students. Scores on these tests, in turn, are the measures by which teachers are judged and schools are evaluated. State tests determine which schools are desirable, which students will be eligible to transfer out (at least under the 2001 No Child Left Behind Act), and, in some cases, the value of local real estate.

When standards dictate the curriculum, some schools are reluctant to veer from the set standards to allow any degree of differentiation for gifted students. For example, I know one educator who has been teaching for a number of years—I'll call him "Mr. Miller." His classes are enriched with tales of his world travels. Students love him. When studying different habitats, his slides and stories bring the content to life. Unfortunately, he is considering leaving the teaching profession. Mr. Miller admits that teaching is no longer as fun as it used to be. "Learning has become regimented," he confided. "The focus is strictly on meeting the standard and passing the test." Content coverage is important for "the test," making it difficult to teach any extra content or do creative activities. Mr. Miller fears that we are raising a nation of test takers, not good thinkers and problem solvers.

Recent focus has been on meeting the needs of students who do not pass the tests, and little recognition has been given to those who have already mastered and exceeded the standards. Rather than ignoring the standards or circumventing them in the curriculum, the standards must be acknowledged and incorporated. Of course, standards must be clear so that teachers are aware of what is required for mastery of the knowledge and skills. However, standards should also allow enough flexibility for educators to use their professional judgment rather than prescribe lesson plans, materials, and instructional methods. Professionals do that, and we need the latitude to use best practice to meet the needs of all students. Rather than focusing on minimal expectations, schools need to assist students in not just meeting, but reaching for and exceeding, the highest standards possible. Isn't it time to focus on strengths? Shouldn't we begin to remove the glass ceiling that denies advanced learners opportunities for growth?

ACCELERATING STANDARDS

One way to meet the needs of gifted students is to use standards to create an ever-evolving learning continuum, rather than one narrow, single path. For example, rather than focusing on first-grade math standards, look at the math standards as they progress through the grades. When students master the grade-level standard, we can accelerate their learning process by introducing the next level standard and helping these students work to master it.

To begin accelerating standards for gifted students, determine what skills and knowledge the students are required to have in each content area at the beginning of the year. You might use pretests or other pre-assessments to determine whether a student has exceeded these knowledge and skill areas, whether she or he is at grade level, or whether she or he needs additional support to meet the standards. For those students who have already mastered the knowledge and skills, list the skills to be developed at the next level or grade (see Chart 8.1).

Early elementary math standard: I know about numbers: I can add and subtract them.

One-to-one correspondence	Simple addition with manipulatives	Simple addition, paper and pencil	Simple subtraction with manipulatives	Simple subtraction, paper and pencil	Two-place addition

Chart 8.1

INCREASING DIFFICULTY

A continuum such as Chart 8.1 addresses the standards but simultaneously allows students to progress as rapidly or slowly as meets their individual needs.

Standards can be expanded well beyond the early elementary level, as demonstrated in Chart 8.2. Multiple skills can be combined to make a far more complex continuum. If your goal is to get a broader picture of the student's ability, then the format below may be one with which you wish to work.

Extension of early elementary science standard: I can understand how to study science, do experiments, and solve problems using science.

I wonder why, look carefully, write down what I see, ask questions, and discover patterns.	I can ask questions, make observations, collect and record information, construct charts, make explanations, and display results.	I can make a prediction, conduct an experiment, interpret and report results.	Using the scientific process, I can conduct investigations that help me understand what I am observing and can explain what I have learned.

Chart 8.2

SOURCE: Adapted from Illinois State Board of Education (1997).

INCREASING DIFFICULTY

When test scores are so important to schools, it only stands to reason that schools would want students to score as highly as possible. To achieve this end, the ceiling placed on standards must be removed and allowances for acceleration must be encouraged. Once students have mastered the content and skill required at their grade level, they must not be allowed to stagnate. There should be nothing to stop the learner from trying to reach the next level, even if the accelerated level goes beyond their current grade.

Taylor, a second grader, was an excellent reader. She had been reading since age four. In her state, the language arts standard for early elementary reading states, "Can read with understanding." For early elementary students, the standard is then broken down further (see Chart 8.3).

Use word analysis and vocabulary skills to comprehend selections.	I can use what I know about letters, sounds, and words to help me figure out new words and phrases.
Use reading strategies to improve understanding and fluency.	I can ask questions about what I have read and predict what might happen later in a story.
Understand a broad range of reading materials.	I can read and comprehend many different kinds of books.

Chart 8.3

SOURCE: Adapted from Illinois State Board of Education (1997).

Taylor's reading ability far exceeded the early elementary standards. Upon realizing this, her teacher examined the late elementary standards. Although the broad standard was much the same—"Can read well with understanding"—the skills were expanded and were more applicable to Taylor's reading ability. For example, for word analysis the standard states, "I can read and understand words I do not know by looking at words and sentences around the word; by using what I know about letters, sounds, and parts of words; or by using a dictionary and thesaurus" (Illinois State Board of Education, 1997). This type of skill-based standards acceleration allows Taylor to work within the context of the standards without being penalized for her ability.

ACCELERATION POLICY

Policies are adopted plans of action composed of a set of rules. School policy is influenced by state policies as well as professional leadership, attitudes of both school and public, bureaucracy, rules and regulations, personal relationships, economics, court actions, reforms, and projects. In dealing with special populations, flexibility in policy design is essential. Flexibility allows schools to make decisions based on student need rather than on set dates or rigid criteria. Ideally, local districts should make decisions about how their gifted students' needs are met and take responsibility for doing so. In reality, gifted education policy at the state level directs what local districts are able to do. At the state level, gifted education policy is tied to rules and regulations that the state legislature has passed and is controlled by how state funding is allocated.

Because gifted students do not enjoy the same level of statutory protection as students with disabilities, it has taken time and effort for states to recognize and assist gifted children. In many states and districts, gifted programming is still viewed as a luxury. Despite years of research and volumes of statistically reliable information (Kulik & Kulik, 1991; Office of Educational Research and Improvement, 1993), the mistaken notion that "bright kids don't need anything extra because they'll do fine on their own" continues to be the received dogma. Research has documented that this conventional "wisdom" is not correct (Colangelo et al., 2004; Kulik & Kulik, 1991; Office of Educational Research and Improvement, 1993). In fact, results from years of research reveal that gifted students could be termed "exceptional" because they have real, persistent, and substantial individual differences and educational needs that regular education is unable to accommodate.

Program Design

Designing a comprehensive acceleration program is like putting together a quilt piece by piece. It will look different for every school because the design of an acceleration program must be based on the unique population each school serves. Program options must extend well past normal instructional boundaries; they need to reach across disciplines, grade levels, and types of intelligence. The program needs to incorporate specific plans for concurrent enrollment at all levels, when appropriate. In addition, counselors are important in different capacities: assessing students for program appropriateness, assessing student progress, addressing social and emotional needs specific to gifted students, and assisting with career and college choices.

Essential to the design of any acceleration program is the guiding principle that gifted learners should be allowed to begin any learning program (subject area or grade) based on their readiness and exit based on their proficiency (see National Association for Gifted Children, 1998). In addition, the program should encourage hands-on, project-based learning that deepens content areas by using the methods of inquiry used by scholars in the field. Community resources can be tapped, linking students to professional leaders to develop internships and mentoring relationships. Community organizations, civic groups, museums, and arts organizations can all become part of the policy that allows educational options to extend outside the classroom walls.

This section highlights the most crucial elements that must be present in any policy designed to create a successful acceleration program: program management, student identification, program services, curriculum/instruction, learning assessment, personnel preparation, and program evaluation.

Program Management

Strong, knowledgeable, professional leadership is key, not only for the application of policy but also for the program's success. When possible, it is helpful to have coordinators of the program involved in the planning stages.

Student Identification

Identification is the process of determining who is eligible for gifted programming. In order to avoid labeling, we technically do not identify giftedness in schools; rather, we identify the need for and appropriateness of different kinds of programming. The potential of the learner needs to be determined so that there is a "match" to programming and services. Consider the following questions in the identification process:

- How are students identified for gifted programming?
- Are multiple measures used? (There is not a single kind of intelligence or a single instrument for measuring intelligence.)
- Is the identification process fair, valid, reliable, and sensitive to the needs of gifted and talented students with regard to special populations?
- What considerations are made for children who are culturally diverse, twice exceptional, economically disadvantaged, or highly creative?
- Are there instruments used that respect each population?
- Are there screeners who speak the child's native language?
- Has consideration been given to children's different learning styles and different ways of processing information?
- Are young students given the opportunity to be identified for gifted services? (Too often young children are not given opportunities to be identified or are tested for gifted programs with paper-and-pencil instruments, which fall far short of tapping their true potential.)
- Is out-of-level testing available for students who consistently score at upper percentiles?
- Does the identification policy incorporate a long-term commitment to finding children who need gifted programming?

Program Services

The following questions can be used as guides when delineating the services an accelerated program will offer.

- Are program services aligned to the needs of the students for whom the program is designed?
- Are services provided for the social and emotional needs specific to gifted students, as well as their academic needs?
- Do the program services allow gifted students from non-majority cultural, economic, and/or ethnic populations to have a successful experience?

Over time, program services will evolve to take into account individuals and their needs. To meet these needs, additional resources and expertise at the local level may be necessary. For example, one district had the commitment to ensure that the city's diverse cultural population was reflected within the school's gifted program. Their problem was not how to get culturally diverse students into the program, but how to retain them in the program once they were identified. Many of the students had to be bussed to the program and leave their neighborhood schools. Some did not have the needed background and skills to be successful in the academically rigorous program—they came from homes that did not have computers, books, or resources that others took for granted. Many of these children felt out of place and wanted to exit the program. Acceleration exacerbated the problem further. Standing out, reaching for more, and going beyond the norm made them shrink back to peer pressure.

Obviously, additional help was needed. The gifted school had a wise administrator who set up a summer program to help the culturally diverse students become acclimated to the rigors of the curriculum before the beginning of the school year. Students who were currently enrolled became "buddies," walking the new students through the hoops and assisting them academically with the aid of the teachers. A full-time tutor was hired to work with students who needed additional support during the school year. Family activities were instituted to give the school a sense of community.

Curriculum and Instruction

Curriculum and instruction are the meat and potatoes of the program. They are the *what* and *how* of school. Beyond containing opportunities for advanced learning, curricula for accelerated students should allow students to make interdisciplinary connections, use advanced resources, stimulate different learning modalities, and employ group inquiry. The following questions must be considered in selecting the curriculum and instruction:

- Is the curriculum appropriate for the needs of the learners?
- Does it allow for those with gifts and talents to move at an appropriate pace?
- Is there a scope and sequence that is planned to avoid gaps in knowledge and at the same time allow for advancement when appropriate?
- Is pre-assessment used to avoid redundant learning?

- Is the curriculum for gifted students tied to the curriculum of the regular classroom?
- Is the curriculum related to the standards?
- Are advanced resources available and used?
- Are the teachers who are responsible for gifted children prepared, supported, and retained?

Assessment of Learning

In order to ensure that an accelerated program is keeping pace with the needs of each student, it is necessary to build in periodic assessments of student performance. There are a number of questions that can help formulate an assessment or evaluation plan:

- Is assessment both formative (continuous) and summative (final or at completion)?
- Is assessment ceiling-free so that educators know the actual level of achievement of the gifted student? Too often the gifted child is at the 99th percentile. Without out-of-level testing or assessments, educators may never know how far above the grade level or how far above the 99th percentile the child may reach.
- Are there accommodations that go beyond the grade level when needed?

One example of a successful assessment plan that evolved to meet the needs of the student is John's story. John was precocious in math. His first-grade teacher was not exactly sure what to do with him; this also was true of his second-grade, third-grade, and fourth-grade teachers. In order to have some gauge of his mathematical knowledge, his fourth-grade teacher enrolled him in a talent-search testing program. This program usually tests sixth graders who are at the 95th percentile or higher on an academic test in math or language arts in order to determine what they know and can do on a measure that takes off the ceiling: the SAT. This test is typically given to juniors in high school.

John was thrilled to take the SAT. When the scores came back, his teacher was amazed to discover that he fared better than most students in high school. In fact, he received the top score for his region, a better score than any of the 700 sixth-grade students tested in his region of the state at the same time. His language arts scores were age-appropriate and, in some cases, even lagged behind his age peers. So it was clear that acceleration to the next grade level was not appropriate in all academic areas.

The teachers decided that the most feasible option was to telescope his math curriculum. He learned the middle school math curriculum in the next two years and began a study of high school geometry. As a sixth grader, John again took the SATs. He even projected his score because he completed the test early. On the scale of 200–800, John estimated that his score would probably be 750. He was disappointed to learn that his score was only 740. He wanted to know who scored the test and would have wanted to know the number of questions missed, the scoring system, and so on.

For the rest of sixth grade and the remainder of middle school, John was allowed to attend the local high school for his math classes. He did well and mastered all of the accelerated classes. However, John's education needs were a problem when he got to high school. What do you do with the student who has mastered all of the math offerings and wants to learn more? The solution was to continue acceleration in math by doing distance learning with a math professor at a leading university. A mentor relationship and respect developed that led to John's attendance at the university after completing high school.

Personnel Preparation

Each acceleration program must include policy that outlines how educators will be prepared to work with gifted and talented students. Every classroom should have a competent, caring, qualified teacher. Without background on the characteristics of the gifted learner, the classroom teacher may have no knowledge of how to make accommodations. Teachers must have an understanding of the gifted learners' characteristics and needs, differentiation of curriculum, and assessment practices. Acceleration of content, process, and products must be supported with a record-keeping system that monitors student growth. Professional development should be a continuous process for all involved and can employ courses available through local colleges and universities.

Program Evaluation

Is the program working? So often we forget to ask this question in a rigorous way. Ideally, an evaluation plan should be developed as the program is being developed. In this way, it is possible to establish baseline data so that program success can be monitored for the duration of the program. For the sake of our gifted students, we must create acceleration programs that recognize their right to be challenged, match their potential, and allow them to learn at their own pace. Of course, these programs need to be based on best practice and current research, but they must also be flexible enough to take into account the needs of individual students. For this reason, policies affecting acceleration programs should be reviewed and evaluated on a regular basis.

Policy and Advocacy

Acceleration policy is often based on misinformation, inaccurate beliefs, and hearsay. Fortunately, policy can be changed by dedicated parents and educators working together to provide accurate information and challenge erroneous beliefs. Part III of this book explores such efforts at advocacy in depth. Chart 8.4 is a brief list of frequently asked questions regarding acceleration, along with appropriate answers.

But if we do it for one student, won't we have to do it for all of them?	Not all students are ready to move at an accelerated rate, and not all will want to accelerate their learning.
What will they do at the next grade level? Shouldn't there be a limit on what is taught and how far to accelerate learning?	One never runs out of knowledge and skills to teach. Look at the work of a professional in the field. What skills and dispositions are necessary for success? Open the door to learning for the field of knowledge. Artificial boundaries are detrimental to learning.
Don't students need to be kept together in the class with their age peers?	Why? It is only in the school setting that students are kept with age peers. Staying with age mates and being discouraged from learning more than the standard curriculum encourages underachievement and poor learning habits. It is much more appropriate and advantageous for students to be with their intellectual peers rather than their age peers. When gifted students are forced to be with age mates in a lower-level curriculum they may become alienated and socially withdrawn over time.
Won't the slower children feel badly if some are accelerated?	Struggling children do not feel good about themselves when grouped with students who appear to learn with little or no effort, know the answer before the question is completed, blurt out the answer, or take over the whole discussion. All children deserve to learn material at a rate and style that meets their needs. This may require grouping and regrouping in classes to keep the students flexible and working toward making achievement gains for all.
Shouldn't we concentrate our efforts on helping the slow children?	We *are* helping the slower children to meet standards. Most teacher training, money in education, and sympathy of the public supports all kinds of adaptations for struggling students. Very little is done to assist the learners who have already mastered the course content.
Aren't gifted programs too expensive?	In 1998, The National Association for Gifted Children found that "less than $.02 of every $100 spent on elementary and secondary is devoted to providing programs for our gifted and talented students" (NAGC, 1998). This is but a pittance of what goes toward educating special needs students. It is time to recognize that the gifted student is just as different from the average student as the child with special needs. In fact, some gifted students also possess special needs. Their handicapping condition may receive attention and support long before their giftedness is recognized.

Chart 8.4

Isn't gifted education the result of having pushy parents?	Why is it that when parents of special needs students speak out, they are seen as legitimately asking for what their children need, but when parents of gifted children speak out they are accused of being pushy? Both sets of parents are only asking for what they feel their children need to have an appropriate education. They are helping their children by trying to have their children's needs met.
Won't acceleration place a label on the accelerated child? Aren't labels bad?	Students are labeled whether we like it or not. Don't we refer to the child with age- appropriate knowledge and skills as average? Those who take longer to master those skills are often said to be below average; those who learn easier and faster are said to be above average. Special needs children may have their disability referred to as mild, moderate, or severe, depending upon the degree and severity of the disability. Why is it we hesitate to recognize the talents and gifts of students? These gifts may appear to be mild, moderate, or severe. The needs of the gifted students are reflected in the degree to which their gift is present. All students deserve an appropriate education. For the gifted students, this does not mean that they receive a label, but rather an opportunity to learn through acceleration.
Aren't gifted students content to stay in the class and help struggling students?	Gifted students should never be used as unpaid teachers. The questions should be, "What new learning is available for the gifted student? Does the gifted student have the opportunity to struggle?" When the levels of instruction for the gifted student are inappropriate and expectations are minimal, intellectual laziness may develop. This can be very difficult to overcome.
Can't gifted students wait to get to college to be challenged?	Is it fair to waste 12 years waiting for college? What about the students who give up and don't play the school game? Some may even go so far as to drop out of school. Those who are not age-eligible to drop out may become behavior problems in their classrooms, resort to negative behaviors to express their anger, or adapt to classroom expectations and never approach their potential. Finally, college may also not provide enough stimulation and challenge for some of these students.
What if we choose not to accelerate a gifted student?	Gifted children who are forced to tolerate boredom in classrooms, where they already know and can do the work, are at risk of developing poor study habits, losing their motivation,

Chart 8.4   *(Continued)*

(Continued)

	underachieving, and losing interest in school. They may become behavior problems, become the class clowns, or mistakenly assume that if you work hard, you must be stupid. Some withdraw, comply with regular classroom expectations, and never use their potential.
As a teacher, how can I accommodate the needs of the gifted learner? What steps do I need to take to begin acceleration?	Review material that is to be learned for the content area at your grade. List essential skills and knowledge. Determine how you will pre-assess students. Examples include, but are not limited to, end of the year assessment, end of the chapter assessment, formal testing, observation checklist, performance assessment, interview, and portfolio. List supporting, relevant, and accessible materials appropriate for the content by grade levels. Match the materials to the standards. Assess appropriateness. For those pre-assessed students who know the standard curriculum, begin to develop a differentiated plan of instruction.

Chart 8.4

PART III

Social and Emotional Aspects of Effective Acceleration

9

Obstacles to Acceleration

CHALLENGE, MASTERY, AND DELIGHT: IT'S AN INSIDE JOB

To understand the learning needs of gifted children, it may be helpful to consider how special education programs for children in the cognitively delayed range adjust teaching expectations and experiences in accordance with their students' learning capacities. Educators make scrupulous attempts to move their students along at their particular appropriate levels of knowledge and pace. But do our brightest students receive the same careful encouragement to experience new learning? There are still popular notions that our most intelligent students will learn no matter what school situations they are mired in. As sensitive teachers know, the internal experience of a child is a determining measure of success in any learning environment. This chapter focuses on how differences in performance and behavior can mask the need for acceleration.

ASYNCHRONY AND INDICATIONS OF MENTAL MALNOURISHMENT

Giftedness is asynchronous development in which advanced cognitive abilities and heightened intensity combine to create inner experiences and awareness that are qualitatively different from the norm. This asynchrony increases with higher intellectual capacity. The uniqueness of the gifted renders them particularly vulnerable and requires modifications in parenting, teaching, and counseling in order for them to develop optimally (Silverman, 1993, p. 3).

Often our young candidates for acceleration have various interests, sensitivities, and personalities. Usually they are too complex to define succinctly. Describing all of these children is like trying to describe a symphony in a sentence. A characteristic "true" for one will be a "false" for another. Jasmine likes to work alone; Maria thrives in groups. There is enormous diversity in the pool of children who would benefit from some type of academic acceleration.

What are the manifestations of mental malnourishment? Some can seem paradoxical: falling below grade-level performance, or being unable or unwilling to play the "school" game. Underachievement, a discrepancy between ability and performance, is pervasive among gifted children. Although some children acquire high achievement, they are still underachieving relative to the level at which they are capable of learning. Regardless of the expressions, any child who is not challenged, immersed in mastering new things, and delighted with the learning process is being intellectually and creatively starved.

Slipping Away: Poor Performance in Highly Capable Students

Many of our little first timers in a classroom can't imagine that their school experience could be any different than it is. They may just settle into accommodating the rules and expectations and get rewarded for being such good children. For them, "goodness" is equivalent to fitting in, and they may make a conscious (or not so conscious) effort to stifle their curiosity in order to not bother anyone. This may manifest in less-than-stellar performance. Others act out behaviorally or fail to do assignments out of boredom, cultural expectations, and/or familial situations. Some of these children suffer from physiological conditions that can affect performance and mask their giftedness, such as ADD/ADHD, allergies, or depression. This section attempts to help you understand and identify different kinds of underachievement traps in exceptionally bright children.

Trapped by Goodness

Gino raced home from the school bus. Waving a small first reader high above his bouncy blonde curls, he dove into Mom's eager arms. "Mommy, look! We got our own reading books today! I'll read some for you!" As he nestled himself on Mommy's lap, Gino proudly opened his early reader and gingerly placed his index finger under the first word he said. As he tentatively moved his guiding finger to the next word, Gino carefully pronounced the single syllable. After a few pages of this laborious effort, Mom puzzled, "You usually read your books much faster; why are you taking such a long time to read each word?" Gino answered, "Oh, that's the way we read in school!"

After her first few weeks in kindergarten, Amy went to spend a weekend with Grandma. The proud kindergartner was brimming with delight to introduce Grandma to all of the wonders of her new world. Grandma beamed as she displayed the materials she gathered up so Amy could play school. Amy raced to the really big sheets of drawing paper and the new crayons! But when she proudly reappeared to show off her clutched bundle of drawings, Grandma didn't know how to respond. She expected to see some development in Amy's unusually advanced fine motor control and drawing abilities. Instead, Amy proudly displayed arrays of scribbled colors! Thankfully, Amy volunteered her own interpretation. "You see, Grandma, at school the other children don't know how to draw very well yet so I just scribble so they don't feel bad."

Often exceptionally intelligent children will not or cannot explain why they develop a gnawing reluctance to be in school. They don't have any other comparison experiences to show them that school could be any different. Meanwhile, their parents and teachers often experience satisfaction that they are great students.

When Gabriella started kindergarten, she realized that she needed to sit quietly through The Letter of the Week—the same letter every day for the whole long week. Meanwhile, she was contentedly reading to herself at home. After a few tedious months, she literally could not stomach it any longer. Gabriella started waking up with stomach aches. She whined, moaned, curled up on the floor, and stayed home with too much pain to go to school. Headaches can also be an indication that enduring the tediousness of going over what gifted learners already know may leave their brain starving for nurturing intellectual calories. After appropriate educational arrangements are made for restricted students, the lively child usually bounces back. In this age of mind-body awareness, many of us appreciate the reality of body as metaphor for what is going on in our psyches.

The greatest vulnerability of extremely intelligent children may be that they have *no visible distinguishing need.* They can become discouraged when not challenged. Their sense of self may not be based on their true abilities, needs, and desires, but on expectations and perceptions of others that require them to not make trouble for their parents or teachers.

Trapped by the Environment

Some children from marginalized cultures may feel out of place in their earliest school years. Stepping into foreign territory can be a terrifying challenge for children from a culture that is out of the mainstream. Perhaps there is a language barrier or educational void that discourages parents from integrating their family with local school culture. They don't want to embarrass themselves by not knowing how to be part of their school society. Other children may feel guilty about setting goals for themselves that are not possible for other people in their family.

Exceptional intelligence can be camouflaged by poverty. Sadly, many students' socioeconomic foundation is a keystone for their academic achievement. When we examine states' student academic achievement scores in various demographics, the low income sinks achievement. Table 9.1 shows third-grade ISAT reading scores for the percentage of students who met or exceeded the Illinois Standards in 2004.

To view similar results for states and individual schools throughout the United States, go to http://www.greatschools.net and see for yourself why we need to sensitively explore what circumstances sustain or impede bright students at critical risk of deceleration. Without critical focus and financial and cultural support for academic programs, bright students are at risk of being mired in their impoverished environments without opportunity to excel.

Trapped by Physiology

Learning Disabilities

High intelligence masks disabilities, and disabilities depress intelligence and achievement scores. Gifted students with unrecognized and undiagnosed learning weaknesses and disabilities tend to appear more "average" in school and are less likely to be identified as needing accelerated programs. Perhaps ignored, misdiagnosed, and underserved learning disabilities are the most frequent subtle barriers to serving highly intelligent students. We hear comments such as, "William isn't gifted; you can't even read his handwriting." Some school districts continue to resist

Table 9.1

	% meeting or exceeding reading standards
All third-grade students	65.0
Not low income	77.9
Low income	46.2
Math, science, and writing score discrepancies are more dramatic.	

SOURCE: Illinois State Board of Education (2004).

accommodating learners' high intelligence with as much fervor as personnel are apt to focus on students' dyslexia, dysgraphia, or other learning difficulties. We are becoming more aware that many gifted students need learning disabilities remediation as well as accelerated curriculum. Fortunately, more school systems now accommodate the special needs of gifted children with learning disabilities and provide support for their dual—or multiple—diagnoses.

To accommodate twice or multiply exceptional gifted students, start at http://www.uniquelygifted.org. You will find helpful information on serving gifted children with learning difficulties in the following references:

- *Different Minds: Gifted Children With AD/HD, Asperger Syndrome, and Other Learning Deficits* (Lovecky, 2004)
- *Misdiagnosis and Dual Diagnosis of Gifted Children and Adults: ADHD, Bipolar, OCD, Asperger's, Depression, and Other Disorders* (Webb et al., 2005)
- *Uniquely Gifted: Identifying and Meeting the Needs of the Twice Exceptional Student* (Kay, 2000)
- *Upside-Down Brilliance: The Visual-Spatial Learner* (Silverman, 2002)

Allergies

Allergy-induced misbehaviors can thwart selecting young children for more vigorous academic experience. What about that squirming kid who can't sit still, who is continually fidgeting with his pencil or enthralled with what's going on out on the playground? Manny doesn't appear to thrive on his seatwork or find your lessons fascinating. You wonder how he could possibly be a candidate for acceleration—a trampoline, yes; intensified schoolwork, no. On the other hand, Karlie is so lethargic and withdrawn you wonder if she is sleep deprived. She's not really obstinate, but just sort of vacant; she doesn't want to be bothered by class participation.

Research performed by the National Talent Search Program of Johns Hopkins University found that children with high intelligence have a high incidence of allergies. Compared with a rate of about 10% in the general population, 55% of the children with precocious mathematical or verbal reasoning ability had allergies or other autoimmune disorders such as ulcerative colitis, celiac disease, and migraine headaches (Benbow & Benbow, 1986). If you observe a child who is lethargic, impossible, oppositional, and/or hyperactive, examine the possibility of allergies, especially if there is a family history of allergies. Sometimes eliminating one allergen, such as red dye from foods or perhaps petroleum solvents from their environments, can create a dramatic difference in attitude and behavior. Although allergy detection and management are cumbersome, unalleviated symptoms can be devastating.

Depression

Depression can mask a dire need to adjust a bright child's school experience. Over the years, I have heard many interpretations of early school experience resulting in statements such as, "School just zapped the life out of her." Mason attended a private preschool and kindergarten and then entered public school for first grade on schedule. Before he acquiesced to spending most of his day in school, he immersed himself in drawing maps: He taped yards of paper together to create his route for road tripping from his home in Vermont to the San Diego Zoo. He kept records of how many miles were traveled from one interesting site to the next. He drew maps of the cosmos showing constellations and planets. As autumn continued, Mason withdrew. He held his focus to his imagination, where he visited Niagara Falls and the Grand Canyon. By October's end, Mason told his mother that he wished he had never been born because at school, no one cares about what he thinks. "They don't even want to get to know me. I just have to sit and wait for the day to be over." In this way, insidious situational depression usurps the spark of our brightest youngsters who are waiting for others to catch up.

If parents or educators observe that any child may be depressed, professional support is needed. If the parents or teachers suspect the child is intellectually mired at school, a child's major source of demoralization may be an inappropriate learning environment. The observations should be discussed with the child's school counselor or therapist. Parents and educators also need to provide supplementary learning materials and experiences for the child, and keep a watchful eye to determine whether these experiences produce some improvement in the child's mood.

SOARING ALONE: AFFLICTION WITH "TOP-OF-THE-CLASS" SYNDROME

Jacob is academically outperforming his classmates; he's at the top of his class. He seems to be doing very well. But is he? We parents and teachers can take personal pride in a student who is "at the top of the class." Conscientious teachers may resist providing a more challenging curriculum for Jacob, explaining, "But then he won't be the best, and he wants to be the best." Well-meaning parents can enable this esteemed status for their child: "Madison always gets 100s on her math tests." Consistently rewarded for her excellent performance, Sydney may never learn to truly test herself. Instead, she feels separate and somewhat excluded from the other children. She may not realize that her peers have valid insights and ideas, making her less willing to cooperate with others. The top is a precarious position that may not offer the benefits we think it does.

Misplaced students may rarely experience their own strengths because they are stretched the least. They do not learn to "struggle" to succeed at their academic achievements. Too many bright children give up rather than endure exerting effort through a perplexing challenge.

An insidious risk of habitually being "the best in the class" is becoming conditioned to being right. That pinnacle position can lead Joshua to assume he knows better than his classmates. Maybe you know someone like Joshua who still cannot ask for directions or for help out of a difficult situation. That is too great a burden to bear and not an appealing trait.

Sydney's classmates and teachers may assume that she should succeed on her own and expect her to tutor other children. Teachers often say of bright children that "They just love to teach!" However, most children would much rather be learning something new. All of us who have spent years listening to the brighter children also know how much these students resent giving up their time going over and over what they already know. Although positioning children to tutor others can be a tempting convenience and give children the opportunity and satisfaction of serving others, a little of this redundancy is usually enough to affirm their confidence and benevolence. Emphasis on tutoring underscores the hierarchy developing in an exceptionally bright child's mind, placing him or her even more firmly at the top, increasing the isolation and hierarchical structure experienced by the top-of-the-class child. If parents and teachers continue to expect Sydney to outdo her peers, she may develop a need for supremacy and control that produces lifelong resistance to cooperating with those who could help her.

HOW GENDER EXPECTATIONS AFFECT ACCELERATED PLACEMENT

Who Is Gifted?

Astute children can be adept at accommodating expectations and blending into classroom customs. These habits may reveal expectations based on their gender. In counseling sessions or poignant informal conversations, some exceptionally bright adults recall how they felt invisible in school, and that this feeling extends to several facets of their adult lives. Highly intelligent men share how they were expected to be stoically emotionally resilient and often find their relationships inhibiting. Limiting gender impositions are damaging to all students. Because highly intelligent children have such vast consciousness, they tend to inherently exhibit traits usually associated with both genders. Gifted boys and girls are more psychologically and socially androgynous than most other children (Hébert, 2003). Androgynous qualities integrate both male and female characteristic emotional and behavioral traits.

In their interests and activities, gifted girls' personality characteristics are more like gifted boys than they are like average girls. Understandably, our astute girls generally prefer to play with gifted boys than with average girls. By adolescence, our adolescent girls usually seek novel experiences, avoid routine, and enjoy challenging experiences even more than boys (Janos & Robinson, 1985, p. 165). Introverted gifted boys may have an added struggle accommodating some societal expectations. Their generally more passive, demure manner can sometimes create awkward circumstances for them.

Girls

We still find vestiges of male dominance in U.S. society. Over the years, I did rough counts of the more than 600 gifted children I tested; about 60% of the students were boys. Linda Silverman, director of the Gifted Development Center, experiences approximately the same disproportion of referrals (Silverman, 2004). However, generally high intelligence is not more prevalent among boys.

Our gifted girls often find themselves in a dilemma between their own high aptitudes and their social milieu. Some of the barriers to self-fulfillment that they experience include lack of family support, debilitating stereotyping, self-doubt, self-criticism, lowered expectations, and attributing success to effort rather than ability (Reis, 2002). Although generally girls are scoring higher on standardized tests than our boys are, there is still room at the top for our brightest girls.

Classroom teachers need to be especially alert to how they are doling out their encouragement to girls. If girls get called on less often in class, they may become conditioned that they have less to offer. Meanwhile, boys are more apt to just call out answers and show what they know. Their brilliance becomes apparent. Rather than attributing their achievements to their abilities, girls tend to relate their academic success to good luck or hard work. We hear high grades glossed over with, "My teacher likes me." Then, when young girls do not succeed with their school challenges, we might hear, "I'm stupid." Alternately, girls may remain silent rather than risk ridicule for a wrong answer. Young girls tend to use their relationships to glean their self-esteem, asking, "Will he like me? Will I embarrass myself?" We need to give critical care to girls so that they can recognize their competence and confidence. Giving girls choices so that they experience some control over themselves and their lives has life-long benefits. The key is to specifically recognize a valuable quality the girl has taken the risk to display. "Jessica, you were really creative in how you arranged your science display. I hope you took a picture of it." With courage and confidence to show abilities, girls will increasingly become candidates for acceleration.

Boys

Our young brightest boys warrant specific focus. "Important developmental distinctions define boys' readiness for the tasks of elementary school and help explain their generally inferior performance compared with girls. First, boys mature more slowly than girls" (Kindlon & Thompson, 2000, p. 31). Here is succinct affirmation that our young, brightest boys need to be given meticulous consideration for early entrance and acceleration. Our exceptionally intelligent gifted boys tend to be more socially and emotionally advanced than most of their age mates, gleaning further astute insight into situations than do their age peers. Another reason given for boys' generally inferior performance compared with girls is that boys are more active and have less impulse control. We often experience the more exuberant passion and intensity of those who are extroverted. However, restricting our brightest boys cannot be a generalized conclusion. Rather than applying the traditional method of holding back the summer birthday boy from starting school, we need to appreciate his abilities, emotional sensitivity, and empathy.

The most "sensitive" personality type is correlated with the highest intelligence range (Myers, McCaulley, Quenk, & Hammer, 1998, p. 269), a situation that can result in social isolation. Psychologically androgynous qualities multiply the possibilities that a person can experience and can lead to a richer life. The more intelligent a boy is, the more likely he will be introverted and make decisions based upon his personal meaning, with the goal of maintaining harmonious relationships. These characteristics do not reflect our society's stereotype of the "all-American boy." Clearly, when rare personality types combine with extreme intelligence, the probability of finding resonant understanding and companionship among young peers is uncommon. Thus, one golden thread that draws through most of the literature about young gifted boys is their *social isolation*. We find that at a very young age, many of our brightest boys felt detached from their age mates. They soon sensed their classmates could not comprehend what they were thinking, needing, and feeling. Academically, they could soar; when adjustments were made so that these young boys could learn in the company of their intellectual peers, they essentially entered a safe haven to be themselves.

DISCERNING ACCELERATION FOR EXCEPTIONALLY INTELLIGENT CHILDREN

When we first get to know children who do not fit into our expectations, ability-congruent school placement can be an enigma. Although we recognize that students ought to become adaptable and resilient, their learning environment also should respond to their unique optimum learning needs.

Finding what is best for our children requires individual discernment. Although the previous segments described helpful research results and many practical suggestions, these statements may not apply to your Jordan. We need to remember that the "typical composite" child who appears to emerge from research data does not exist in our school. In this book, we are often focusing on children who are in some ways "statistically insignificant," and the modes we learned about optimum teaching methods may not apply.

Standardized Testing

We need to be cautious about how we interpret and impose expectations from test scores. If we are looking at intelligence scores, the gifted segment range alone spans more than 100 IQ points. The term *gifted* is a portal to look closely at children and investigate their idiosyncrasies. It is important not to broadly generalize expectations from test scores.

Intelligence quotient scores represent an average level of several abilities. Depending on the test administered, there could be about 10 different ability scores averaged together to derive the general intelligence quotient. Six-year-old Elizabeth was independently IQ tested, roughly representing a mental age of eight. However, there are numerous components of this score. Perhaps Elizabeth's visual-spatial and math abilities are about average and her memory and vocabulary are extraordinary. Elizabeth's eloquence and descriptive vocabulary are astounding and advertise what she knows. An IQ score can prompt inappropriate expectations because we tend to impose the generalization that a child with a high IQ "should know better," shouldn't makes careless mistakes, and should be motivated to show what she or he knows.

Underestimated Abilities

An intelligence quotient score can be an underestimation of a child's abilities. It is difficult to "fake" a right answer. Students can't pretend to know something they don't. However, there are numerous reasons why scores might not appropriately represent abilities. If the assessment was a group written test, undetected visual disabilities could interfere. True-false and multiple-choice test questions present enigmas for our brightest students. With their vast consciousness and divergent thinking abilities, they can think of instances when each choice could be true or false or when every multiple-choice option might apply.

When using individualized IQ tests administered by an examiner, several factors can invalidate the child's scores. The child's relationship with the examiner can jeopardize validity. For his own reasons, Ethan didn't like Dr. Randall! Sometimes the testing environment is distracting. I've heard of a copy room being used for an IQ testing room where disruptive people came in to copy during the testing session. Fire engines can be gathering outside a window. Another child might be missing a birthday party or his favorite television program. Other times, a child might be coming down with the flu, on the verge of a high fever.

Other motives might sabotage valid IQ or achievement test scores. Anthony worried that if he scored high on this test, more would be required of him. He did not want to let his parents down, nor have the added pressure. Alyssa was concerned that she could be placed in a higher grade or another school and didn't want to leave her friends. Ryan resented missing a skating party at that very moment. Children can rarely "pretend" to know something they do not know, but there are many circumstances that can depress test scores.

Test Ceilings

Another deception inherent in standardized testing is created by scores in the highest percentiles and scaled scores. To demonstrate their abilities, children who score in the upper 90th percentile need to be assessed with tests designed for higher age or grade levels. Standardized achievement test scores near the highest possible indicate that the test ceiling may be too low; there is not enough high-level challenge on the test for the student to show what she knows. Many standardized achievement tests show academic attainment results in percentile or stanine scores for the child's grade placement level. The parents' printout report shows that Grace is achieving at the 99th percentile in four subjects. She's a model student and we are all so proud of her! However, this report does not represent the results Grace would attain if the questions and problems represented higher grade levels. Unless she is given out-of-grade-level assessments, there are no indications that Grace can read three grade levels above her second-grade placement.

Intelligence quotient test scores can also be limited by test ceilings. When a child achieves subtest scale scores in the highest possible rank, it is likely that the questions were not difficult enough to ascertain the full extent of the child's abilities. Therefore, the IQ scores are probably an underestimation of that child's abilities.

Camouflaged Abilities

Introversion

Most people with high intelligence are introverts. Introverts have the highest mean intelligence scores (Myers et al., 1998, pp. 268–269). In assessing over 4,000 gifted children at the Gifted Development Center, it was found "over 60% of gifted children are introverted. . . . Over 75% of highly gifted children are introverted" (Silverman, 2003).

This has pervasive implications for identifying children needing acceleration. People with introverted preferences generally generate their life energy from being alone and are usually comfortable working independently. Unlike extroverts, who sometimes think by talking, introverted people do not have a great need to tell people what they think, know, and feel in their rich and full inner life. They often prefer peace and quiet and can resent being invaded when friendly extroverts use their receptive silence to fill with their own ideas, observations, and activities. Introverts can appear to be "off in their own world."

Thus, introverted children are often overlooked for participation in gifted or accelerated programs. While extroverted Kayla is eager to tell what she is thinking, introverted John is still ruminating about the possibility of embarrassing himself by having the wrong answer. If you don't know what an extrovert is thinking, you haven't been listening; if you don't know what an introvert is thinking, you haven't asked.

Debilitating Social Isolation

Mrs. Miller: "They know by second grade that they aren't like everyone else, so he [David] would do anything to be part of a group. He submerged himself to blend in; the real suicide of self-denial."

Phil Donahue: "What would have helped you most?"

David Miller (highly gifted student who attempted suicide in high school): "Less alienation. In your head you were an ugly duckling. . . . I didn't understand why other people didn't see things the way I did." (Donahue, 1981)

Although we generally consider girls to be more sensitive to social relationships, insightful gifted boys can adeptly submerge their outstanding abilities to merge into their groups. We find that at a very young age, many gifted boys, as well as girls, feel detached and psychologically obscured from their age mates. Some soon sense their classmates cannot comprehend what they are thinking, needing, and feeling. If our brightest children are not allowed to share their school experience with other children who enjoy learning at their levels, by the third grade they are probably getting teased for their great grades. Many smart girls and boys have frantic needs to be accepted by their classmates. Rather than allow themselves to be ridiculed and stand out as a nerd, they can turn inward, becoming depressed or exhibiting psychosomatic disorders such as headaches or stomach aches. Some perceive that what they are is not what is wanted.

There can be tremendous peer pressure to conform to low-achieving norms, especially among marginalized children who already stand out from their cohorts: minorities and other children who desperately want to fit in and be accepted by their peer group. If they show that they know more than what is being taught, they risk being further ostracized. Thus, they often remain silent and dare not show that "they are coming from somewhere else." Some of these children soon settle into their local standard social and academic paradigm. However, when adjustments are made for students to learn in the company of their intellectual peers, they essentially enter a safe haven to be themselves and began to rise academically.

Inner Drives

Although our highly intelligent students usually have voracious cravings to learn, you know they may not be enthused to perform assigned classroom tasks. While these subdued scholars are enticed by their own evident and unconscious motives, their rationale for tepid participation is often incomprehensible to frustrated parents and educators. We'll explore some obscure motives that might lure our brightest students to pursue their personal priorities.

Brianna has her own reasons to punish her parents. She thinks she can make them feel like bad parents if she makes poor grades. Besides, it seems like her mom and dad own her good grades; they seem to usurp her achievements and flaunt them. Alex wants his parents and educators to pay more attention to him and show that they care about him by helping and encouraging him more. Even punishing would prove that he is valued, so he contrives problems and inadequacy. Taylor doesn't get any perks from excelling in school; she has no idea why she needs to be doing this! Sydney wants her teacher to expect less of her and get off her back to do better. Brandon doesn't have a sense of how to manage his time and set priorities.

Various other motives impede academic investment.

- Containing restricted energy that needs release before she or he can focus on imposed tasks
- Gaining power and self-control through noncompliance
- Seeking peer acceptance by submerging into their group
- Being in physical pain
- Being worried about family members' health, alcoholism, drug abuse, marital strife, violence
- Resenting redundancy
- Seeing no value in practicing what she or he already knows
- Trying to protect his or her pride from failure
- Fearing success will impose higher expectations and pressure

Objections to Acceleration

A frequent objection to permitting a child early entrance to kindergarten, to be advanced a grade, or even to be allowed to learn a subject she or he has already mastered in his or her grade level is "But what about socialization? Jennie doesn't know how to make friends in her class. She just seems to be in her own world!" or "How will Zeke tolerate being the smallest kid in first grade when he didn't even have any friends in preschool? I don't want him to be a complete social outcast." However, educators, counselors, and psychologists have amassed convincing evidence that advanced learners' social comfort zone basically corresponds to their comparable mental age, not their chronological age (Colangelo et al., 2004). Actually, a good indication that a student would benefit from academic acceleration is if she or he is naturally drawn to older playmates. If you are considering early entrance or other type of academic acceleration for a young child, you might think how doing nothing, just allowing this child to drift with age mates, could ensnare his or her abilities. Allowing "underage" children to associate with classmates who understand and appreciate their academic abilities and emotional concerns seems more benevolent.

An objection to whole-grade acceleration is that exceptionally smart students aren't super-intelligent in all areas, or that their behavior is not universally advanced. Although sometimes only subject acceleration is more appropriate, instead of keeping a child back because she or he is not gifted in every area, with careful observation and assessment accelerated students can receive additional support and differentiated expectations in their various personal and academic domains.

In general, gifted students learn faster, absorb more, and understand—or at least perceive—greater depth in issues they encounter. A good educational program must respond to these differences and provide a faster pace and greater depth and complexity. Miraca Gross has pioneered research on radical acceleration, which is advancing more than one grade at a time. She has widely documented the enormous social and emotional advantages—even cures!—that come from placing exceptionally gifted children with their intellectual peers.

10

Adaptations to Personality

THE BRAIN THAT DRIVES THEM

Many highly intelligent children are permeated with a unique intensity. This intensity amplifies nearly everything they think, feel, experience, and create. Sometimes we wonder how a seemingly minute detail can matter so much to them. We may think they overreact, but some are adamant about the profound significance of their concern. We include this section so you will be more familiar with behaviors of children who need to be accelerated and will not interpret some of these typical behaviors as immaturity. Intensity lends crucial energy and significance to their intelligence, creativity, and wisdom. Our exceptionally bright children's passion manifests itself in overexcitabilities and through their personality type. Because acceleration imposes learning about "gifted education" on a regular classroom teacher, we include this section that likely would be part of a gifted education teacher's training.

WORKING WITH OVEREXCITABILITIES

Overexcitabilities, abbreviated as OEs, were defined by Polish psychologist/psychiatrist Kazimierz Dabrowski, who studied the lives of highly self-actualized people to learn more about their development. An overexcitability is like a selective lens that intensifies life experiences. Although such behaviors may seem quirky and "too much," these manifestations of inner intensity contribute a framework children will use to develop their talents. We will briefly explore each one.

Psychomotor

Gifted children tend to exhibit relatively higher energy. Parents frequently report that their exceptionally bright young children tend to need less sleep than their age mates. Sometimes special activities for gifted preschool children are scheduled during the other children's nap time. When you hear rapid speech, especially accompanied by animated hand gestures, you have a good clue how psychomotor overexcitability affects children. Parents of bright children who usually display high physical activity tend to report that if their children experience a mentally engaging day at school, the children are much calmer than when they are required to do redundant tasks and endure waiting while other classmates listen to the third version of the week's lesson. Nervous habits such as finger tapping, tics, compulsive talking, and acting out are other manifestations of psychomotor OE.

These young children can release their surplus of unspent physical energy in untimely, inappropriate ways. Their actions can give you the impression that the child is immature or out of control because his or her self-expression is so animated and physical, sort of "antsy." Psychomotor OE can deter identifying children who are intellectually appropriate for participation in special programs they need; the calmer bright children are more likely to be selected for gifted programs.

Although sitting still is a goal for children's early school years, allowing bright children with psychomotor OEs to move about, as long as other students are not disrupted, can facilitate their learning. These children are usually not deliberately trying to irritate us; they are wired for moving. Our wish to subdue their lively expression is futile. Rather than trying to squelch their energy release, we can negotiate with them ways to release their energy that are congruent with the classroom situation. They can stand up while reading, or perhaps quietly play with a silent object. These children tend to be kinesthetic learners, so let them *do* the subject. Other lessons can be embossed in body memory, as in, "Pose in the form of California!"

Some parents and educators are extra protective of these gifted children's time. Some "hothouse" their exceptionally bright child and prefer that she or he invests in enriching, intellectual activities rather than "wasting time" on a playing field. On the contrary, it is essential that children who innately need to be on the move have appropriate action opportunities. However, it would be helpful if physical activities were more cooperative than competitive. Otherwise, our young, bright accelerated children may feel physically inadequate and avoid playground games that demonstrate their relatively inferior physical development. This can be particularly devastating for gifted children with psychomotor overexcitability; every cell in their bodies wants to participate. Their bright minds imagine a high standard of performance, but their fragile pride may restrict their participation. For this reason, individual sports appeal to children who are younger and smaller than their companions. Many gifted children find that martial arts classes such as karate or Tae Kwon Do offer an appealing merger of mental concentration, body control, and energy release.

Emotional

Emotional overexcitability is common in gifted children. Many highly intelligent children live an expanded emotional life. Writings by Annemarie Roeper are replete with this theme. A common poignant plea from parents of gifted children is, "I just wish my child weren't so sensitive." Their intense feelings manifest themselves in extreme, complex, positive, and negative ways. Many of these children seem to have extra emotional antennae and are impacted by emotions; everything gets inside of them.

Bright children's emotional intensity permeates their lives. From people who are surrounded by young, exceptionally intelligent children, we hear estimates such as, "Her emotional life is 10 times richer and deeper than most children's," or "It's like he wears his heart on his sleeve," or "Josie seems to carry the weight of the world on her shoulders." A memorable example of how many competent children are extremely emotionally aware comes from a story of first grader Garrett, who cried at school. Garrett is extra aware of emotional meanings and is especially emotionally permeable. Not much just "rolls off his back." Garrett's family sought professional help, and their behaviorist psychologist prescribed that Garrett be punished by various restrictions whenever he cried at school. This was not helpful. When a compassionate teacher asked Garrett what it was like for him to be in the classroom, he began by explaining, "Well, you see, other kids just have one feeling. I have lots of feelings. I have millions of feelings and I have them all at once! I feel so embarrassed when Leah calls Riley 'fat girl,' and when Jordan's fish died I was so sad that I cried." Clearly what would have worked better for Garrett is an invitation to talk about his perfectly legitimate, if strong, emotional reactions with an empathetic listener. The key is to listen to these children and to accept that an extreme emotional response may be an indicator of intense awareness rather than "immaturity."

Children like Garrett can simultaneously experience an entire range of contradictory emotions. They may be riveted in an approach-avoidance dilemma. Sometimes they feel so many complex emotions that they are almost paralyzed to act for fear that they might act wrongly or get a negative reaction from someone. They may be bearing emotional loads that accumulate from fears, concern about death, anxieties, love, loneliness, deep caring for others, and excruciating self-scrutiny.

Emotional overexcitability can manifest in somatic expressions. Young children seldom find the words they need to describe what they are feeling because they have not yet learned how their deep feelings represent responses to what they are experiencing. Their little bodies can take over and beg for comfort for headaches, stomach aches, and rashes.

Being especially emotionally sensitive can be particularly devastating for boys. At an early age, they may wonder about their supposed masculinity. Boys, as well as girls, need to be reminded that their being so sensitive is a precious, rare quality that may not always be appreciated by others.

Intellectual

Intellectual overexcitability is another hallmark of many gifted children. They are driven to discover and have a voracious appetite for intellectual effort and stimulation. You hear, "Why?" until you beg Haley to stop. In class, they may drift into speculations, wondering how many words they can make from the letters in *chocolate*. These bright children need to nourish their intellectual void. Many of our acceleration candidates already know much of what they are being taught in the classroom. To give herself the intellectual calories she needs, Haley may construct complex mental projects, such as building a space station for her American Girl doll.

Students who need acceleration have minds that urge them to restlessly probe the unknown. Their brain activity is intense and quick. Brooke asks questions in class that seem to be way off topic; however, she has made connections far beyond the material that has been presented. Intellectual OEs cannot stop wondering, and they can be relentless in seeking answers. Elijah *has* to know how dust balls are created, and then he needs to create an experiment to prove that he knows. Melissa thrives on thinking up new and different ways to do things. Their divergent thinking abilities usually make true/false questions an enigma for them; they can think of instances when each choice could be true or false, or when every multiple-choice option could apply. Just as someone with a hyperactive thyroid has more energy than other people without trying, these intellectually alert children are not trying to be so absorbed in their intellectual pursuits; their consciousness is prolific with questions and facts.

These insatiable children need to have their genuine inquisitive nature honored by taking their questions seriously and helping them find sources for their answers. Finding a mentor can relieve parents and teachers and engage children in work or play that supports their passions. By encouraging activity in an interesting field, mentoring relationships can develop great confidence in young children. Having a mentor often determines life success more than does intelligence or creativity. It might be a fertile pursuit to inquire in your local high school about connecting with an appropriate high school student, or National Honor Society member, who could work with a young child on a shared project of interest. For example, if the child is obsessed with bugs, you might contact the high school science department and inquire whether a student would like to do some afterschool activities with your budding entomologist.

Imaginational

Imaginational overexcitability is congruent with how most gifted people think; it extends into the intuitive realm and plays with possibilities. Kim and Annie gravitate to each other at every opportunity. They create their own universe and walk in. "Let's play office! Let's play millionaires!" No props, no problem; they're all in their imaginations! These kids are often avid readers and content with long periods of solitary wondering and thinking. In class, they may go off into their own fascinating quandaries.

Appreciating imaginational tendencies can help draw out a child's ideas that initially may seem too "farfetched" for the child to share. Logan looks at the stars and wonders what kind of animals and humanoids are living a more peaceful life than he hears on the news. Young, bright children with keen imaginations can assume that parents and educators share—or are at least aware of—their imaginary experience. By creating an environment that is safe for elaborate wonderings, teachers allow imagination to become a creative source rather than a cause of uncertainty and fear.

Young gifted children particularly develop imaginary companions (Webb, Meckstroth, & Tolan, 1982). These pretend friends offer solace and company, especially to exceptionally bright children who may not have anyone in their accessible vicinity who can keep up with what they think or join in their elaborate visions. By "practicing" activities with their fantasy friends, young children can create courage to venture into more actual social situations.

Sensual

Sensual overexcitability gives people heightened response and satisfaction from experiencing taste, smell, touch, sight, and sound. Usually these sensual experiences are a great source of pleasure. Rachel will gravitate to a velveteen cushion and covertly stroke it. A small piece of her "blanky" is still available in her pocket. For many, smells are more pungent, tastes are more intense, and sounds resonate with their souls. Some children hold vivid memories of sensory experiences. Children with sensual OEs become enveloped in sensual experiences. The morning sun on the trees that waltz in the wind creates playful shadows that dance around the school yard. This sight sends shivers through Jennifer. She absorbs the view in every cell. You find Blake immersed in sucking on an orange segment; he's still holding it in his mouth after five minutes. He detects taste more than most and enjoys it immensely.

Another aspect of sensual OE is a negative experience of sensory input—even a seemingly benign environment may feel offensive, grating, repulsive. Julia refuses to taste anything she thinks has onions in it. Morgan will not go near the goat exhibit at the county fair; the stench makes him gag. Tony needs to wear a white noise headset during some parts of a movie, definitely during the previews, because the sound is too invasive. Some of these children cannot endure the barraging din of cafeteria noise.

Many gifted children have low sensory thresholds; thus, they are conscious of more sensation than most others experience. We can help them learn to manage their experiences. When I mention to parent groups that many kids insist on having the tags cut from the neck of shirts and wear their socks inside out because seams are too distracting, there are lots of laughs and groans of recognition. These children's extreme responses are usually genuine, not attempts to manipulate us.

We can, however, let children know how their exaggerated reactions affect us. We can work with them to come up with a repertoire of responses they can use to self-soothe, depending on the situation. Engage children in brainstorming different ways they can manage circumstances, including various ways they can respond to annoying or pleasurable, but overstimulating, input. Unless the situation is severe, rather than rescuing our hypersensual children from difficult conditions, we can teach them to creatively manage themselves.

UNDERSTANDING PERSONALITY TYPES

In an educational age of differentiation and honoring diversity, a key factor to enhancing children's learning is respecting and accessing their personality types. Especially during the initial transition period, a child adjusting to a different learning environment will accommodate the change better if the experience is compatible with his or her innate personality and learning style. *Entelechy* means becoming what you are, actualizing your vital force—just as an acorn becomes an oak tree. Similarly, personality type is a significant and largely innate aspect of how we relate to people, facts, situations, and perceptions. Personality type influences everything from motivation to social preferences and learning styles. We need to remember that "type" refers to preference, not ability.

Understanding others' and your own type can help you appreciate and cooperate with your students' different needs and inclinations. You may remember years when dominantly left-handed children were required to write with their right hand. It can be similarly awkward for children to take in information and produce evidence of their learning if their inferior personality functions are required for the processes. Allowing children to learn and demonstrate what they know in congruence with their learning style preferences sparks their enthusiasm and enables their cooperation.

Here are succinct descriptions of personality type components as well as some suggestions to help you create learning experiences congruent for each type. Although various learning style and personality type definitions have developed over the past few decades, here we base our classifications on the standard Myers-Briggs types (Myers et al., 1998). Your sensitive attention and observation will reveal much about your children's learning style preferences. Accommodating learning styles eases accelerated children into their new classroom experiences.

EXTROVERSION-INTROVERSION

The Extrovert-Introvert (E-I) scale describes to what extent individuals prefer to focus on their outer or inner worlds.

Extroverts (E) focus on the outer world of activities, people, and spoken words; they are energized by being in on the action.

- They think by talking; what they start out saying may not be their final idea.
- They communicate more by talking than writing.
- They enjoy group projects; they function best in the context of relationships.
- They experience an activity to understand it; they like trial-and-error learning.

- They act impulsively, then reflect.
- They show and tell others what they are doing.
- They tune in to their environment; they are acutely aware of other people and activities.
- They seek action and activity.

Introverts (I) focus on the inner world of ideas, dreams, and feelings; they essentially recharge their energy by being alone.

- They try to understand an activity before experiencing it.
- They process ideas by thinking; they think reflectively before answering or acting.
- They have an intense need for privacy; they resent interruptions.
- They crave time alone.
- They feel lonely when around others; they want only one or two close friends.
- They mask their feelings; they often hide what is most important.
- They stay with one project for a long time.
- They dislike background noise.

Introverts are not aberrations of extroverts!

SENSING-INTUITIVE

The Sensing-Intuitive (S-N) scale describes how people prefer to use their physical senses or their intuition and imagination to determine what is going on in their world. These differences create the greatest chasm between people's realities.

People with a *Sensing* (S) preference predominately use their eyes, ears, and other senses to discern what is happening inside and outside them.

- They try to understand how information will be used.
- They want examples of abstract ideas.
- They enjoy learning in a linear, one-step-at-a-time fashion.
- They tend to be realistic and practical.
- They tend to be acutely aware of their surroundings.
- They like things to be definite and measurable.
- They take care with facts.
- They want to do things in the way they first learned them.
- They live in the present and focus on the reality of a situation.

People with an *Intuitive* (N) preference draw on information from their five senses and rely on imagination and inspiration to show them meanings, relationships, and possibilities.

- They focus on concepts; they like to understand the big picture first.
- They tend to jump in anywhere and leap over steps in a nonlinear fashion.
- They ignore directions once they get a feeling about what is to be done.
- They pass quickly over details, then forget them or make factual errors.
- They work off hunches and flashes of insight.

- They go "off the subject, off on a tangent," although to them, it's all relevant.
- They enjoy learning new skills and looking for new ways of doing things.
- They enjoy imagining "What if?"

THINKING-FEELING

The *Thinking-Feeling* (T-F) scale describes to what extent individuals prefer to make decisions based on considering the facts versus personal meaning.

Those with *Thinking* (T) preferences attempt to decide objectively on the foundation of facts, basing their choices on the distinct logical consequences of each action.

- They make decisions by analyzing and weighing the evidence, including all facts, pleasant or unpleasant.
- They seek an objective standard of truth; they desire fairness and justice.
- They excel at analyzing what is wrong with something.
- They find it difficult to say, "I'm sorry" because they know they are right; those are just the facts!
- They tend to be most convinced by logic.
- They express themselves directly, with honesty and clarity.
- They hold themselves and others to consistent standards.

Feeling (F) preference people usually make choices based on personal values and meaning, not necessarily feelings or emotions.

- They make decisions not wholly based on logic or fact, but on the need to protect a relationship.
- They tend to be most convinced by how they feel.
- They have permeable boundaries and usually take situations personally; "It was my fault."
- They express themselves with warmth, acknowledging other people's feelings.
- They place a high value on relationships.
- They sacrifice their own needs to preserve harmony in a group.
- They want to be recognized for their personal qualities and cooperative skills.
- They make exceptions to rules to accommodate other people's dignity and feelings.
- They tend to be driven by wanting to be liked and to take care of other people's emotions.

JUDGING-PERCEIVING

The *Judging-Perceiving* (J-P) scale describes to what extent individuals prefer to organize their life based on plans versus the desire for experience.

Individuals with a *Judging* (J) preference tend to live in a planned, orderly way, wanting to regulate life and control it.

- They want to know what to expect; they want things settled and routine.
- They like precise assignments and rules; they are decisive and seek closure.

- They create boundaries and structures for their projects.
- They need exact directions so they can feel assured about doing the right thing.
- They tend to work with a deadline.
- They complete one project before going on to another.
- They limit their involvement to what they think they can get done.

Individuals with a *Perceiving* (P) preference intend to understand and experience life rather than control it; they trust their ability to adapt to the moment.

- They prefer working on flexible ideas without a plan.
- They wait and see what develops before making final decisions.
- They tend to change course and adapt ideas on a whim.
- They enjoy and create novelty and change.
- They tend to involve themselves in too many projects.
- They seek open-ended assignments; they like to play with possibilities.
- They procrastinate in case something more interesting comes up along the way.
- They periodically hand in late assignments.

USING TYPE PREFERENCES FOR CHILDREN NEEDING ACCELERATION

One of the most critical values for understanding personality type is acknowledging your own type preference. Although most of us like our own type best, no trait is superior to another. Being aware of our own type preference bias helps broaden our appreciation of personality differences.

Teachers tend to teach in ways consistent with their own personality type (Meisgeier & Murphy, 1987). As teachers and parents, we need to understand, balance, and function in all modes. It is an obscure discernment to recognize our own prejudices against qualities that do not reflect us. We have to be careful to not inflict our own type preference bias on children and adults who are not like us: "Roger is a loudmouth. Carl has his head in the clouds. Helen is too sensitive. Ruth can't get her act together."

Again, it is also essential to keep in mind that these personality descriptions are preferences, not abilities. Andrea, an introverted accountant who enjoys sitting alone most of the day and meticulously focuses on numbers, can also tell fascinating extemporaneous stories. She is certainly capable of being the life of the party; however, Andrea prefers to return to her quiet space in order to rest and recharge. Here we are concerned with natural preference or "comfort zone." Each of these predominant qualities varies by degree and situation; there is no constant standard for how a person exhibits his or her personality traits.

Meta-analysis of 52 research analyses correlates personality type preferences and high IQ or academic achievement scores, such as the SAT. "When statistically significant, the correlations were in favor of Introversion, Intuition, Perceiving, and sometimes, Thinking" (Myers et al., 1998, p. 268).

Looking at each learning style preference, here are a few ideas to help you use type preferences to facilitate accelerated children's accommodating to advanced environments.

Introverts:

Provide them with a quiet place.

Allow them to work alone and with a partner, rather than in a larger group.

Give them more thought processing time before expecting them to start speaking.

Extroverts:

Arrange for them to work in small groups.

Allow trial and error learning.

Let students talk through their learning process with a partner.

Sensing:

Use concrete, real-life examples.

Provide hands-on materials for the child to experience.

Use audiovisual aids.

Intuitive:

Present the global, large setting conditions before the detailed facts.

Offer open-ended problem situations to be creatively solved.

Explore alternative solutions.

Thinking:

Clarify necessary criteria for accepted behaviors and grade scale.

Offer real-life problems to solve.

Highlight cause and effect.

Feeling:

Give the students personal attention—a tap on the shoulder as you pass.

Ask how they feel about a project, what is important.

Write appreciative notes on graded papers.

Judging:

Clarify classroom schedule and anticipated changes with lead time.

Write out assignment expectations and grading criteria.

Provide opportunity for students to organize a project with your approval.

Perceiving:

Give students choices for projects and assignments.

Suggest a timeline for projects, starting with a due date and going backwards.

Give free release time as a reward.

APPLYING TYPE PREFERENCE PRINCIPLES

There are several ways we can enable accelerated students to transition into new challenges. We can offer options that allow for opposite type preferences, asking,

"Would you rather work with a group or do an independent project? What do you think or feel about your project? Would you like to start now, or at the latest possible time you could still do a great job? Do you prefer to have a quiet place to work on your project, or are you comfortable at the table in the back of the room?" We can remember to give Introverts the processing time they need. Wait at least three seconds—10 is better—after asking a question before answering it yourself or going on to other students. We can give Feelers individual recognition that we care about them. This could be a smile and a focused, "I'm glad you're here," when they enter the classroom.

When you meet your transitioning students half way, you will be facilitating their progress and comfort in their accelerated program. There are several excellent guides to supporting children relative to their personality type.

- *People Types and Tiger Stripes* (Lawrence, 1993)
- *The Developing Child: Using Jungian Type to Understand Children* (Murphy, 1992)
- *Effective Teaching, Effective Learning: Making the Personality Connection in Your Classroom* (Fairhurst, 1995)

For younger children, The Murphy-Meisgeier Type Indicator for Children can be used to identify children's type preferences. The Myers-Briggs Type Indicator is a widely used and well-researched tool to identify and understand personality types. A person needs to be certified to administer, score, and interpret these instruments.

11

Facilitating Acceleration

ADAPTING TO A CHILD'S NATURE

As parents and educators, we must understand the nature of children in order to develop their innate strengths and help them compensate for their weaker qualities. Gifted children can be exhausting, demanding, perplexing enigmas. They veer from normal in many, sometimes subtle, ways. Few counselors and school personnel have had specific training to meet gifted children's particular needs. However, by understanding some characteristic qualities of young bright children's personalities and inner drives, we can gear their learning experiences to access their enthusiasm.

PERIOD OF ADJUSTMENT

Bright children often embark on a collision course upon starting school. Some children who are candidates for acceleration are wired with qualities that, as well as contributing to their inner drive to learn, can exacerbate debilitating stresses for them and the people who care about them. Because of these differences, their initial change into an accelerated program can be rocky. These children will probably experience more stress than other children as they tentatively face new challenges and unknown circumstances. In adjusting to a new environment and new expectations, an accelerated child can take one step forward, then two steps back during the first few weeks. This section offers some suggestions that can be especially valuable to use with young children who are adjusting to the transition into an accelerated program.

Enter Hilary. An excellent way to embrace her world is to tell her that you want to get to know her better, and ask her to please select about a dozen photographs to show you. The key factor is that Hilary selects the photographs so that she can portray herself to you on her terms. It is helpful to inform her family of your request via a note home. When the photos arrive, if you show enthusiastic interest in getting to know her, she may let go of feeling that she has been placed in a precarious position. When you provide a few moments of separate space for an intimate session, children will lead you into their inner worlds. They will feel more in control of the situation if you add interest and enthusiasm to what they present. We tend to trust people who are interested in us and want to listen to us. This overture will help transitioning children feel safe in their unfamiliar placement.

Another means to convey courage and care for your young, apprehensive transferring students is to arrange a short interview with them. You can invite their participation by telling them, "I want to get to know you better and find out what you are interested in and like to do." You may wish to use the following opening questions:

- What are some activities that you most enjoy doing?
- What are some things about you that other people like a lot?
- How would you spend a weekend if you could do anything you wanted to do?
- What are some things you would like me to know about you?
- What would you like other people to know to get along better with you?
- How do you hope that your time in my class (in your AP reading group, etc.) is different from your other classroom experiences?

At the end of your interview, thank the child for his or her time.

MANAGING PERFECTIONISM

Perfectionism can acutely affect gifted children. Many tend to be frustrated and disappointed unless the results of a project match their imagined expectations. However, what looks like perfectionism could actually be a manifestation of this child's voracious drive to create and understand. Still, if a child is unhappy, anxious, or seems to be developing a negative, over demanding sense of self, it is useful to look further into the stresses that perfectionism can create.

We need to acknowledge that there is a continuum of perfectionist qualities. Positive perfectionism involves receiving real satisfaction, pleasure, and empowerment from conscientiously investing effort in worthwhile tasks and discerning when a project permits or requires meticulous effort, concern, and time. Perfectionist ideals can be encouraging and inspire children to persevere—vivid expectations cause them to strive for a worthwhile goal. Emma is determined to learn to jump rope and willing to listen to helpful coaching. She tries to run into the whirling rope over and over, disentangling herself again and again. She has been nurtured to expect that achievement comes with practice and effort. However, anxious detrimental perfectionism is based on shame, guilt, or fear of not doing well enough; it strips a person's satisfying gratification. This section addresses potentially wounding and constricting perfectionism.

Gifted children are especially vulnerable to feeling valued for what they can produce, for being smart and right. Sometimes they may think they have to be perfect to be acceptable. Initially, youngsters who have been selected to move beyond their age peers could have in mind that they need to perform perfectly to justify this change. This may begin with a sense that they must make their parents proud. They may subconsciously think, "The better I perform, the more I am loved."

There are various views on perfectionism.

1. Innate and high achievement standards are driven from within a person.

2. Parenting pressures can produce distressing perfectionism.

3. Debilitating perfectionism could arise from persuasive media messages to be perfect.

4. Peers and teachers pressure to be the best.

Regardless of its source, the quest for perfection can sometimes paralyze gifted children. Young children might expect that they "should" be able to produce what they conceive internally. When children are compulsively seeking perfection, their resources, experience, and fine motor control are often not able to accommodate the intricacies of their mental model. Sometimes their lack of experience coaxes them to stay smug and safe in their familiar ways. Because he knows he has not mastered skipping, Thomas's mandate that he should do things exactly right won't even let him try to learn to enjoy skipping around the room. Evelyn saw a hummingbird in her hollyhocks almost every day last summer, and now she wants to draw that fascinating little bird. Evelyn's internal image of what she wants to draw is far too intricate for her hand-eye coordination development. Though she vividly imagines how this beautiful bird appears, her rendition shows little resemblance. Failure looms in every attempt. She is devastated, continuing to trash several more trials, before slumping into her dejected self.

Because our brightest students have been conditioned to learn more easily than their age mates, they can expect most activities to be relatively effortless. As an adult, Jacqueline reflected, "I never had to study to get A's until I took AP classes near the end of high school. I'm a perfectionist now because I never failed at anything when I was young and expectations to do things perfectly just followed me." Remembering his experiences in school, Chase realized, "I gained my identity and reputation for being the best. I was the really smart guy who never got a B." Integrating young high-achieving students in an accelerated program could require them to exert themselves, and they may resist this at first. However, the benefits of appropriate academic challenges are lifelong.

Ways to Soothe Wounding Perfectionism

Read biographies of accomplished people. Delving into the details of famous people's lives reveals how many trials and disappointments they endured and how persistence contributed to their success. How many filaments did Edison try before he was able to create an electric light bulb? Kettering ordered 2,000 batteries when he set out to develop the self-starter because he knew there would be many trials.

Help children distinguish between their feelings of self-worth and their performance. Self-worth is always present, but performance varies over time. Encourage by statements such as, "It must feel good to know that you tried something new," or "It took a lot of courage to experiment with this design without knowing how your airplane would turn out."

Expect progress, not perfection. Ask, "What did you learn while you were doing this? How might you do it differently next time?"

Acknowledge the value of completion. Done is better than perfect! Remind the child of all the computers and cars that are redesigned every year in order to improve on the model.

Discover meaning and priorities. Help the child discover what is truly important and satisfying to him or her. Ask, "What parts are you proud of? What part would you do again? How did you decide that? What was it about the Washington Monument that intrigued you enough to build a scale model?"

Reward trying. "Do your best" can be damaging. If we say, "It's OK how it turned out as long as you did your best," we imply that this project represents the child's best effort. Encourage children to try a skill without committing to high performance. Sometimes, its worth is in the learning experience. Bright children especially need to accept the value of practice and persistence; risking an attempt is about motivating themselves and persisting in the face of frustrations. And not everything is worth doing our best!

Find enjoyment. Regardless of the results, remind the child that seeking joy is crucial to developing any talent. Ask, "What part of your project did you enjoy most?"

Applaud persistence. "I bet you learned a lot from working on this." Successful people keep on working at something even when their efforts are not immediately rewarding—heroes keep working on their project even though it is hard to do.

Help children set realistic goals. Sense of failure comes from inappropriate goal setting. Honor and admire that James wants to make a model of the Eiffel Tower from toothpicks, but mention to the four-year-old that this might be a task that he would need to practice to perform well, and suggest making the model out of popsicle sticks.

Break tasks down into small, attainable successes. Help a child reduce his or her immediate expectations. "Inch by inch, it's a cinch. Yard by yard, it's hard." Learn to play two measures a day. How do you eat an elephant? One bite at a time!

Model self-acceptance. What we do imprints our children the same way they learn to speak our language. If you live in a house where English is spoken, you will learn to speak English. *Be aware of how you react to your own mistakes.* As you move from one activity to another, you can speak your processing aloud. Let the children hear you mentally making corrections as you think through a project step-by-step. "I was wondering how we could have fun while learning about why we celebrate Thanksgiving. First, I planned to make a mural. Then I realized that we did not have enough space to display it. Next, I thought about individual reports, but that would take too much time to give everyone a turn to report. Thanksgiving would be over by then!"

DEVELOPING SELF-EFFICACY

Alexis's parents are perplexed, embarrassed, and feel inadequate. Her teachers are frustrated that Alexis won't participate in class activities. Alexis seems so apathetic, which confuses everyone. Before she was identified to participate in an advanced grade, Alexis was intellectually starved. What's going on? It is likely that even in this accelerated environment, she lacks opportunities to develop self-efficacy. Without confidence in her new surroundings, without the sense that she has some control over her learning experience, Alexis resists participating, regardless of her classroom placement.

Even when we set our bright young students on an appropriate, faster track, they must have two crucial qualities to participate in these programs: confidence and an ability to make choices that affect their lives. Confidence and a sense of control are essential for self-efficacy. Without confidence, students *won't* assert themselves; without some perceived control over their situation, they *can't* assert themselves. In his groundbreaking book *Emotional Intelligence*, Daniel Goleman (1995) reports that about 20% of success in life is determined by IQ, but the other 80% is determined by an individual's level of emotional intelligence, a key component of self-efficacy.

Confidence

Achievement is greatly determined by confidence. What you tell yourself about a situation and your attitude are essential components of confidence. "I can" is often more important than IQ. With this insight in mind, it is important to realize that placing children on an accelerated learning path can significantly decrease their confidence level. In their previous class, they knew all the answers to the questions that were asked (and many of the answers to those that weren't), but in an accelerated program their confidence may sink when they realize that they must put forth effort to understand new ideas.

Caring adults sometimes innocently inflict "You should know better" on children we seek to inspire. Would you be motivated to greater achievements if your partner or coworker observed, "You *should know better*"? Or even worse, "The flower border you planted looks pretty good, but you could *do better*." This judgment suggests that we are evaluating people based on some prearranged expectation that puts them on a higher level than they experience. Critical judging conveys that they are failing this test.

Unlike these kinds of shaming statements, two of the most essential confidence builders are encouragement and empathy. Both must be used together; encouragement sounds empty when we don't empathize with the concerns students have, while empathy without encouragement allows students to sit in a problem and not find a way out. When our children are overly cautious to try new activities, we can suggest, "Remember when you didn't know the difference between left and right? Soon you will be glad you have learned how to do this too!" In this way, we remind them of a time when they did not know how to do something (empathy), and then remind them of how they mastered that task (encouragement).

When students feel that their teachers have high empathy for them there are some significant effects: academic achievement, positive self-concept, attendance, and positive peer relationships in the classroom are all improved. These children also commit less vandalism and have fewer discipline problems. Further, there is a significant relationship between perceived teacher empathy and the student's value of that teacher's competence, which, in turn, affects a child's willingness to put forth effort. Empathy is a key to many psychological principles to effectively modify behaviors.

One of the most potent ways to convey empathy is to become an effective listener. First grader Anna wailed that she had lost her favorite bear pencil. Wanting to soothe Anna, her teacher gently told her, "Just go play with something else and your bear pencil will show up when you least expect it." Anna retorted, "Then I least expect it right now!" With an astute child, platitudes don't work. Empathy does. Empathy is not just a nice idea; it is a real force. These bright kids need some compensatory emotional support, a real connection with us, to encourage their full participation in the classroom.

Here is a brief menu of techniques to help develop empathetic listening skills.

- If you cannot take time to listen at the exact moment a child wants to tell you something, make an appointment. A few intimate minutes a day is usually more meaningful than longer, less frequent periods to convey that you think what the child feels is important.
- When you are ready to listen, pay attention with your entire body and mind as if nothing else at that moment matters as much as this child's thoughts and feelings. Listen with the intention of discovering the insightful gift the child is giving you.
- As you listen, keep eye contact as much as possible, and try to have your eyes at the same level as the child's.
- Listen to understand what a situation means to the child, rather than to explain what it means to you.
- Take the child seriously. Respond with mirroring behaviors and statements: slight head nods, "Mmmm . . . Uh huh . . . I see." Reflect essential bits of the

child's thoughts and feelings. Be careful to use the child's words rather than interpret them.

- Ask for clarification and amplification. "I'd like to know how you felt about that. What are some of the things you are feeling now?"
- Remember that when you accept and understand a feeling, you don't have to agree with it. "I can really tell that you are so angry you feel like hitting Tommy," does not mean that you agree with the urge toward violence. Feeling something does not necessarily lead to doing something. Recognizing this is part of a process of making constructive decisions about behaviors (which is covered in the next section).
- Respond to the child's feelings with affirmation and identification. "I'm in a bad mood," can be affirmed with, "It doesn't feel good to be in a bad mood." A "bad mood" might mean the child is feeling "inadequate" or "embarrassed" because she or he cannot fit everything into a schedule. If you can help a child identify his or her feelings, then the child can take the next step.
- Ask what the child perceives to be the source of the problem, then probe with, "What else could be going on that troubles you?" Brainstorm alternatives to try.
- Strive to give life to a child's ideas. In any situation, be aware of your positive to negative response ratio and the ways you have the power to give life or death to a child's thoughts.
- Finally, a simple gesture such as a smile or greeting a child by name can speak volumes of encouragement and personal interest. As a habit, invest a few seconds in recognizing and appreciating each child as he or she leaves or arrives in your home or classroom.

Control

Our students are rarely motivated by gold stars and smiley faces if they resent that their self-determination was usurped. Our brightest children tend to have a strong internal sense of control. It is not that they are driven to control other people, but they are apt to operate from their own central station. Brandon found it a great adventure to maneuver himself onto the roof of his house. He had received enough threats and scolding not to play on the roof, which was just what he needed to know. The next time his father caught him walking on the roof, Dad chewed him out. "Didn't we tell you not to play on the roof?" Brandon came back with, "I wasn't playing on the roof, I was seriously on the roof!"

Highly intelligent children of all ages exhibit the need for free choice. Qualities such as a determined sense of autonomy, independence, self-sufficiency, self-direction, and nonconformity are in that mix. To generate perceived control and internal motivation, offer the child choices within limited options. Our brightest students are driven by how they experience control over their educational choices. Intrinsic motivation is a key to their enthusiastic participation (Clark, 2002b, pp. 413–414).

Gifted students' axis of control turns them toward projects and tasks that have meaning. You find that when working to achieve *their* goals, our students with voracious minds show more persistence, perseverance, enthusiasm, and even self-sacrifice. Happily, these qualities are predictive of future success.

You can use various techniques to appeal to children's need for control.

- Tell them what to expect.
- Allow lead time and give notice before an activity is to be started or terminated.

- Give options within defined limits, allocating different levels of choice depending on a student's competencies.
- Arrange independent study projects in which children can fall in love with a subject.
- Create learning contracts. The contract will include what students will learn, how, by what time, and how they will be evaluated. This creates a sense of freedom as students assume more ownership of their learning.

Most of our students who transition into higher-level academic experiences need to learn that their choices can work for them or against them. It is essential that they realize that they can choose behaviors and attitudes when they face challenges and recognize that most of their results are self-produced. Seeing the connection between what they do and what happens to them gives a sense of control. When we keep them aware of their past decisions and behaviors, students are less likely to develop a victim attitude and make excuses for their setbacks. Bright children's astute awareness, vivid imaginations, and excellent memories enable us to work *with* their self-control tendencies, helping them learn to make wise choices so that they develop self-esteem and rewarding relationships. Prufrock Press (http://www.prufrock.com) offers user-friendly publications on teaching the lifelong skills of creative decision-making processes.

Motivation

We often confuse "underachievement" with not being motivated to learn. Students identified for acceleration usually have a voracious craving to learn; however, they may appear to lack purpose. Why? Because children are always motivated, though usually by their own perceived priorities. Gabriela may have incentives to punish her parents. Jack could need his parents and educators to give him more attention and help, so he contrives inadequacy. Autumn may not feel rewarded by her school experience—she has no idea why she needs to be doing this. Lilly wants her teacher to expect less of her. Mark may not have lived long enough to know how to set priorities. Then there are always the unknowns: home situations, peer pressures, outside interests and hobbies, fear of failure, fear of success.

Children's motivation to participate in a particular learning project can be fueled by relating the project to some meaningful idea. Ask, "What are all the things you might like to do when you are an adult? You have so many years ahead of you and probably many jobs that you will be doing when you are older that do not even exist yet. When I was your age, home computers and cable television didn't exist. Now many people work with computers, with other advanced technology, and produce television shows. Write down all of the types of activities you would like to do in your lifetime. Include ideas for your job, for vacations, for hobbies, and for fun, too."

You might ask your students whether they can remember a time when they were glad that they had persisted to learn something, like determining to struggle hard to know north, south, east, and west directions. You can help relate new learning trials to students' needs if you invite them to predict how this lesson could be helpful to them in their future.

To develop motivation to learn, another approach could be to ask your students to pretend that they are the directors of a foundation. You may need to invite someone to explain what a foundation is. Tell the children that their foundation has to give away a million dollars every year. Next, explain what a "cause" is, such as clean air, world hunger, stray dogs, and so on. Ask students to make two lists: one of all the causes to which they would like their foundation to give money and another list of causes that they would not fund. Then you can elaborate that to do projects that are important to them later in life, they will need to know so many more things than they know now. You can remind the children that when they do what is important to them in the future, they could be glad that they practiced these skills here in school. What skills might they need to make money and wisely distribute it for their cause?

Here are more ideas to help you facilitate constructive motivation.

- **Express trust that children will act intelligently and responsibly.** Use anticipatory praise; expect positive behavior. "I know you can do it; just try the first step!"
- **Respond to children's inner needs, not to their negative behavior.** Needs may not be verbally expressed. Interpret their behaviors and bodily expressions in order to ascertain their inner needs. "Are you worried you'll feel silly when you try to do this?"
- **Agree on the consequences of not complying** and adhere to establish trust and security.
- **Explore alternatives and choices.** Allow learning choices within defined limits.
- **Encourage cooperation** rather than competition.
- **Clearly distinguish between who a child is and what she or he accomplishes.** "I love having you in my class; your interesting questions make me learn too."
- **Stimulate creativity and responsibility** by asking, "What do you think might happen if you . . .? What else might you try? How might you feel then?" Have the child explore the question, "In what ways will my decision help me or hurt me?"
- **Ask children to suggest ways in which they would like to learn.**
- **Encourage children to express how they feel.** Establish a complaint department to avoid explosive revolts. Keep a Suggestion Box in which children can deposit opinions, even anonymously.
- **Help a child to find a peer so that he or she can enjoy cooperative experiences.**
- **Review suggestions in the Perfectionism section.**

12

Social Relationships

Appropriate academic acceleration is one of the best ways to encourage bright children to soar into their unfettered possibilities. A golden thread that connects every aspect of acceleration is a chance to make compatible friends. Not only do these children need academic challenge, they need the opportunity to associate with emotional and intellectual peers. We have found that the brightest children generally have spent their youngest years gravitating to older children for compatible play. Martha, mother of precocious six-year-old Paige, laughed when she confessed that before Paige went to Jade's house for a play date, they had to discuss that a "play date" meant that Paige was supposed to spend her time with Jade, not Jade's mother! Generally, social development is determined significantly more by mental age than chronological age. When exceptionally bright children are with their intellectual peers, they develop and maintain a higher self-concept.

In Hans Christian Andersen's story "The Ugly Duckling," a young swan's surrounding pond mates, all ducks, ridiculed him because he wasn't like them. The swan did not know that he was different from his flock; because he was placed in that pond, all of the flock thought he should look and be like the others. As we all know, it was finally discovered that this misplaced bird was of a different feather, and he eventually settled into where he could be appreciated. "The Ugly Duckling had found his true home at last. He lifted his long, graceful neck and returned the caresses of his new brothers. He thought he would die of happiness"(Carruth, 1987).

We've seen that feeling estranged is one of the greatest stressors for our children who need to be in an accelerated program. It is widely accepted that by age five or six, gifted children are quite aware of being different. Sometimes they interpret this "weirdness" as something wrong with them. They may ask, "Why do things bother me that don't bother other children? Why do I have so many questions? Maybe I'm not as smart as the others; they seem to already know things." Our misplaced students have fewer opportunities to experience understanding and empathy because of the many influences that complicate their chances for finding friends. Attempts at social engagement and making friends can go awry due to the intensity of the ideas coming into a gifted child's brain.

With eyes sparkling and words punctuated with flailing arms, Tony eagerly enters a small group in the dress-up/play corner, "Hey! Let's pretend we're dolphins and talk to each other in signals. I've got the code all figured out! Four beeps mean 'There's danger approaching,' three short hums mean, 'I see something to eat.' And dolphins change colors like chameleons—let's camouflage ourselves with these different clothes!" Meanwhile, a classmate replies, "You're weird, Tony."

This kind of social mismatch can be prevented with careful acceleration. According to *A Nation Deceived*, by age 18, students who had been accelerated reported high focus of control and self-esteem; acceleration did not contribute to social and emotional problems (Colangelo et al., 2004). Students who are satisfied with their school experience have better social relationships, and vice versa. "There is no evidence that being younger than one's classmates is associated with social or psychological difficulties. Often it becomes obvious during the first year or two of school that a bright student needs a higher-level, faster-paced instructional setting" (p. 63). Here is our call to action!

FINDING COMPATIBLE FRIENDS

Gratifying social relationships are crucial for a happy life. Our social relationships provide the context, meaning, support, and vitality for the rest of our experience.

However, experiencing satisfying social relationships is often an enormous task for exceptionally intelligent people. The more a person's intelligence exceeds the norm, at any age, the more difficult it is to find sincerely compatible companions. As intelligence increases, so does the potential for misunderstanding.

Due to some of their relatively rare characteristics, gifted children have fewer chances to find friends who can fully relate to them.

- They may make up intricate rules for games and create complex play.
- They may gravitate to children who also crave complicated play and leave others who don't.
- They may come across as bossy because they can be so creative and want to organize the play to suit their new ideas.
- They may realize that they sometimes see, feel, know, and do things that others do not.

It is essential for adept learners to feel accepted and understood. Children with exceptionally active, astute minds can't be like everyone else. Their friends and feelings have an essential, intense influence on their lives; they can't tone it down and not take things seriously. The brain that drives them permeates everything they are and do. For example, you would not expect a child who functions in even the mildly developmentally delayed range to thrive in an average school program without specific support. We would not expect a child with an IQ of 60 to be like any other child his or her age, except with a slower ability to learn.

Judy Galbraith's research identifying the "Eight Great Gripes of Gifted Kids" was popularized in *The Gifted Kids' Survival Guide for Ages 10 & Under* (Galbraith & Espeland, 1983). This list continues to be widely featured in literature and counseling of bright students.

1. No one explains what being gifted is all about! It's kept a big secret.

2. School is too easy and too boring.

3. Parents, teachers, and friends expect us to be perfect all the time.

4. Friends who really understand us are few and far between.

5. Kids often tease us about being smart.

6. We feel overwhelmed by the number of things we can do in life.

7. We feel different and alienated.

8. We worry about world problems and feel helpless to do anything about them. (p. 4)

Examining this familiar list, you can determine that grouping exceptionally competent children with their peers would reduce most of these familiar protests.

ADJUSTMENT VERSUS ACCELERATION

To a certain extent, children must learn to adjust to their environment. However, questions arise about where the fulcrum of "adjustment" lies. Paring yourself down in order to "fit in" constitutes a living suicide. Our goal must be to inspire our children to maintain their sense of self as they learn to interact successfully with other people. We now know that we need to look at "adjustment" from their point of view, honoring their abilities both to accommodate and to maintain integrity. What does it feel like to be gifted? For gifted children, it's normal to be abnormal. Just as a plant can't help turning toward light, these children can't deny their extreme awareness, sensitivity, curiosity, and intensity.

In the process of deciding whether to accelerate a child into a higher grade or class, sometimes acknowledging that more compatible social peers are available in the alternative class determines the "social skip." Given the opportunity, if Dominic gravitates to older children, you have significant assurance that his intellectual comfort zone is in an advanced grade. Children's needs for a social skip can be subtle, imperceptible to themselves and their caregivers. Just as we know that young children sometimes cannot discern that their academic school experience could be any different than it is, imagining that they could have more suitable friends may be a thought that exists beyond their realm of possibilities. We've discussed how high intelligence tends to amplify exceptionally bright children's experiences, complicating and intensifying what goes on within and around them. If Bryan is surrounded by students who hold him back, he can become disappointed and frustrated with classmates who he thinks "could do better if they only tried." It can be frightening and alienating for Brian to realize that he sees and knows things that other children do not.

Although it is not the norm, there are times when grade acceleration needs to occur sometime mid-year. If this were done to accommodate only one or a few appropriate subjects, there can be even less apprehension about making this adjustment sometime after the academic year begins. We know that inappropriate school conditions can be truly damaging to a child. When a child wants to venture a mid-year skip and the receiving teachers agree to support this change, there are great advantages to taking this leap out of a stagnant or damaging school situation.

For example, Taylor was lonely in his second-grade class, where the only person to whom he could relate was his teacher. Even though he needed to move to another building mid-year, he was much happier in Mrs. Goldblatt's classroom. She had taken some gifted education classes and had one other student who shared Taylor's extremely high intelligence. In the beginning, although Taylor's limited life experience made it a little awkward for him to join in, his sweet manner and generous kindness with his new social group was a magnet for the help and good will of his new classmates. Mrs. Goldblatt also assigned a "Buddy for the Day" to Taylor, who would be available to guide him through his day. His daily Buddy explained routine activities to him and sat with him at lunch; every child in the class played the Buddy role.

A common objection to grade skipping or grouping with academically compatible colleagues is the sentiment, "Jacob needs to learn to live in this world and get along with everybody. I don't want him to become elitist!" But despite this sentiment, keeping Jacob back in the name of populism can take his time and add resentment. When we hear from the Jacobs who remain with their age mates though performing two grades ahead of them, we hear more of the Great Gripes. Some of them acquire the top-of-the-class syndrome, and some feel as if their environment is telling them, "What you are is not what's wanted." Instead, allowing children who share academic competence levels to also share the same classroom deters elitism.

Here, these children can receive help from and offer help to one another. They can learn to cooperate—and compete—in a congruent environment.

FACILITATING THE SOCIAL SUCCESS OF ACCELERATION

"Every day I come to school I look for a friend. Sometimes I find one, but the next day I have to look all over again." Our young, bright children want to feel accepted and liked by their educators and classmates, but effectively negotiating their way through a school day takes competent interpersonal skills. Skipping a grade requires even more social proficiency to accommodate their new classmates. They need to proactively assimilate into their new situations.

Alex feels that lunch and recess are the worst parts of his day. This is when he is "on his own" to navigate the impermeable clusters of kids who seem to be doing just fine without him. He learned to bring his handheld electronic game to feign fascination with his desolate status. Especially during the first weeks of an acceleration adjustment, educators may need to maneuver situations to include children like Alex until they become accustomed to the availability of like-minded children. Although Alex is academically astute, the challenge of integrating with classmates on his own can gnarl his confidence. Because acceleration often involves disrupting children from staying with their regular classmates, we need to understand how to facilitate gratifying social relationships for our children with exceptional abilities who are navigating the acceleration process.

It's the fifth day of the new, advanced grade placement. David is eager to get outside for recess. But when he's out, he lingers at the playground's edge. David plays with his favorite action figure and shifts his focus from the shrieking commotion of his classmates to a wandering, random gaze, then back to the bedlam. Observing this scene, parents and teachers may wonder whether they've made the wrong decision: Does David not have enough social confidence? Because expanded consciousness is congruent with high intelligence, many of our young Davids stand back, surveying the new situation, learning the ropes of recess. They need to understand what is expected before risking participation. Although they may appear withdrawn, children like David are consciously participating, preparing to join in. He is likely observing to learn appropriate plays and associations. Although these sensitive, intense students may initially lack courage to engage in unfamiliar social relationships, acceleration offers a foundation for developing friendships. Now they are among a group of potentially fulfilling friends.

Let's look at ways to facilitate mutually satisfying peer relationships when a student shifts to an accelerated mode and enters a new social situation.

Reduce Competition

Most highly intelligent children desperately want to fit in. Refrain from showing that José was "the best" or better than his classmates. He can be humiliated if his work is held up as a model. For little José, to be above others may mean that he turns his back on them and leaves them behind. Again, because most gifted children are acutely sensitive and introverted, they feel that outperforming someone else hurts too much and do not want to inflict this humiliation on classmates. For these reasons, it works best to try to motivate by cooperation rather than competition.

Find Components of Relationships

Help your children search for friends by interest and activity match; everything doesn't have to "fit" to create a friend. Sam may delight in someone who shares his passion for rocks—maybe the high school student who works at the local rock shop on weekends. However, his emotional best friend can likely be someone much younger. Sam gravitates to the preschool Sunday school room to play with children who have not learned to inhibit their fright, disappointment, or delight. Sam is safe to unleash all his emotional expression with these little friends who like and look up to him however he feels. In another third-grade classroom, Olivia keeps up with him when he surfs the Internet and absorbs fascinating facts about astronomy. Olivia's head is in the stars, too. She enthusiastically shares her astral explorations with Sam. Angelina is Sam's best friend for bike riding around the neighborhood; she explores any route with him. Perhaps one of these connections can develop into a treasured best friend.

Participation in community lessons, interest groups, or activities where there are no age or grade specifications can open peer possibilities. For example, you might look for lessons at a science museum or community theater.

Role-Play Social Situations

Let children experience the impact of their own behaviors. In some of these processes, you occasionally might have each child speak through a "character." That is, a student can be the voice for a stuffed animal, hand puppet, or toy figure. This rehearsal helps intercept personal embarrassment. You might also encourage participation in drama classes or amateur plays so that children can try out different roles.

Remember that their minds are geared toward trying out new experiences. You can turn mentally "walking through" anticipated experiences into a game. "I'm going to a new class for advanced Spanish. What should I do if I'm lost and don't understand the grammar? Should I interrupt the teacher or wait until after class and ask for an explanation?" To create self-assurance, anticipate the probable encounters and role-play different ways to respond. Encourage children anticipating change in their school life to imagine possible expectations, anticipate consequences, and practice some behaviors—first in their minds, then aloud, then as a role play.

Help Them Understand Their Feelings and Relationships

Children who think and know outside of their age-range accepted "box" may need your help accepting that, in many situations, other people cannot understand their feelings and perceptions. To this end, asking children to keep a journal or talk into a tape recorder can help them discover and be more aware of how they think and present themselves. They can also be working out management strategies to develop behaviors they want to use. Help them expand possibilities by incorporating reflections such as "Part of me feels . . ." or "Another part of me thinks. . . ." Ask children, "What do you look for in a friend? In what situations do you have these qualities?" Let students describe these traits in operational terms, step-by-step, in ways that suit their personality and goals.

When navigating social conflicts, "How are we going to work this out?" can become our students' theme for getting along with each other. We must help them learn to engage in problem solving and conflict resolution without blame. Censuring leaves the blamer without responsibility to seek options to resolve a dispute. Our young fumbling students are just practicing, trying to learn how to express their needs and get along with others who can potentially help them. A great confidence builder is for a child to experience over and over that "If I make a mistake in the way I treat someone else, or if someone hurts my feelings, it is the way I resolve the situation that endures."

Rehearse resolving adverse situations through reading, telling, and acting out wonderfully rich stories that let children mentally try out different encounters. Give them creative opportunities to change the story so that it can evolve into practicing their own experience. Changing the story changes their perceptions and ideas, and changing their perceptions and ideas changes their lives and their world. In this vein, it is worth helping your students create their own affirmations. "At the party, I can manage and I will have a wonderful time. Mimi invited me because she likes me and wants to be with me. I can tell her how I feel. That's how you make friends: telling them how you feel."

Analyze the Situation

Because children often generalize awfulness, it is helpful to analyze a problem situation rather than be a victim. Look at Madison, who feels rejected by two classmates: Help her identify the dynamics and components of the stressful relationship being experienced. Whose needs are not being met? What were each person's intentions? Together, determine what Madison can try to do the next time she encounters a similar situation, focusing on learning from experience. Consider some conflict resolution practices. Ask Madison whether her behavior and attitude will work for her or against her. Remind her that she can only change herself.

Supplement Peer Relationships

Whatever activity strengthens a child's confidence and identity fortifies his or her ability to create successful relationships. Carmen finds acceptance and solace in the music she listens to; she relates to it. Adrianne connects to her artwork. She hones her sense of self as she expresses herself through her drawings. A pet cat or hamster can be a confidant. Pet therapy works along these lines—children can gain trust in themselves and others. Just the process of silently or verbally expressing their thoughts to a pet is valid practice and builds self-confidence.

Mentors or tutors can significantly strengthen a child's confidence and skills in relating to other children. Call the high school and ask whether there is a student who shares Diego's interest in chess, the Civil War, or rock and roll—however esoteric that might be. This match might develop into a valuable link that allows Diego to experience a cooperative relationship. Sometimes National Honor Society members are required to do some community service; tutoring may meet the requirement.

Create and Perform a "Makes Me Happy" Show

On sections of paper, ask students to draw and/or paste illustrations of things they are happy about or like to do. Another focus for this display can be "Good Works." Activities they have enjoyed or their good deeds can include what they've tried hard to do; how they've helped a friend, a pet, or the environment; or something they've shared with others. Each child can interpret his or her images to the group. This is a great way for children to introduce themselves in a positive way.

Conduct Interviews

Create pairs in a novel way, perhaps by lining up students alphabetically. Then progressively join by first and last in line until the middle two (or three) are matched. Each has a limited time to answer the query, "Tell me about yourself" or other probing question. The interviewer can write down some notes, switching roles after time is up. During following days, each interviewer presents a newly discovered classmate to the class.

Eliminate Bullies

Sometimes bullies harass our younger accelerated students. Established classmates might want to take advantage of their junior status, lower stature, and, perhaps, more docile nature. Pairing your vulnerable student with a Buddy deters bullying.

Here are a few ideas to suggest to your little target of teasing and bullying.

- Don't try to get even. Is it wise to let someone who is mean decide how you behave? You don't want to be someone who acts the same way as a bully, right?
- Ignore the bully. Do not allow the bully to get what she or he wants. Walk away.
- Remain calm and rational. Respond to a mean request, "That wouldn't make any sense. Would you do that?"
- Reflect back to the bully what she or he is doing. "You want me to give you my place in line or you'll tear up my papers? Why do you need to act this way? You must be having a really bad day!"
- Ask a teacher or a helpful friend for help and ideas, with the goal of becoming able to manage most situations yourself.
- Stand up straight, look the bully in the eye, and say in a firm, confident voice, "Leave me alone!" or "Stop it!" Then stay calm and walk away, toward a group, if possible.
- Try saying, "I'm wondering whether you're getting what you need by acting this way."

Two books can be comforting companions to our children who endure being taken advantage of and pushed around by other children. If you buy only one, make sure to get *Stick Up for Yourself! Every Kid's Guide to Personal Power and Positive Self-Esteem* by Gershen Kaufman, Lev Raphael, and Pamela Espeland (1999). It is written for and appeals to bright children aged 8 to 12 because the authors skillfully explain the reasons for behaviors and suggest responses. Another useful source is *Settle*

Conflicts Right Now! A Step-by-Step Guide for K–6 Classrooms by Jan Osier and Harold Fox (2001).

Many exceptionally bright children can become angry because they think that other people just don't care. They may take other people's relatively lower level of sensitivity as an intended attack on them. We must help them understand that it's not that other children don't care, but that sometimes they just don't see and feel the same way. One way to explain this to a child is to use a microscope metaphor. "Henry, you know some of us have to wear glasses to see well. Others see very well without glasses. Some people even see and feel more, as if they are looking through a magnifying glass. And you, Henry, sometimes see and feel like you're looking through a microscope. You notice things that other people just don't see or feel. And sometimes other people notice and feel things that you do not."

Informing parents about your focus on congenial social skills may engage their awareness and support. Perhaps your most potent influence for teaching harmonious, encouraging social relationships is how you interact with young children. Maybe your reading this chapter will make your professional and personal life sparkle!

13

Facilitating Acceleration for Parents and Educators

"When I already know something, I can't learn it again."

—Corey, age six

Although there is evidence that acceleration greatly promotes a child's opportunity to learn in school, there has been a cultural lag dragging these bright kids back into their same-age classroom rut. Often our smartest children's learning needs are marginalized. Accommodating special education for accelerated learning should be honored as fervently as we provide for other crucial special education conditions. Advocacy for special education continues to cast a wider net. It is hoped that acclaim for the authoritative volume *A Nation Deceived* (Colangelo et al., 2004) will facilitate allowing children to learn at their capacities. What appears in *A Nation Deceived* is essentially what our colleagues in the field of gifted education have been advocating for decades: The dearth of teacher training programs for gifted education also limits the options for these children to be recognized and served. Inadequate funding, partially because of a limited constituency, constrains appropriate services.

It takes advocacy to create accelerated programs. Serving exceptionally intelligent students reaps great benefits for families, in classrooms, in schools, and in the community. Families, neighborhoods, and commercial enterprises want to associate with and attract a population with bright children. Competent professionals inquire about which schools provide special programs for highly capable students.

Coming to appreciate the benefits of acceleration has been a bumpy, winding road. Rather than considering it an assault on childhood, we recognize how universal our goal of selective acceleration is—to provide appropriate learning experiences at the pace and stage of a child's readiness. However, any book can only go so far toward creating a successful acceleration experience; parents and teachers must do the rest. This chapter focuses on how we can assist acceleration as a viable alternative for a single advanced learner or for all of the exceptionally able children in a school.

GOALS OF ADVOCACY

During the Hollingworth Center for Highly Gifted Children 1996 Conference, I led a session with the children's group; most were adolescents. The students' goal was to create a handout for the participating parents and teachers informing them "what works" for them. We created this handout from their discussion.

For Parents

- Assume that you need to educate educators. You can't just go along with everyone else.
- Work with the school system if you can; work against the system if you have to.
- Don't give up; stick with it. The only thing worse than not trying is not finishing.
- Consult your child and let your child take some of the responsibility for change.
- Allow yourself, teachers, administrators, and your child exploration, discovery, and trials.
- No one may *know* what to do.

For Teachers

- You don't have to know what to do for gifted children; just be open to learning.
- If we're not challenged with hard enough work, we can't concentrate because there's not enough to engage our minds. Then we just want to get through the assignment and make careless errors.
- Demonstrate that you believe that the student can accomplish more advanced work. Perhaps arrange for a few students to apply the class assignments to a more advanced text.
- Listen to the kids.

About Acceleration

- Don't assume that the child won't succeed by being accelerated.
- There can be worse problems due to *not* accelerating!
- Listen to the student's views, to what the student has to say.
- There are advantages to accelerating a child with a companion.
- Select a teacher who demonstrates that he or she welcomes the accelerated student into the class. The receiving teacher's attitude and philosophy is reflected by the other students.
- Acceleration is more fun!

From these insights and previous research, we concluded that the following main factors are needed to make acceleration successful.

- Children must be informed about the decision and want the change.
- Receiving teachers need to be carefully selected for their flexibility, positive attitude, training concerning acceleration, and willingness to help children adjust to the new situation.
- Parents must want this placement, agree to cooperate with teachers to assist in initial tutoring to fill any learning gaps, and communicate with teachers about children's reactions to this change.
- Administrators need to provide support services for students, teachers, and parents involved in acceleration processes.
- There needs to be ongoing evaluation for all involved; expect to adjust to discovered needs.

Although the misconception that a bright child will thrive in any school situation still permeates the popular field, you can be an agent to change the future.

BARRIERS TO ACCELERATION WITHIN THE SCHOOLS

Acceleration typically becomes the scapegoat for many difficult issues. Almost any future flaw in a child's life can be blamed on the "dire consequences" of having skipped a grade. Reflections I've heard from high school students' parents include, "Caria skipped a grade. She's done really well in school and has lots of friends and enjoys sports, but she has acne. I think that the stress from skipping caused it." "Jason started kindergarten when he was four. He made good grades all through school and was involved in many activities. But I think it made him shy. He doesn't have many good friends and it is hard for him to meet people."

Think about the objections to grade-skipping that you have heard. What do they usually reflect? Often it's the sentiment that separating a child from his or her age peers causes some sort of social rejection or maims him or her emotionally.

- "She'll feel inferior because she is smaller. Besides, she won't have the same interests."
- "What about the prom when everyone else is driving?"
- "He'll be smaller for sports and feel incompetent!"
- "Would you want your 10-year-old associating with kids who are going through puberty?"

What other concerns do you have? How many times have you heard the classic objection, "What about socialization?" to deny any type of acceleration? Let's briefly look at some intrinsic barriers to acceleration found in the schools. In the next section, we'll take an in-depth look into the range of responses to acceleration found in the families of exceptionally bright children.

Personal Beliefs

Thoughts of acceleration can conflict with your personal beliefs. When personal beliefs conflict with research evidence, personal beliefs win out almost every time. In the United States, most people believe that it is inappropriate to eat dog meat. Eating dogs is inconceivable—almost cannibalism! This is a belief. Yet in other lands, responsible, kind, intelligent people feast on dog meat. I saw "field rat" on the menu of a large, popular restaurant in a Vietnamese city. Before you continue reading this chapter, please pause and become aware of the beliefs you have about acceleration. What remnants of your experiences might maintain a fortress against children academically moving ahead of their age peers? I invite you to examine and openly discuss your beliefs about acceleration in the light of experience and research. Then gain courage to try some different practices.

Peer Relations

No one seeks to look foolish among his or her peers, and many educators fear that this might be what acceleration will accomplish. It is likely that acceleration processes were not encouraged in their administrative or teacher training. Many school administrators resist "going out on a limb" to accommodate exceptional learning needs of children if their "diagnosis" is not acknowledged in the realm of special education or if there is no precedent for such veering off the traditional path. They may be thinking, "What if the child proves that it was a bad idea? Who will be blamed? *Me?*" If you open yourself to acknowledging some other relatively recent teaching techniques, such as differentiating visual-spatial learners, you gain appreciation for how the education field is evolving. In the process of learning how and why one may accelerate children who have been denied learning at their ability levels, it becomes apparent that *not* allowing children to learn at their competency level can do more harm than restraining them to their chronological age learning level.

Personal Experience

Even personal experience can become a barrier to acceleration. Emma S. taught many grades in a few schools. She became an administrator, yet she continues to teach some science classes. Decades ago, her daughter Sue skipped a grade. As can happen even in the most loving, conscientious families, this daughter's life story is sad and disappointing. Emma's conscience tries to rectify her daughter's life experiences by "blaming" Sue's problems on grade acceleration. Thus, Emma assumed the position of guardian against grade acceleration in her district. As many of us have done, Emma took her personal disappointment and pain and applied it where she had professional power, and exceptional talent was deserted.

FAMILY APPREHENSION ABOUT ACCELERATION

Issues for families of gifted children are complex and intense. Adopting a school acceleration program means recognizing qualities of giftedness in a child. Thus, considering acceleration possibilities can stir up deep feelings in families. This paradigm shift into stepping outside the lines of traditional education affects the roles and relationships of an entire family system. When one bright star is identified, the whole family constellation shifts to accommodate that child's exceptional attributes. Each family member will have a unique reaction in resonance with his or her particular history, temperament, personality, interests, and abilities. Once a child is recognized as exceptionally intelligent, parenting seems to become a greater and more complicated responsibility. Parents experience confusion and anxiety about their ability to perform their new roles.

When a child embarks on an accelerated path, a range of responses is evoked in his or her parents. Some are wholly enthusiastic; they are profoundly grateful that educators recognize what they have experienced at home. Hilda and Richard endured Katya's waning interest in school. Although Katya acquiesced to all of her school assignments, she quietly resented being the class "example." Her parents appreciate the acceleration opportunity that their school has provided. Other parents recoil with apprehension; like their children, they often have a keen sense of justice and fairness, and they do not want themselves or their child ostracized for claiming to be better and more deserving than others.

Many factors complicate recognizing and coming to terms with one child's exceptional abilities. Ethnic, racial, gender, economic, geographical, and age components also define how acknowledging exceptional ability—even giftedness—in the family is welcomed, accepted, and resented. In blended families, stepparent and noncustodial parent roles amplify the intricacy of assimilating giftedness. Some parents will be hesitant to take a cultural leap. "How will I explain this to my parents or neighbors?" These kinds of responses were briefly discussed in Chapter 5.

Understanding how parents respond to their child's proposed acceleration program is essential for mutual family-school empathy and support. When parents are informed and feel understood, they can encourage their children's adjustment and facilitate the process. At the other extreme, if parents and school personnel do not collaborate prior to an acceleration shift, the opportunity can be sabotaged. This section will focus further on understanding the range of responses that parents may experience when acceleration is considered as an option for their child.

Doubts About Giftedness

We have found that about one-third to one-half of parents disagree with their child's assessment of giftedness. When only one parent concurs with the identification, this discrepancy is a probable source of marital conflict (Keirouz, 1990). It is usually the mother who is the most invested in accommodating her child's exceptional learning abilities. When there are discrepancies, it is most often the father who wants his child to stay within normal age expectations. Reasons behind these doubts often center on a parent finding it difficult to accept his or her own high intelligence. Although "most studies have shown IQ to be highly (though never 100 percent) heritable" (Winner, 1996, p. 174), "many gifted adults have no idea that they are more intelligent than the norm" (Alvarado, 1989, p. 78).

Parents of first-born children may not be aware of how exceptional their child is. At family gatherings, Petra fits right in with her young cousins, who might have similar genes. Some of these parents are likely to offer excuses when neighbors and friends suggest that their first-born child is especially bright.

- "Well, Mitzi quit work when she knew she was pregnant and has spent a lot of time with Petra."
- "Scotty's had a lot of advantages; he used to be glued to all the Baby Einstein videos, and we bought educational toys for him."
- "Sam's Granny read to him a lot; that put him ahead."
- "It's just because we always talked with him like we would to any adult; you know, never used baby talk."

As long as the children are meeting their parents' expectations, they may not be seen as exceptional. However, genes and lifestyle prevail. As Carlina explained, "If you plant a potato, you get a potato."

Further, if concerns permeate some parents' thoughts about accepting accelerated programs for their children, they may be less likely to acknowledge their child's outstanding abilities.

- "Oh, I've seen those gifted kids on TV. I know what they act like and Jimmy's not like them." (Television programs often sensationalize prodigies.)
- "No, don't put Carlie in that gifted program. Just let her be a normal child so she can have friends and won't feel different from the other kids."
- "When you tell me that Jeremy is gifted, I worry that he'll grow up to be like Ted Kaczynski; you know, the Unabomber."
- "No, Rachel's not gifted. She hates school and I have to fight with her all the time to get her homework done."

Many parents need to make an initial transformation of acknowledging their own giftedness. One of the most prevalent responses I hear from people who read *Guiding the Gifted Child* (Webb et al., 1982) is something similar to, "I saw myself on those pages. Now I know why I never seemed to fit in. I always thought there was something wrong with me." For many parents, identifying giftedness in their child initiates a process of grieving for what might have been and of evolving their self-concept. One winter I worked and played with Kathi Kearney in a southern, rather rural part of Maine and visited her self-contained classroom for highly gifted elementary students. The school building's large, near ground-level front porch/deck was scattered with snowshoes. Cross-country skis rested against the front wall. My guest role was to discuss any issues these kids wondered about. Sometime into our morning gathering, Matthew asked, "Where does giftedness come from?" I elaborated on the influences of heredity and environment. Matthew interjected, "No, you're wrong! Our parents get it from us! First we're identified to be in a gifted class, then our parents start reading books and going to meetings and they decide they're gifted too!"

Parents of children needing acceleration probably have natures that characterize gifted children: acute sensitivity; intense focus, feelings, and reactions; strong internal sense of control; keen awareness; creative imagination; probing, analytical curiosity; and an extraordinary memory. Professionals who work with gifted kids can assist parents to honor these exceptional assets in themselves so that they can advocate more effectively for their children.

Higher Standards for the Child

Parents can worry and object that their Angela will risk "losing ground" because after her acceleration, she will be evaluated on a higher scale. Parents may become confused about what being gifted means and what it does not mean. They might fear that being taught and tested at a higher level will "rob" their child of her childhood.

When parents are told that their child scores in the top 1%, what kind of expectations might they impose on their child? Often they believe that the label "gifted" applies to all parts, and they know that their child is not particularly gifted in math, for instance. Parents need to be reminded that the acceleration can be focused to respond to the student's particular learning needs.

Higher Standards for the Parents

When a child is formally identified as needing an accelerated program, parents encounter various ambivalent emotional reactions, which often include confusion and anxiety about their new "job description." They are sometimes stunned to find that their child deserves special care, and they wonder whether they can measure up to the challenges. In various levels of consciousness and tumult, parents may grieve for the loss of their "normal" child. Parents may have some apprehensions that even more will be required from them than they have already given to their child.

Shame and Guilt

I called Carol to report her son's testing results: Eli's intelligence scores were in the 99th percentile, and his academic achievement levels were two to three years above his grade level. Now she had some evidence to understand why Eli was so miserable in school and some hope to negotiate a more appropriate program for him. Her response was revealing. "This is almost the best news I've ever had, and, you know, there's no one I can call." Parents are usually cautious about admitting that their children might surpass their peers by being brighter and more accomplished. Some families experience social rejection if their children are too different from their relatives and neighbors. Exceptional children may teach themselves to read before they start elementary school. One young mother grieved that her own mother scolded her with, "Now you've gone ahead and ruined first grade for Cindy by teaching her to read, just like it was spoiled for you."

Shifts in Power Structure

Sometimes power and dominance roles are shifted in a family with a highly intelligent child, especially when parents feel intimidated that their child may "outsmart" them. Some parents attempt to "hothouse" their adept child. They exempt him or her from cooperative family tasks like taking out the garbage because his or her mind is "worthy of higher pursuits." In the worst case, there can even be a tendency for a child who is recognized as having exceptional academic abilities to rise to virtually being head of the household; the family generally revolves around his or her needs. Of course, that is too much of a burden for a young child to bear.

Sibling Responses

When parents compare one child's exceptionally high scholastic achievements with his or her siblings' academic accomplishments, these parents tend to view their lower-achieving children as less competent than they actually are. Marion was concerned that her younger daughter was a "late talker" because she did not converse in sentences until she was 18 months old, four months later than her older sister. Relative comparisons may also be apparent to the siblings themselves. Thus, parents have a crucial role to be sensitive and to appreciate each child's unique qualities. Personal qualities like being helpful, a good finder, on time, and knowing how to repair things are some features to recognize with appreciation. Parents must recognize increments of competence rather than glorify being the best or the first. High mental achievements should not be more acclaimed than acts of kindness, empathy, and service.

Parents can become deeply concerned about the insidious wounding effect of one child being labeled exceptionally competent and becoming a candidate for acceleration, especially if an older sibling does not demonstrate comparable abilities. These parents may worry that if a younger child matches or surpasses a sibling in a subject or a grade, the older child—or any sibling not selected for special recognition of high academic ability—will become resentful and lose self-esteem. Brothers and sisters who are appropriately accommodated in their classrooms might become more accepting of their sibling's scholastic shift if it is interpreted as a response to having different learning *needs*.

Remember that intelligence is highly determined by genetics. Miraca Gross (2004) presents findings of several studies that all show strong genetic intelligence resemblance. However, intellectual strengths may not be in the same domains. Some are highly verbal, others have mathematical strength, and others exceptional visual-spatial abilities. Sometimes highly intelligent children are verbally adept and skilled at claiming a large portion of their parents' power, attention, and time, leaving less for their siblings.

Some accelerated students' siblings may become inspired that this opportunity to learn in more appealing conditions could relieve their classroom tedium and will enthusiastically pursue this possibility for themselves. Precedent is powerful! A bottom line for parents to consider when arranging for one child in a family to exceed another's academic pace is that it is not fair to hold one child back to make another child feel better. Instead, caring adults can explain to siblings, aunts, and neighbors that they were advised that Annie had *different learning needs* that could be met in another classroom or program.

ADVOCACY TIPS FOR PARENTS

We have looked at a few family responses to accelerating students in academic programs. Many parents will experience huge variations from these examples. Parents are often aware that their child requires a more challenging school experience, and the most empowering response that a parent can have is to develop into an advocate for some mode of acceleration.

- "When do you think this review will be over?" seven-year-old Chase asks his parents nearly every day after school.
- "Twelve more years of THIS?" from five-year-old Brian, after the first six months in his long-awaited kindergarten class.
- "Mom, when will the REAL SCHOOL start?" asks Sarah, age five (IQ 155), after two months of kindergarten.
- "I can't stand this snooze-fest!" says seven-year-old Andrea about her first-grade classroom.

Sometimes parents consider home schooling as an antidote to their child being stifled in an age-locked classroom. One parent shared, "After trying to negotiate some changes with his kindergarten teacher and still experiencing Seth coming home depressed and impossible, we decided to home school. I asked him whether he thought he might miss being with kids more, and if so, maybe want to go back to school. But he said, 'Well, the problem is, there's just so much to learn in this world, and I couldn't really learn that much in school.'" In some cases, it might be an advantage to arrange a combination of home school and classroom program to accommodate unusual learning needs.

Acceleration advocacy usually starts with early entrance. A synthesis of research results on (1) early entrance to kindergarten, (2) grade skipping, and (3) acceleration clearly shows that these are positive interventions, although educators continue to resist these practices. There was a high rejection rate of early entrance applicants by school principals (seven out of ten rejected all candidates for early entrance) who justified their decision using arguments such as, "The socialization process and the ability to get along with one's early entrancers is far more valuable to a child's progress than any academically gifted program at this stage of his/her development" (Vialle, Ashton, Carlon, & Rankin, 2001, p. 15). This attitude reflects the typical uninformed assumptions of educators about the socioemotional adjustment of early entrants, and it is in direct contrast to the literature on early entrance, which shows that early entrants are at least equally well adjusted, if not better adjusted, than similar children who did not enter school early.

There were other reasons cited for rejecting early-entrance applicants:

- Principals maintained that parents wanted their children to "fit in," to progress at normal rates, and to avoid the problems of "early exit."
- The child was considered to be too physically small and immature.
- Principals were not familiar with the policy and its practice.
- Administrators or educators had personal opposition to early entrance, without specific arguments.
- Most principals did not deem exceptional academic ability to be a convincing reason for early entrance. (Vialle et al., 1991)

Sometimes there is a cultural lag among educators to facilitate this process. Adverse negative attitudes of teachers can seriously affect a child's progress. Some attitudes are based on misconceptions and trivial information. Parent advocacy can inform educators and facilitate accelerated programs. If parents want excellent handholding encouragement and step-by-step guidance, please invest in *Stand Up for Your Gifted Child* by Joan Franklin Smutny (2001).

ADVOCACY TIPS FOR EDUCATORS

Just as parent advocates must learn to appreciate the struggles of the educators they are working to affect, administrators and school personnel involved in developing accelerated programs in a school or classroom must understand the difficulties parents have when their child has been identified as a candidate for acceleration. This section focuses on what educators can do to advocate for acceleration. Like their children, parents need to understand the reasons for acceleration practices and policies. Otherwise, they may unintentionally sabotage what educators desire to accomplish.

Hold an Orientation Meeting

- Initially, parents need to be notified that their child has been identified to participate in an accelerated program. The notice can convey as much relevant information as suitable.
- Include a request for a short personal or telephone interview with a parent of each participating child to answer further questions. It is helpful to define the anticipated interview duration in this announcement, perhaps five to ten minutes.
- A short personal or telephone interview with every child's parent can have enormous benefits. A personal interview is ideal because you can pick up body language to give depth to your information. Although many predictable questions should be answered in the initial announcement, you can reach out to diffuse apprehensions and misconceptions about this opportunity.
- Lead with a list of questions, and really listen to the answers.
  o Do you have any questions about this program?
  o How do you hope the accelerated program will serve your child?
  o Do you have any information that can help your child benefit from this program?
  o What can you tell me about your child's strengths and weaknesses?

- If schedules are too tight, or if certain parents are not available to meet with you, offer the option of a written "Help me understand and support your child" questionnaire.
- *Approach parents in a spirit of collaboration.*
- Re-read the above section about family apprehension, and remind yourself that parents may have many feelings and misconceptions.
- Remember that parents do not want to harm their child. Even if they have some knowledge of acceleration, they are not confident that they know *how* to implement it. They also wonder whether they *could* manage the essential cooperation of all people and facilities that would be involved.

- If feasible, arrange a meeting for parents of all children who have been identified for accelerated curriculum. Remember that many parents will feel estranged from their general school-parent group. When parents speak to parents, they integrate, understand, and accept the information you give them more thoroughly. They can then assist you further.
- Identify two or three involved parents as "Parent Liaisons" who agree to liaise with the parents involved in your acceleration program. The acronym APT (Accelerated Program Team) can be used for this kind of parent-led group.
- Give status and credibility to your parent constituency.
- Seek parent support in every way possible.

Effective advocacy for your acceleration endeavors starts at home. Informed parents can convey to their children that their strengths and high abilities are recognized and appreciated and that exercising their aptitudes will serve them their entire lives. By affirming their competency, their self-expectations are raised. We have all noticed that self-affirmations influence children's performance significantly more than their teachers' expectations.

It is also essential that parents and teachers communicate their concerns and intentions to each other. Some form of regular messaging needs to take place. A significant number of parents are reluctant to voice any worry or complaint to their child's teachers. Although they may have severe concerns about some classroom situation, many parents remain mute rather than risk complaining to their child's teachers. They may rationalize, "I don't want to complain because I'm afraid that Zoe's teachers will take it out on her."

Perhaps the single most important factor in allowing bright students to appreciate their abilities is to have well-trained teachers who are able to understand both the cognitive and affective needs of young gifted students and to counsel parents to work in partnership with them. Remember, you can only change yourself and what you do. Then perhaps what you choose to think and do will influence others positively.

Usually, no one really *knows* what to do, but you can always *try* something. We need to let go of the idea that we can determine *the best* plan for all of our students, or even for one of them. We can only *consider* possibilities and *try* options. That is better than doing nothing for a child who is stifled by academic expectations.

Bibliography

Agne, K. J. (2001, Summer). Gifted: The lost minority. *Kappa Delta Pi Record.* Retrieved March 2, 2006, from www.findarticles.com/p/articles/mi_qa4009/is_200107/ai_n9004086/

Alvarado, N. (1989). Adjustment of adults who are gifted. *Advanced Development, 1,* 77–86.

Amabile, T. M. (1996). *Creativity in context.* Boulder, CO: Westview Press.

American heritage dictionary (2nd college ed.). (1985). Boston: Houghton Mifflin.

Arieti, S. (1976). *Creativity: The magic synthesis.* New York: Basic Books.

Arnold, K., & Subotnik, R. (1995, Spring). Mentoring the gifted: A differentiated model. *Educational Horizons, 73*(3), 118–123.

Assouline, S. G., Colangelo, N., Lupkowski-Shoplik, A. E., Lipscom, J., & Forstadt, L. (2003). *Iowa acceleration scale: A guide for whole-grade acceleration K–8* (2nd ed.). Scottsdale, AZ: Great Potential Press.

Baldwin, A. Y. (2003). Lost and found: Achievers in urban schools. In J. F. Smutny (Ed.), *Underserved gifted populations: Responding to their needs and abilities* (pp. 83–91). Cresskill, NJ: Hampton Press.

Baldwin, A. Y., & Vialle, W. (Eds.). (1999). *The many faces of giftedness: Lifting the masks.* Albany, NY: Wadsworth.

Benbow, C. P. (1991). Meeting the needs of gifted students through use of acceleration. In M. C. Wang, M. C. Reynolds, & H. J. Walberg (Eds.), *Handbook of special education: Research and practice* (pp. 23–36). Oxford: Pergamon Press.

Benbow, C. P., & Benbow, R. M. (1986). Physiological correlates of extreme intellectual precocity. *Mensa Research Journal, 21,* 54–87.

Benbow, C. P., & Lubinski, D. (1996). *Intellectual talent.* Baltimore: Johns Hopkins Press.

Benbow, C. P., & Stanley, J. C. (Eds.). (1983). *Academic precocity: Aspects of its development.* Baltimore: Johns Hopkins University Press.

Betts, G. T. (1986). The autonomous learner model for the gifted and talented. In J. S. Renzulli (Ed.), *Systems and models for developing programs for the gifted and talented* (pp. 27–56). Mansfield Center, CT: Creative Learning Press.

Black, P., & William, D. (1998, October). Inside the black box: Raising standards through classroom assessment. *Phi Delta Kappan,* 139–148.

Bloom, B. S. & Krathwohl, D. R. (1984). *Taxonomy of Educational Objectives.* Boston, MA: Pearson Education.

Bloom, B. (1985). *Developing talent in young people.* New York: Ballantine Books.

Bredekamp, S. (Ed.). (1987). *Developmentally appropriate practice in early childhood programs serving children from birth through age 8* (Exp. ed.). Washington, DC: National Association for the Education of Young Children.

Bredekamp, S., & Rosegrant, T. (Eds.). (1992). *Reaching potentials: Appropriate curriculum and assessment for young children* (Vol. 1). Washington, DC: National Association for the Education of Young Children.

Brody, L. E., & Benbow, C. P. (1987). Accelerative strategies: How effective are they for the gifted? *Gifted Child Quarterly, 3,* 105–110.

Burmark, L., & Fournier, L. (2003). *Enlighten up! An educator's guide to stress-free living.* Arlington, VA: Association for Supervision and Curriculum Development.

191

Canfield, J., & Wells, H. C. (1994). *100 ways to enhance self-concept in the classroom: A handbook for teachers and parents.* Upper Saddle River, NJ: Pearson Education.

Carbo, M., Dunn, R., & Dunn, K. (1986). *Teaching students to read through their individual learning styles.* Englewood Cliffs, NJ: Prentice Hall.

Carruth, J. (1987). *My giant treasury of fairy tales.* New York: Exeter Books.

Carson, R. (1965). *The sense of wonder.* New York: Harper & Row.

Clark, B. (2002a). Assessment that empowers teachers and learners. *Gifted Education Communicator, 33*(2), 10–11, 31–32.

Clark, B. (2002b). *Growing up gifted: Developing the potential of children at home and at school* (6th ed.). Upper Saddle River, NJ: Prentice Hall.

Coil, C., & Merritt, D. (2001). *Solving the assessment puzzle: Piece by piece.* Marion, IL: Pieces of Learning.

Colangelo, N., Assouline, S., & Gross, M. (2004). *A nation deceived: How schools hold back America's brightest students. The Templeton national report on acceleration.* Iowa City: The University of Iowa.

Colangelo, N., & Davis, G. (2003). *Handbook of gifted education* (3rd ed.). Needham Heights, MA: Allyn & Bacon.

Coleman, M., & Gallagher, J. (1992). *Report on state policies related to the identification of gifted students.* Chapel Hill, NC: University of North Carolina at Chapel Hill, Frank Porter Graham Child Development Center, Gifted Education Policy Students Program.

Crawford, R. P. (1964). *Techniques of creative thinking.* Flint Hill, VA: Fraser Publishing.

Daurio, S. P. (1979). Educational enrichment versus acceleration: A review of the literature. In W. C. George, S. J. Cohn, & J. C. Stanley (Eds.), *Educating the gifted: Acceleration and enrichment* (pp. 13–53). Baltimore: Johns Hopkins University Press.

Davidson, J., & Davidson, B. (2004). *Genius denied: How to stop wasting our brightest young minds.* New York: Simon & Schuster.

The Davidson Institute for Talent Development. http://www.ditd.org. (Offers full text articles on early childhood, perfectionism, and underachievement.)

Davis, G. A., & Rimm, S. B. (1988). *Education of the gifted and talented* (3rd ed.). Englewood Cliffs, NJ: Prentice Hall.

Delisle, J., & Galbraith, J. (2002). *When gifted kids don't have all the answers: How to meet their social and emotional needs.* Minneapolis, MN: Free Spirit.

Donahue, P. (1981, January 16). Gifted children and suicide [Television broadcast]. In *The Phil Donahue show.* New York: NBC.

Doty, G. (2001). *Fostering emotional intelligence in K–8 students: Simple strategies and ready-to-use activities.* Thousand Oaks, CA: Corwin Press.

Eberle, B. (1982). *Visual thinking.* Buffalo, NY: D.O.K. Publishers.

Eberle, B., & Standish, B. (1997). *Be a problem solver: A resource book for teaching creative problem-solving.* Waco, TX: Prufrock Press.

Elkind, D. (1981). *The hurried child: Growing up too fast too soon.* Reading, MA: Addison-Wesley.

Elkind, D. (1988a). From our president. Acceleration. *Young Children, 43*(4), 2.

Elkind, D. (1988b). Mental acceleration. *Journal for the Education of the Gifted, 11*(4), 19–31.

Fairhurst, A. M., & Fairhurst, L. (1995). *Effective teaching, effective learning: Making the personality connection in your classroom.* Gainesville, FL: Center for the Applications of Psychological Type.

Feldhusen, J. F. (1989). Synthesis of research on gifted youth. *Educational Leadership, 46,* 6–11.

Feldhusen, J., & Kollof, P. B. (1986). The Purdue Three-Stage Enrichment Model for gifted education at the elementary level. In J. S. Renzulli (Ed.), *Systems and models for developing programs for the gifted and talented* (pp. 126–152). Mansfield Center, CT: Creative Learning Press.

Feldhusen, J. F., Proctor, T. B., & Black, K. N. (2002). Guidelines for grade advancement of precocious children. *Roeper Review, 24*(3), 169–171.

Fisher, M. D. (1988). *Fisher comprehensive assessment of giftedness scale.* Manassas, VA: Gifted Education Press.

Fisher, M. D. (1998). A sensibility approach to identifying and assessing young gifted children. In J. F. Smutny (Ed.), *The young gifted child: Potential and promise, an anthology* (pp. 52–61). Cresskill, NJ: Hampton Press.

Freeman, C. (2003). Designing math curriculum to encourage inductive thinking by elementary and middle school students: Basic principles to follow. In J. F. Smutny (Ed.), *Designing and developing programs for gifted students* (pp. 69–85). Thousand Oaks, CA: Corwin Press.

Galbraith, J. (1999). *The gifted kids' survival guide: For ages 10 & under* (Rev. ed.). Minneapolis, MN: Free Spirit.

Galbraith, J., & Espeland, P. (1983). *The gifted kid's survival guide for ages 10 & under.* Minneapolis, MN: Free Spirit.

Gallagher, J. J. (1969). Gifted children. In R. L. Ebel (Ed.), *Encyclopedia of educational research* (4th ed., pp. 537–544). New York: Macmillan.

Gallagher, J. J. (1985). *Teaching the gifted child* (3rd. ed.). Boston: Allyn & Bacon.

Gallagher, J. (1996). Educational research and educational policy: The strange case of acceleration. In C. Benbow & Y. D. Lubinski (Eds.), *Intellectual talent: Psychometric and social issues* (pp. 83–92). Baltimore: Johns Hopkins University Press.

Gallagher, J. (2004). Public policy and acceleration of gifted students. In N. Colangelo, S. G. Assouline, & M. Gross (Eds.), *A nation deceived: How schools hold back America's brightest students. The Templeton national report on acceleration* (Vol. II, pp. 39–45). Iowa City: The University of Iowa.

Gallagher, J. J., & Gallagher, S. A. (1994). *Teaching the gifted child* (4th ed.). Boston: Allyn & Bacon.

Gardner, H. (1993). *Frames of mind: The theory of the multiple intelligences.* New York: Basic Books.

Gilman, B. J. (2003). *Empowering gifted minds: Educational advocacy that works.* Denver, CO: DeLeon.

Goertz, J. (2001). Searching for talent through the visual arts. In J. F. Smutny (Ed.), *Underserved gifted populations* (pp. 459–467). Cresskill, NJ: Hampton Press.

Goleman, D. (1995). *Emotional intelligence: Why it can matter more than IQ.* New York: Bantam Books.

Gordon, W. J. J. (1961). *Synectics.* New York: Harper & Row.

Gordon, W. J. J. (1974). *Making it strange.* Books 1–4. New York: Harper & Row.

Gregory, G. H., & Chapman, C. (2002). *Differentiated instructional strategies: One size doesn't fit all.* Thousand Oaks, CA: Corwin Press.

Gross, M. U. M. (2004). *Exceptionally gifted children* (2nd ed.). New York: RouteledgeFalmer.

Gross, M. U. M., & van Vliet, H. E. (2003). *Radical acceleration of highly gifted children: An annotated bibliography of international research on highly gifted children who graduate from high school three or more years early.* Sydney, Australia: University of New South Wales.

Guilford, J. P. (1968). *Intelligence, creativity and their educational implications.* San Diego, CA: Robert R. Knapp.

Hébert, T. P. (2003). Gifted males. *Gifted Education Communicator, 33*(4), 16–18.

Heinbokel, A. (2002). Acceleration: Still an option for the gifted. *Gifted Education International, 16,* 170–178.

Heller, A. (2004, January 29). At 14, she's working for a Ph.D. in engineering. *Philadelphia Inquirer.* Retrieved January 29, 2004, from http://www.philly.com

Hennessey, B. A. (2004). *Developing creativity in gifted children: The central importance of motivation and classroom climate.* Storrs, CT: The National Research Center on the Gifted and Talented.

Hoagies' Gifted Education Page. http://www.hoagiesgifted.org. (Excellent articles relating to every aspect of gifted children, including a collection on acceleration.)

Illinois State Board of Education. (1997). *The Illinois learning standards.* Springfield, IL: Author.

Illinois State Board of Education. (2004). *ISAT 2004 aggregate results.* Retrieved November 15, 2005, from http://www.isbe.state.il.us/pdf/2004_assessment_results.pdf

Information Center on Disabilities and Gifted Education. http://ericec.org/fact/stateres.html. (State resources for gifted education.)

Isaksen, S. G., Puccio, G. J., & Treffinger, D. J. (1993). An ecological approach to creativity research: Profiling for creative problem solving. *Journal of Creative Behavior, 27*(3), 149–170.

Janos, P. M., & Robinson, N. M. (1985). Psychosocial development in intellectually gifted children. In F. D. Horowitz & M. O'Brien (Eds.), *The gifted and talented: Developmental perspectives* (pp. 149–195). Washington, DC: American Psychological Association.

Johnsen, S. K., & Goree, K. K. (2005). Teaching gifted students through independent study. In F. A. Karnes & S. M. Bean (Eds.), *Methods and materials for teaching the gifted* (2nd ed.). Waco, TX: Prufrock Press.

Jones, E., & Southern, T. (1992). Programming, grouping, and acceleration in rural school districts: A survey of attitudes and practices. *Gifted Child Quarterly, 36,* 111–116.

Kaltman, G. S. (2005). *Help! For teachers of young children: 88 tips to develop children's social skills and create positive teacher-family relationships.* Thousand Oaks, CA: Corwin Press.

Kanuka, H. (2005). An exploration into facilitating higher levels of learning in a text-based Internet learning environment using diverse instructional strategies. *Journal of Computer-Mediated Communication, 10*(3). Retrieved February 12, 2006, from http:jcmc.indiana.edu/vol10/issue3/kanuka.html

Kaplan, S. (2001). Layering differentiated curriculum for the gifted and talented. In F. A. Karnes & S. M. Bean (Eds.), *Methods and materials for teaching the gifted* (pp. 133–158). Waco, TX: Prufrock Press.

Karnes, F. A., & Bean, S. M. (Eds.). (2005). *Methods and materials for teaching the gifted* (2nd ed.). Waco, TX: Prufrock Press.

Kaufman, G., Raphael, L., & Espeland, P. (1999). *Stick up for yourself! Every kid's guide to personal power and positive self-esteem* (Rev. ed.). Minneapolis, MN: Free Spirit.

Kay, K. (2000). *Uniquely gifted: Identifying and meeting the needs of the twice-exceptional student.* Gilsum, NH: Avocus.

Keirouz, K. S. (1990). Concerns of parents of gifted children: A research review. *Gifted Child Quarterly, 34*(2), 56–63.

Kerr, B. A. (2001). *Smart girls: A new psychology of girls, women, and giftedness.* Scottsdale, AZ: Great Potential Press.

Kerr, B. A., & Cohn, S. J. (2001). *Gifted boys: Talent, manhood, and the search for meaning.* Scottsdale, AZ: Great Potential Press.

Kindlon, D., & Thompson, M. (2000). *Raising Cain: Protecting the emotional life of boys.* New York: Ballantine.

Kingore, B. (1990). *The Kingore observation inventory.* Des Moines, IA: Leadership Publishers.

Kingore, B. (1993). *Portfolios: Enriching and assessing all students, identifying the gifted grades K–6.* Des Moines, IA: Leadership Publishers.

Kingore, B. (1998). Seeking advanced potentials: Developmentally appropriate procedures for identification. In. J. F. Smutny (Ed.), *The young gifted child: Potential and promise, an anthology* (pp. 31–51). Cresskill, NJ: Hampton Press.

Kingore, B. (1999a). *Assessment: Time-saving procedures for busy teachers.* Austin, TX: Professional Associates.

Kingore, B. (1999b). *Teaching without nonsense: Activities that encourage high-level responses.* Austin, TX: Professional Associates.

Kingore, B. (2002). *Rubrics and more!* Austin, TX: Professional Associates.

Kitano, M. K., & Kirby, D. F. (1986). *Gifted education: A comprehensive view.* Boston: Allyn & Bacon.

Kulik, J. (1992). *An analysis of the research on ability grouping: Historical and contemporary perspectives.* Storrs, CT: National Research Center on the Gifted and Talented.

Kulik, J. A., & Kulik, C. C. (1984). Synthesis of research on effects of accelerated instruction. *Educational Leadership, 42*(2), 84–89.

Kulik, J. A., & Kulik, C. C. (1987). Effects of ability grouping on students' achievement. *Equity and Excellence, 23*(1–2), 22–30.

Kulik, J., & Kulik, C.-L. (1991). Ability grouping and gifted students. In N. Colangelo & G. A. Davis (Eds.), *Handbook of gifted education* (pp. 230–242). Needham Heights, MA: Allyn & Bacon.

Kurcinka, M. S. (1991). *Raising your spirited child: A guide for parents whose child is more intense, sensitive, perceptive, persistent, energetic.* New York: HarperCollins.

Landrum, M. S., & Shaklee, B. (Eds.). (1998). *Pre-K–grade 12 gifted program standards.* Washington, DC: National Association for Gifted Children.

Lawrence, G. (1993). *People types and tiger stripes.* Gainesville, FL: Center for Applications for Psychological Type.

Lovecky, D. (2004). *Different minds: Gifted children with AD/HD, Asperger syndrome, and other learning deficits.* New York: Jessica Kingsley.

Margolin, L. (1994). *Goodness personified: The emergence of gifted children.* New York: Aldine de Gruyter.

Marland, S. P. (1972). *Education of the gifted and talented.* Washington, DC: U. S. Government Printing Office.

Maslow, A. H. (1968). *Creativity is self-actualizing people. Toward a psychology of being.* New York: Van Nostrand Reinhold.

Mathieson, K. (2004). *Social skills in the early years: Supporting social and behavioral learning.* Thousand Oaks, CA: Corwin Press.

May, R. (1975). *The courage to create.* New York: W.W. Norton.

Meckstroth, E. (1997). Complexities of giftedness: Dabrowski's theory. In J. F. Smutny (Ed.), *The young gifted child, potential and promise: An anthology* (pp. 295–307). Cresskill, NJ: Hampton Press.

Meiners, C. J. (2003). *Share and take turns.* Minneapolis, MN: Free Spirit.

Meisgeier, C., & Murphy, E. (1987). *Murphy-Meisgeier type indicator for children manual.* Palo Alto, CA: Consulting Psychologists Press.

Morrison, G. S. (1995). *Early childhood education today.* Upper Saddle River, NJ: Prentice Hall.

Murphy, E. (1992). *The developing child: Using Jungian type to understand children.* Palo Alto, CA: Davies-Black.

Myers, I. B., McCaulley, M. H., Quenk, N. L., & Hammer, A. L. (1998). *MBTI manual: A guide to the development and use of the Myers-Briggs type indicator* (3rd ed.). Palo Alto, CA: Consulting Psychology Press.

Myers, I. B., & Myers, P. B. (1995). *Gifts differing: Understanding personality type.* Palo Alto, CA: Davies-Black.

Nash, D. (2001, December). Enter the mentor. *Parenting for High Potential,* 18–21.

National Assessment of Educational Progress. (1992). *Writing portfolio study.* Washington, DC: National Center for Statistics.

National Association for Gifted Children. (1998). *Pre-K–grade 12 gifted program standards.* Washington, DC: Author.

National Association for Gifted Children. (2004). *Position paper: Acceleration.* Retrieved March 14, 2005, from http://www.nagc.org/index.aspx?id=375

National Association for Gifted Children. (2005). *State of the states 2004–2005: A report by the National Association for Gifted Children and the Council of State Directors of Programs for the Gifted.* Washington, DC: Author.

National Association for Gifted Children and Council of State Directors of Programs for the Gifted. (2003). State of the states: Gifted and talented education report 2001–2002. Washington, DC: Author.

National/State Leadership Training Institute on the Gifted and Talented. (1976). Principles of a differentiated curriculum for the gifted/talented. In *A new generation of leadership* (p. 1). Los Angeles: Office of Ventura County California Superintendent.

Neihart, M., Reis, S. M., Robinson, N. M., & Moon, S. M. (Eds.). (2002). *The social and emotional development of gifted children: What do we know?* The National Association for Gifted Children Service Publication. Waco, TX: Prufrock Press.

Nowicki, S., & Duke, M. P. (1992). *Helping the child who doesn't fit in.* Atlanta, GA: Peachtree.

Oakes, J. (1985). *Keeping track: How schools structure inequality.* New Haven, CT: Yale University Press.

Obrzut, A., Nelson, R. B., & Obrzut, J. E. (1984). Early school entrance for intellectually superior children: An analysis. *Psychology in the Schools, 21*(1), 71–77.

Office of Educational Research and Improvement, U.S. Department of Education. (1993). *National excellence. A case for developing America's talent.* Washington, DC: U.S. Government Printing Office.

Osborn, A. F. (1963). *Applied imagination* (3rd ed.). New York: Scribner's.

Osier, J., & Fox, H. (2001). *Settle conflicts right now! A step-by-step guide for k–6 classrooms.* Thousand Oaks, CA: Corwin Press.

Our Gifted Online Conferences. http://www.neiu.edu/~ourgift/index.html. (Conferences about specific topics such as underachievement, differentiation, and advocacy presented by nationally known experts. Parents can also ask questions and dialogue with professionals.)

Our Gifted Online Conferences Yahoo Group. http://groups.yahoo.com/group/OGTOC. (A discussion group for the parents and teachers of gifted children.)

Parnes, S. J. (1967). *Creative behavior guidebook.* New York: Scribner's.

Parnes, S. J. (1981). *The magic of your mind.* Buffalo, NY: Creative Education Foundation.

Passow, A. H., Goldberg, M., Tannenbaum, A., & French, W. (1955). *Planning for talented youth.* New York: Teachers College Press.

Passow, A. H., & Rudnitski, R. A. (1993). *State policies regarding education of the gifted as reflected in legislation and regulation.* Storrs: University of Connecticut, National Research Center on the Gifted and Talented.

Paul, R. (1997). *Critical thinking: What every person needs to survive in a rapidly changing world.* Conoma, CA: Center for Critical Thinking.

Piirto, J. (1998). *Those who create* (2nd ed.) Scottsdale, AZ: Great Potential Press.

Piirto, J. (2004). *Understanding creativity.* Scottsdale, AZ: Great Potential Press.

Poincaré, H. (1913). Mathematical creation. In B. Ghiselin (Ed.), *The creative process: A symposium.* Berkeley: University of California Press.

Polette, N. (1997). *Research reports to knock your teacher's socks off!* Marion, IL: Pieces of Learning.

Reis, S. M. (2002). Developing the talents and gifts of girls: 20 strategies that work. *Gifted Education Communicator, 33*(4), 12–15, 32–35.

Reis, S., Burns, D., & Renzulli, J. (1992). *Curriculum compacting.* Mansfield Center, CT: Creative Learning Press.

Renzulli, J. S. (1977). *The enrichment triad model: A guide for developing defensible programs for the gifted and talented.* Wethersfield, CT: Creative Learning Press.

Reynolds, M. C., Birch, J. W., & Tuseth, A. A. (1962). Review of research on early admissions. In M. C. Reynolds (Ed.), *Early school admission for mentally advanced children* (pp. 7–18). Reston, VA: Council for Exceptional Children.

Riley, T. L. (2005). Teaching on a shoestring: Materials for teaching gifted and talented students. In F. A. Karnes & S. M. Bean (Eds.), *Methods and materials for teaching the gifted* (2nd ed., pp. 657–700). Waco, TX: Prufrock Press.

Roeper, A. (1995). *Annemarie Roeper: Selected writings and speeches.* Minneapolis, MN: Free Spirit.

Rogers, C. (1962). Toward a theory of creativity. In S. I. Fames & H. F. Harding (Eds.), *A source book for creative thinking* (pp. 63–72). New York: Charles Scribner's Sons.

Rogers, K. (1991). *The relationship of grouping practices to the education of the gifted and talented learner* (Research-Based Decision Making Series). Storrs: University of Connecticut, National Research Center on the Gifted and Talented.

Rogers, K. B. (2001). *Re-forming gifted education: Matching the program to the child.* Scottsdale, AZ: Great Potential Press.

Rogers, K. B. (2003). *Reforming gifted education: How parents and teachers can match the program to the child.* Scottsdale, AZ: Great Potential Press.

Rogers, K., & Kreger Silverman, L. (1997, November). *Personal, social, medical, and psychological factors in 160+ IQ children.* Paper presented at the National Association for Gifted Children 44th Annual Convention, Little Rock, AR. Available online at www.gifteddevelopment.com.

Romain, T. (1997). *Bullies are a pain in the brain.* Minneapolis, MN: Free Spirit.

Schiever, S. W., & Maker, C. J. (1997). Enrichment and acceleration: An overview and new directions. In N. Colangelo & G. A. Davis (Eds.), *Handbook of gifted education* (2nd ed., pp. 113–125). Boston: Allyn & Bacon.

Schilling, D., Johnson, R., & Wentz, Z. (1996). *50 activities for teaching emotional intelligence: Level I elementary.* Torrance, CA: Innerchoice.

Seeley, K. (1989). Arts curriculum for the gifted. In J. VanTassel-Baska, J. F. Feldhusen, K. Seeley, G. Wheatly, L. Silverman, & W. Foster (Eds.), *Comprehensive curriculum for gifted learners* (pp. 300–313). Boston: Allyn & Bacon.

Shore, B., & Delcourt, M. (1996). Effective curricular and program practices in gifted education and the interface with general education. *Journal for the Education of the Gifted, 20,* 138–154.

Siegle, D., & McCoach, D. B. (2005). Extending learning through mentorships. In F. A. Karnes & S. M. Bean (Eds.), *Methods and materials for teaching the gifted* (2nd ed., pp. 473–518). Waco, TX: Prufrock Press.

Sinetar, M. (2000). *Spiritual intelligence: What we can learn from the early awakening child.* Maryknoll, NY: Orbis Books.

Silverman, L. K. (Ed). (1993). *Counseling the gifted and talented.* Denver, CO: Love.

Silverman, L. K. (2002). *Upside-down brilliance: The visual-spatial learner.* Denver, CO: DeLeon.

Silverman, L. K. (2004). *What we have learned about gifted children 1979–2003.* Retrieved May 17, 2005, from http://www.gifteddevelopment.com/What_is_Gifted/learned.htm

Smutny, J. F. (2001). *Stand up for your gifted child: How to make the most of kids' strengths at school and at home.* Minneapolis, MN: Free Spirit.

Smutny, J. F. (Ed.). (2003). *Underserved gifted populations: Responding to their needs and abilities.* Cresskill, NJ: Hampton Press.

Smutny, J. F., & von Fremd, S. E. (2004). *Differentiating for the young child: Teaching strategies across the content areas (K–3).* Thousand Oaks, CA: Corwin Press.

Smutny, J. F., Walker, S., & Meckstroth, E. (1997). *Teaching young gifted students in the regular classroom: Identifying, nurturing, and challenging ages 4–9.* Minneapolis, MN: Free Spirit.

Southern, W. T., & Jones, E. D. (1991a). Academic acceleration: Background and issues. In W. T. Southern & E. D. Jones (Eds.), *The academic acceleration of gifted children* (pp. 1–28). New York: Teachers College Press.

Southern, W. T., & Jones, E. D. (Eds.). (1991b). *The academic acceleration of gifted children.* New York: Teachers College Press.

Southern, W. T., Jones, E. D., & Fiscus, E. D. (1989). Practitioner objections to the academic acceleration of gifted children. *Gifted Child Quarterly, 33,* 29–35.

Stanish, B. (1988). *Lessons from the hearthstone traveler: An instructional guide to the creative thinking process.* Carthage, IL: Good Apple.

Stanley, J. (1978). SMPY's DT-PI model: Diagnostic testing followed by prescriptive instruction. *Intellectually Talented Youth Bulletin, 4*(10), 7–8.

Stanley, J. C. (1979). The study and facilitation of talent in mathematics. In A. H. Passow (Ed.), *The gifted and talented: Their education and development. 78th year book of the National Society for the Study of Education* (pp. 169–185). Chicago: University of Chicago Press.

Starko, A. J. (1995). *Creativity in the classroom: Schools of curious delight.* White Plains, NY: Longman.

Storfer, M. D. (1990). *Intelligence and giftedness: The contributions of heredity and early environment.* San Francisco: Jossey-Bass.

Subotnik, R. (1995). Joshua Lederberg: Scientific risk taker and innovator. *Journal for the Education of the Gifted, 18*(2), 210–218.

Swartz, R., & Parks, S. (1994). *Infusing critical and creative thinking into content instruction.* Pacific Grove, CA: Critical Thinking Press & Software.

Swiatek, M. A., & Benbow, C. P. (1991). Ten-year longitudinal follow-up of ability-matched accelerated and unaccelerated gifted students. *Journal of Educational Psychology, 83,* 528–538.

Sykes, C. (1995, August 27). The attack on excellence. *Chicago Tribune*, pp. 17–20, 22–23.

Taba, H. (1962). *Curriculum development: Theory and practice.* New York: Harcourt, Brace & World.

Thompson, M. C. (2000). *Curriculum as profound engagement with the world.* Keynote speech to the National Curriculum Networking Conference, The College of William and Mary. Retrieved May 10, 2005, from http://cfge.wm.edu/documents/CurriculumProfound. html

Tieger, P. D., & Baroron-Tieger, B. (1997). *Nature by nature: Understand your child's personality type–and become a better parent.* New York: Little, Brown and Co.

Tomlinson, C. (1999). *The differentiated classroom: Responding to the needs of all learners.* Alexandria, VA: Association for Supervision and Curriculum Development.

Tomlinson, C., Kaplan, S., Renzulli, J., Purcell, J., Leppien, J., & Burns, D. (2002). *The parallel curriculum.* Thousand Oaks, CA: Corwin Press.

Torrance, E. P. (1974). *Torrance tests of creative thinking: Norms and technical manual.* Lexington, MA: Personnel Press/Ginn-Xerox.

Torrance, E. P. (1979). *The search for satori and creativity.* Buffalo, NY: Creative Education Foundation.

Torrance, E. P. (1980). Growing up creatively gifted: A 22-year longitudinal study. *Creative Child and Adult Quarterly, 5*(3), 148–158, 170.

Torrance, E. P. (1995). *Why fly: A philosophy of creativity.* Norwood, NJ: Ablex.

Treffinger, D. (1986). Fostering effective, independent learning through individualized programming. In J. S. Renzulli (Ed.), *Systems and models for developing programs for the gifted and talented* (pp. 429–460). Mansfield Center, CT: Creative Learning Press.

Treffinger, D. J., & Firestien, R. L. (1989). Update: Guidelines for effective facilitation of creative problem solving. *Gifted Child Today, 12*(4), 35–39.

VanTassel-Baska, J. (1986). Acceleration. In C. J. Maker (Ed.), *Critical issues in gifted education* (pp. 179–198). Rockville, MD: Aspen.

VanTassel-Baska, J. (1988). *Comprehensive curriculum for gifted learners.* Needham Heights, MA: Allyn & Bacon.

VanTassel-Baska, J. (1992). Educational decision making on acceleration and ability grouping. *Gifted Child Quarterly, 36*(2), 68–72.

VanTassel-Baska, J. (1993). Linking curriculum development for the gifted to school reform and restructuring. *Gifted Child Today, 16*(4), 34–37.

VanTassel-Baska, J. (1996). Contributions of the talent-search concept to gifted education. In C. P. Benbow & D. Lubinski (Eds.), *Intellectual talent* (pp. 236–245). Baltimore: Johns Hopkins University Press.

VanTassel-Baska, J. (2003). *Curriculum planning and instructional design for gifted learners.* Denver, CO: Love.

VanTassel-Baska, J. (2005). Acceleration strategies for teaching gifted learners. In F. A. Karnes & K. Stephens (Series eds.), *Practical strategies series in gifted education.* Waco, TX: Prufrock Press.

Vialle, W., Ashton, T., Carlon, G., & Rankin, F. (2001). Acceleration: A coat of many colours. *Roeper Review, 24*, 14–18.

wa Gacheru, M. (1985). Children of Nairobi. *Illinois Association for Gifted Children Journal, 4*, 5–7.

Walker, S. Y. (2002). *The survival guide for parents of gifted kids: How to understand, live with and stick up for your gifted child.* Minneapolis, MN: Free Spirit.

Wallas, G. (1925). *The art of thought.* New York: Harcourt, Brace, and World.

Webb, J. T., Meckstroth, E. A., & Tolan, S. S. (1982). *Guiding the gifted child: A practical source for parents and teachers.* Scottsdale, AZ: Great Potential Press.

Webb, J. T., et al. (2005). *Misdiagnosis and dual diagnosis of gifted children and adults: ADHD, bipolar, Asperger's, depression, and other disorders.* Scottsdale, AZ: Great Potential Press.

Wiggins, G., & McTighe, J. (1998). *Understanding by design.* Alexandria, VA: Association for Supervision and Curriculum Development.

Winebrenner, S. (1992). *Teaching gifted kids in the regular classroom.* Minneapolis, MN: Free Spirit.

Winner, E. (1996). *Gifted children: Myths and realities.* New York: Basic Books.

Index

Corwin Press